GW01185788

BUYING A BRIDE

Buying a Bride

AN ENGAGING HISTORY *of* MAIL-ORDER MATCHES

Marcia A. Zug

NEW YORK UNIVERSITY PRESS

New York

NEW YORK UNIVERSITY PRESS
New York
www.nyupress.org

© 2016 by New York University
All rights reserved

References to Internet websites (URLs) were accurate at the time of writing. Neither the author nor New York University Press is responsible for URLs that may have expired or changed since the manuscript was prepared.

ISBN: 978-0-8147-7181-5

For Library of Congress Cataloging-in-Publication data, please contact the Library of Congress.

New York University Press books are printed on acid-free paper, and their binding materials are chosen for strength and durability. We strive to use environmentally responsible suppliers and materials to the greatest extent possible in publishing our books.

Manufactured in the United States of America

10 9 8 7 6 5 4 3 2 1

Also available as an ebook

For my husband, Geordie,
and my girls, Willa & Lucy

CONTENTS

ACKNOWLEDGMENTS

An earlier draft of the first chapter, "Lonely Colonist Seeks Wife," was initially published in the *Duke Journal of Gender Law & Policy* 20 (2012): 85. Similarly, an earlier draft of "Mail-Order Feminism" was first published in the *William and Mary Journal of Women and the Law* 21 (2014): 153. I would also like to thank the following people for their help and support: James Dwyer, Martha Ertman, Mark Graber, Michael Greenberger, David Schleicher, Robin Wilson, Kevin Noble Maillard, Aziz Rana, Inge Lewis, Vanessa Byars, Madhavi Sunder, Jana Singer, Carol Young, and Joan Yablon.

Introduction

Mention the term "mail-order bride," and you are likely to conjure up two very different, very contradictory images. One is a sad and gritty portrait of an abused and desperate woman, probably very young, and almost certainly foreign, while the other is the rosy image of a strong and brave pioneer bride, possibly older, and quintessentially American.[1] *Buying a Bride* attempts to reconcile these two images. Looking at the history of mail-order brides from the early years of the Jamestown colony to the present, this book examines how we arrived at these conflicting depictions and why the perception of mail-order marriages as formerly good but now bad is both simplistic and inaccurate.

Mail-order marriage has always contained competing elements of risk and reward. These marriages offer women an opportunity to improve their lives, yet they must abandon the security of their homes and families and marry a stranger. Today, women willing to take this chance are considered desperate and helpless, but this was not always true. Historically, mail-order brides were regarded as courageous due to their willingness to embrace the risks and uncertainties of mail-order marriage. The 1934 short story "Object, Matrimony" exemplifies this view.[2]

"Object, Matrimony" was written by Rose Wilder Lane, the daughter of the iconic American author Laura Ingalls Wilder,[3] and depicts the twenty-year mystery surrounding the marriage of Jed Masters and his mail-order bride, Clarinda. The story opens in the late 1870s, in Sioux County, South Dakota, in a half-built town at the "end of the line."[4] A young woman, clearly a lady, but also a stranger, emerges from one of the passenger cars of an arriving train. She is described as pale and seemingly frightened, but it soon becomes clear that she is also brave and determined. As Clarinda exits the train, she turns to the crowd of gawking townspeople and brazenly asks where she can obtain a marriage license. The crowd is stunned. One of the townswomen declares she has never "heard of a woman so bold and brash."[5]

After receiving her answer, Clarinda rounds up a justice of the peace and a carriage and sets out for Jed Masters's house. Upon meeting Jed, Clarinda informs him that she is accepting his offer of marriage and insists on marrying him right away. Jed reluctantly agrees and the two are married. Then, immediately after the ceremony, Jed demands an explanation. He wants to know why Clarinda was in such a rush to marry and accuses her of being pregnant. She denies it, but refuses to explain herself. Instead, she simply states, "It's a fair bargain. You advertised for a wife because you wanted a woman, any woman. I married you because I wanted a husband." When Jed continues to insist, she tells him, "You can kill me, but I'll never tell."[6]

"Object, Matrimony" illustrates both the risks of mail-order marriage as well as the strength and determination regularly ascribed to early mail-order brides. Initially, Clarinda's secrecy and Jed's displeasure seem to indicate helplessness and vulnerability. However, at the end, her secret is revealed and it becomes clear that Clarinda is not a victim. Clarinda tells Jed that she had once been engaged to another man, but when she discovered his plan to elope with her friend she left him and came west to marry. She then triumphantly informs Jed that her former fiancé recently lost his fortune and that she has just purchased his farm and evicted him and his wife. Mail-order marriage gave Clarinda the opportunity to reassert control over her life, avoid victimization, and even extract revenge. Nevertheless, the story concludes by suggesting that the most significant benefit Clarinda gained from her mail-order marriage was happiness. After Clarinda's revelation, a stunned Jed asks his wife if she would still have her fiancé if given the option. She lovingly replies, "Goodness no, ... I wouldn't have anybody but you."[7]

Lane's story portrays mail-order brides as strong and resilient and shows how women could use mail-order marriage to cope with their powerlessness in a male-dominated society. At the same time, Lane's story also hints at the connection between mail-order marriage and broader national interests. The location of the town in the story is significant. Its setting at the "end of the line" signifies both the end of the railroad and the edge of U.S. control. Lane's town is reminiscent of the thousands of real towns that were created to secure U.S. control over Indian lands. In all of these border towns, the presence of women was considered crucial to national expansion. Consequently, both the territorial and federal governments routinely offered legal and financial incentives to spur female immigration. These incentives significantly benefited mail-order brides, but they were not costless. The arrival of mail-order brides frequently coincided with the displacement of native women. Unfortunately, this history is rarely acknowledged. Most favorable accounts of mail-order marriage tend to focus on the experiences of white, American women. When men and women of color used this form of marriage, the positive perception of these unions evaporated. Moreover, this shameful history continues to influence modern views regarding the practice.

Buying a Bride demonstrates that many of the widespread concerns regarding mail-order marriage have questionable origins. This book also emphasizes the similarities between historic mail-order marriage and its modern counterparts and demonstrates that the benefits offered by these marriages remain significant. Nevertheless, I think it is important to acknowledge that a focus on the advantages of mail-order marriage was not the original intention of this book. In fact, it was my own negative reaction to a magazine article on mail-order marriage that initially inspired this project. The article described the mail-order experience of a successful fashion photographer named Steven Baillie, who had tired of the American models and actresses he usually dated and decided it was time to "settle down."[8] Baillie wanted a "traditional wife," meaning a woman who would prioritize her husband and family, and he turned to mail-order marriage because he believed foreign women made better wives. When asked to explain his specific concerns with

American women, Baillie stated, "They have entitlement issues. . . . I want to be the entitled one now."[9] After presenting this explanation, the article described how Baillie chose a mail-order bride company, how he selected his fiancée from the hundreds of women available on the company's website, and how he believed he had finally found "the one." The article then revealed that he had been horribly wrong.

The second half of the article detailed the transformation of Baillie's fairytale romance into a nightmare. The smart, beautiful woman he had selected, who liked to cook and clean and dote on him, also had an unexpected temper. She became jealous of his friendships with other women, including the daughter of a female friend, and Baillie quickly realized the relationship was not going to work. By this point, the woman was pregnant, but Baillie didn't care. When her visa expired, he chose not to marry her, and sent her home. The article then ended with Baillie's glib reflection that there are worse problems than dating American models. He stated:

> Look at my life before I had this freaking bitch here. What was the problem? I'm freakin' hangin' out with all these models and strippers. And yeah, it's empty, but like, what's the problem? Why was I willing to give this up? So now . . . I'm just going to enjoy everything that comes my way. My outlook is like, "I'm just going to bone as many of these chicks as I can." I just wanna not worry about anything. My life is pretty fucking awesome.[10]

This article horrified me. It seemed to confirm my worst suspicions regarding mail-order marriage. Here was a man routinely dating beautiful, desirable women yet turning to mail-order marriage because he believed his previous girlfriends had not been sufficiently grateful. Instead of examining his own behavior, Baillie looked to an Internet "catalogue" to solve his relationship problems. When he became displeased with the "product" he received, he "returned" her like an ill-fitting pair of pants. *Buying a Bride* began with this article in mind.

As I started my research, I expected to find that modern mail-order marriages are fundamentally harmful and that these problems are long-standing. I was surprised that this is not what I found. Despite significant risks, mail-order marriages are typically beneficial and even liberating for women. Consequently, after reaching this conclusion, the object of the book changed. *Buying a Bride* no longer aimed to demonstrate the inherent problems with mail-order marriage. Instead, the book examines the changing perceptions surrounding these marriages and seeks to understand why we continue to venerate the mail-order marriages of the colonial and frontier days while simultaneously fearing their modern-day counterparts.

Buying a Bride addresses this puzzle by examining the history of mail-order marriage from the Jamestown Colony to the present. It shows how the laws and policies pertaining to mail-order brides varied drastically over time and how changes in the racial makeup of the brides, the fulfillment of America's manifest destiny, and evolving beliefs regarding love, marriage, and gender in American society all played a part in transforming mail-order marriage from a lauded institution into one that was, and continues to be, vilified. Accordingly, the book is arranged in two parts. The first half examines the importance and respect afforded pre–Civil War mail-order brides. The second half details the continuing benefits as well as the increasing skepticism and criticism directed at mail-order marriage in the post–Civil War period until the present.

Specifically, the first half of the book looks at the role of early mail-order brides with regard to the successful colonization of North America. Chapter 1 focuses on the mail-order brides of the Virginia colony. The Virginia government considered marriage vital to the success of the entire colonial enterprise, and this belief translated into significant social, economic, and legal benefits for the mail-order brides of Jamestown. Chapters 2 and 3 continue the examination of colonial mail-order brides by contrasting the successful mail-order bride program of New France with its disastrous counterpart in the Louisiana colony. Both chapters show how French bridal programs were influenced by concerns regarding population instability as well as fears of Indian/white miscegenation. However, chapter 2 documents the successful filles du roi program and the ways it benefited both the brides and the colony, while chapter 3 examines the failure of Louisiana's bridal program and how it harmed the colony and the women. In addition, chapter 3 highlights the stark difference between mail-order marriage and trafficking while also revealing why these two concepts are so often linked. Chapter 4 then turns to the mail-order brides of California and the Pacific Northwest. This chapter analyzes the immigration incentives offered to eastern women and the legal and social benefits they received after arrival. It further shows how the U.S. and Canadian governments used female immigration to secure their respective control over North America and how this was achieved, in part, by displacing and harming native wives.

Part II of the book considers the circumstances that led to the increasingly negative perception of mail-order marriage. Although concerns regarding mail-order marriage are long-standing, they have intensified significantly over time. Initially, criticisms focused on the possibility of fraud and manipulation. However, once foreign women began using mail-order marriage to circumvent racially restrictive immigration policies, the unease regarding the practice became widespread. Chapter 5 begins with an examination of the first matrimonial advertisements. Matrimonial ads gave women greater control over their marriage prospects. However, because this increased marital choice came at the expense of parental control, these ads were almost immediately considered problematic. This chapter documents the reservations surrounding early matrimonial advertisements and why they became popular despite such concerns. Chapter 6 focuses on the post–Civil War period and demonstrates that the devastation of the war and the continuing need for women on the frontier kept mail-order marriage popular throughout the nineteenth century. This chapter also shows that the negative associations regarding mail-order marriage continued to grow during the postwar period and quickly became widespread once the racial demographics of the brides changed. Chapter 7 explores how "undesirable" groups, such as Asians and Eastern and Southern Europeans, used mail-order marriage to circumvent America's restrictive immigration policies. It demonstrates that the use of mail-order marriage for this purpose created a substantial backlash and cemented the general perception of mail-order marriages as harmful. Chapter 8 then concludes with an examination of modern mail-order marriages. This final chapter addresses the common criticisms of mail-order marriage, particularly the accusation that large numbers of these women are abused and exploited. This chapter also evaluates the equally common claim that such a marriage undermines the purpose of matrimony and perpetuates gender inequality. Finally, after examining these criticisms, the chapter ends by asserting that the harms associated with mail-order marriage have been exaggerated and that the benefits have been underappreciated.

Before proceeding further, I would like to offer an explanation regarding terminology. Mail-order marriage is a highly contentious topic and even the term "mail-order bride" is divisive. In fact, after reviewing early drafts of this book, a number of my colleagues encouraged me to find a substitute expression. These men and women were uncomfortable with the phrase "mail-order bride" and its explicit reference to purchasing women. I share these concerns and do not dispute that the term has these implications. Nevertheless, rather than shying away from the association with female commodification, I decided to confront it. The potential commodification of women is one of the biggest criticisms of modern mail-order marriage. By referring to the women in this book as "mail-order brides," I signal my intention to address these criticisms and explicitly challenge the assumption that such women are exploited.

I would also like to clarify my definition of "mail-order marriage." In this book, mail-order marriage is defined as a marriage resulting from some form of advertisement or other public request, soliciting women to enter into a marriage with a previously unknown man and typically travel a significant distance to complete this union. Pursuant to this definition, I do not consider any arrangement in which a woman is transported against her will or most arranged marriages (meaning marriages between strangers intentionally organized by a common friend or family member) to be mail-order marriages. Nevertheless, I do include marriages arranged by a third party at the request of the couple, particularly when these marriages were arranged to accommodate the immigration desires of the potential bride. In addition, my definition of mail-order marriage also includes marriages that resulted from general calls for brides, and is not limited to marriages created in response to one man's specific solicitation.

Last, I include female-initiated correspondence in my definition of mail-order marriage, but only where the woman traveled to marry the man. I do not include any examples of mail-order husbands in this history. Although there are some modern examples of American women placing matrimonial advertisements in order to attract a foreign husband, typically to find someone of a similar religious or cultural background, the numbers are extremely small. In general, few American women are interested in finding a mail-order husband. However, homosexual men are increasingly turning to this form of introduction. Now that same-sex marriage is recognized nationwide, the number of foreign mail-order husbands is likely to increase, and it will be interesting to see how the experiences of these men resemble those of mail-order brides. Nevertheless, because same-sex mail-order marriages are still exceedingly rare, this book does not include an examination of these relationships.

PART I

When Mail-Order Brides Were Heroes

1

Lonely Colonist Seeks Wife

As Catherine looks out across the water, she wonders what her life will be like when she reaches Virginia. She knows that conditions will be hard, but life in England was also hard. At least in the colony, there is the possibility of advancement. The Virginia Company has assured her and the other women that they will have their choice of marriage partners. They have promised that the men are wealthy, or at least will be with the women's help, and that the women will have a share of this wealth. Catherine knows it is a risk, but she has been assured she can always return home if she changes her mind. Regardless, Catherine expects to stay. There is little for her back in England. She will marry a colonist and help found a nation.

The above thoughts illustrate what I believe one of the first mail-order brides might have felt as she traveled thousands of miles from England to settle in the Virginia colony. There is no actual record of the hopes and fears of these young women. Nevertheless, we do know that their arrival in 1619 was eagerly anticipated and desired.

Marriage was vital to the success of the colony.[1] Wives were needed to create stable family units, produce and care for children, and cement America's racial and cultural hierarchy. However, the difficulty was that few European women were interested in immigrating. In fact, female immigration to the colonies was so rare that when a group of forty women from La Fleche, France, began boarding a ship for Canada in 1659, the townspeople tried to prevent their departure because they were convinced the women were being kidnapped.[2] Mail-order marriage helped resolve this problem. These women immigrated when others would not, and consequently, their presence was considered critically important.

The risks the early settlers faced were substantial.[3] Most potential colonists had heard frightening accounts of disease and famine, and many of these stories seemed to indicate that women were particularly vulnerable. One horrific tale from Virginia involved a colonist who "slue his wife as she slept in his bosome, cut her in pieces, powedered her & fedd upon her till he had clean devoured all her parts saveinge her heade."[4] In the northern colonies, settlers such as the Puritans and the Quakers accepted these risks as the price of religious freedom, and as a result, these areas had little difficulty attracting large numbers of family groups.[5] In contrast, the southern colonies, which lacked this religious draw,[6] had a much harder time finding families willing to accept the dangers and hardships of colonial life. A handful of women came to the colonies shortly after the first male settlers arrived, but their numbers were small, and even fewer came with their children.[7] Moreover, some families, like that of Sir Thomas Gates, sent their daughters back to England if their wives died.[8] As early as 1609, a broadside (poster) produced by the Virginia Company of London demonstrated that the colony's governing body recognized the need to recruit women. The broadside was directed at family groups and specifically emphasized that both men and women were needed for "the better strengthening of the colony."[9] Nevertheless, despite such appeals, few families immigrated to the southern colonies.[10] Instead, the majority of southern colonists were single men, primarily individual speculators and fortune hunters, who came to profit from America's abundant land and natural resources and then return home.[11] As colonial historian Julia Cherry Spruill has noted, these "men were not interested in building permanent homes in Virginia or in cultivating lands to be enjoyed by future generations." They simply "planned to make their fortunes and then return to England."[12]

The transient nature of the southern population was problematic, and it quickly became clear that the lack of women was threatening the future of the fledgling colony.[13] In 1614, the Virginia Company's lawyer, Richard Martin, spoke before the House of Lords and highlighted the threat posed by the colony's gender disparity. He informed the members, a significant number of whom had shares in the company,[14] that Virginia desperately needed "honest laborers, with wives and children."[15] He then recommended the appointment of a committee to consider ways to increase family immigration.[16] Other members of the Virginia Company shared Martin's immigration concerns. However, class politics ultimately prevented consideration of his proposal. Martin was only a lawyer and not a lord, so his requests, which went beyond legal advice, were considered presumptuous. One contemporary described his speech as "the most unfitting that was ever spoken in the house."[17] Consequently, not only were Martin's appeals ignored, they resulted in punishment. The day after appearing before the House of Lords, Martin was arraigned for contempt. He was brought before Sir Randall Crew, the Speaker of the House, forced to kneel, and given following admonishment:

> The case was this a petition relative to the Virginia Company had been presented, and an order for the Council to appear, that he as their Attorney had represented himself with diverse Lords. That the House at first was disposed to listen to him with all due respect and love; that the retrospect of the Virginia Plantation was acceptable, for it had been viewed with the eyes of love. But afterwards, he has impertinently digressed, for it was not his place to censure and advise. The House had therefore brought him before them, and although many were his acquaintances, yet all now looked upon him with the eyes of judges, and not as private friends.[18]

After Martin's censure, the issue of family immigration was dropped, but the lack of women remained a significant problem. Finally, in 1619, the Virginia Company's treasurer, Sir Edwin Sandys, who now controlled the company, decided to address the issue.[19] He warned his fellow shareholders that if immediate action was not taken, the colony's gender imbalance would soon "breed a dissolucon, and so an overthrow of the Plantation."[20] Sandys recommended sponsoring the immigration of single women because he believed their presence would "make the men more setled [and] lesse moveable" and decrease the number of men who, because of the dearth of women, "stay [in the colony] but to gett something and then return for England." This time, the recommendation to address the colony's female immigration problem was met with approval. After hearing Sandys's suggestion, Lord Francis Bacon, a founding member of the company, immediately expressed his public support declaring it "time to plant with women as well as with men; that the plantation may spread into generations, and not ever pieced from without." Shortly after Sandys's request, the company began recruiting single women to marry the Jamestown colonists.[21]

In the spring of 1620, ninety mail-order brides arrived in Jamestown. Their arrival was considered a success, and the next year Sandys requested funds to transport an additional one hundred women. By this time, the company was in financial difficulties and no longer had the necessary money.[22] However, because Sandys insisted that more women were absolutely essential, the company agreed to raise the money by subscription. Due to these efforts, another fifty brides were sent to Jamestown.[23] Altogether, the Virginia Company sponsored the immigration of 140 mail-order brides.[24] The arrival of these women was intended to reduce the number of male colonists returning to England, but this was not the only reason female immigration was considered necessary. Despite the femaleless wasteland described by Sandys, the colony did not actually lack women. America was filled with indigenous women, and relationships between the male colonists and native women occurred almost immediately.

As early as 1608, after disease and starvation wiped out nearly a third of the original Jamestown colonists, a large number of the male survivors began taking Indian wives.[25] By 1612, the Spanish ambassador to England reported that "between 40 to 50 Englishman . . . had married Indian women."[26] He also informed the company that nearly all of these men had abandoned the colony for their wives' villages.[27]

The first group of brides arrives at Jamestown. Courtesy of Picture Collection, New York Public Library, Astor, Lenox, and Tilden Foundations.

Only two years earlier, the entire population of Jamestown consisted of sixty colonists.[28] Consequently, the number of desertions described by the ambassador was shocking. Just as concerning was the fact that these desertions seemed unstoppable. Virginia Governor Dale had already decreed that deserters were "to be hanged, some burned, some to be broke upon wheels, others to be staked and some to be shot to death." This law had little effect, and colonial men continued to leave the colony.[29]

Desertions contributed to the already declining population, while also undermining the moral justification for the entire colonial endeavor. Virginia settlers had rationalized colonization by highlighting the supposed differences between themselves and the country's native inhabitants. Captain John Smith's 1607 report on the native population of Virginia epitomized this trend, characterizing the local Indians as cruel, irrational, vengeful, treacherous, and barbaric. He also accused these tribes of Satanism. He described the Virginia Indians as devil worshippers who prayed to idols shaped "with such deformity as may well suit with such a god" and claimed they practiced child sacrifice.[30] Such accusations seemed to confirm the English colonizers' belief in their moral and religious superiority. However, intermarriage threatened these distinctions.[31]

Britain's recent colonizing venture in Ireland had demonstrated that settlers were extremely likely to adopt the customs and manners of native inhabitants with whom they intermixed. One typical report from the Irish colony bewailed the number of Englishmen who "in small time have grown wild in Ireland, and become in language and qualities Irish." This report also noted the paucity of Irishmen who "do in exchange become civilized and English."[32] Virginia's colonial leaders worried that marriage to Indian women would lead to similar results. Specifically, they feared that intermarriage would cause European men to abandon their "civility"[33] and become indistinguishable from the "heathen savages."[34] This fear was then further exacerbated by the perceived sexual availability of Indian women. In John Smith's 1612 account of life in the early Virginia colony, he wrote about his visit to one of Powhatan's (Pocahontas's father) villages and noted that in any of these villages, an Englishman could expect "a woman freshly painted red with pocones and oil to be his bed fellow."[35] Smith also detailed his own experience. He claimed to have been greeted by "30 young women [who] came naked out of the woods (only covered behind and before with a few greene leaves), their bodies all painted, some white, some red, some black, some partie colour, but every one different." He then described being invited back to their lodging where they "more tormented him than ever, with crowding, and pressing, and hanging upon him, most tediously crying, love you not mee?"[36] Similar, although less colorful, accounts were provided by colonist and company secretary William Strachey, who declared that the local women were "'most voluptious' and eager to 'embrace the acquaintance of any Straunger.'"[37]

In order to prevent desertions to the native villages and lessen the attractions of native women, colonial leaders described white/Indian relationships as religiously prohibited.[38] In his 1609 sermon, the colonial Reverend William Symonds railed against the dangers of miscegenation. Symonds cited the biblical injunction that "God's people in Canaan 'keepe to themselves,'" and "not marry nor give in marriage to the heathen, that are uncircumcized," and he warned that the "breaking of this rule" jeopardized one's chance for eternal salvation and risked "all good succese of this voyage." Symonds's religious admonishment did little to stem the flow of desertions, and even within the colony, some determined men found ways around this prohibition. The most famous intermarried colonist was John Rolfe. In his letter to Governor Dale seeking permission to marry Pocahontas, Rolfe acknowledged "the heavie displeasure which almightie God conceived against the sonnes of Levie and Israel for marrying strange wives." Nevertheless, he argued that this concern was inapplicable to his own relationship, because Pocahontas was converting to Christianity and, thus, their marriage would actually be furthering God's work and assisting with Rolfe's "owne salvation."[39] Rolfe's arguments were persuasive and earned Dale's endorsement of the marriage.[40]

By 1619, it had become clear that neither religious prohibitions nor capital punishment was a sufficient deterrent against intermarriage. The company, therefore, concluded that the best way to reduce desertions and ensure the colony remained racially and ethnically distinct was to provide colonial men with a viable marriage alternative to native women.[41] Understandably, the women recruited to fulfill this important task were chosen with care. They were not prostitutes, criminals, or beggars.[42] In fact, out of the thirty-eight women whose social status is known, eight had links to the gentry. According to the company records, four of the women were the daughters of gentlefolk; two others had uncles and one cousin (once removed) who were knights; and the eighth was described as the daughter of Mr. Gervase Markham, "of the Nottinghamshire gentry."[43] In addition, the company insisted that all

The wedding of Pocahontas and John Rolfe. Courtesy of the Library of Congress.

the women "had been received ... upon good recommendation."[44] One, a young widow named Anne Rickard, was given the following recommendation:

ffor asmuche as itt is a charitable deede to certifie & declare a truthe in all cases especially where the same ys required, Wee therefore the churchwardens & parishoners of the parishe church of St James at Clarkenwell in the countie of Middlesex whose names are hereunder subscribed doe certifie & declare to all whome theis presentes shall come be seene or reade that the bearer hereof Anne Rickard widowe now inhabiting within our said parishe & so hathe don for the space of Six yeres or neere thereaboutes in which tyme shee hathe demeaned herself in honest sorte & is a woman of an honest lyef & conversation duringe the tyme shee hathe lyved amounges us & so is & ever hathe bynne esteemed & reputed for any thinge ever wee heard or knowe of to the contrary, And for that the said Anne Rickard is mynded &

purposed to dwell elsewhere hathe entreated & required of us whose
names are hereunder subscribed this our testymoniall in her behalf. In
witness whereof to this our presente writing or Testimoniall wee have
subscribed our names the xiiith of December 1620.[45]

This letter demonstrates Rickard's "good character," and it confirms
that she came voluntarily. This was not the norm; in the early Virginia
colony voluntary immigration was rare. Each year, hundreds of settlers died from disease and starvation, and new recruits were essential.
However, finding willing immigrants was difficult, and replacement
settlers were increasingly brought to the colony against their will.

In 1615, Governor Dale asked King James I for more colonists, and
the king complied by ordering the transportation of one hundred convicted male felons.[46] Shortly thereafter, Sir Edwin Sandys asked the
Virginia Company for more settlers, and one hundred street urchins
were rounded up and shipped to Virginia.[47] Then, in 1617, the Virginia
Company introduced the headright system, and as a result, colonial
kidnapping eventually became endemic.

The purpose of the headright system was to encourage immigration
by giving settlers who financed their own passage fifty-acre tracts of
land. It also provided fifty acres of land to individuals willing to sponsor
the passage of a new settler,[48] and as a result, speculators and planters
began paying recruiters to "find" settlers they could send to Virginia.
By midcentury, thousands of men, women, and children were being
kidnapped every year. In 1671, a single kidnapper or "spirit" named John
Stewart was accused of kidnapping more than more than six thousand
victims.[49] It is possible this number was an exaggeration, but kidnapping was so pervasive that songs were written about it. One such song,
"The Woman Outwitted: or the Weaver's Wife," popular in the period,
described a wife "cunningly catch'd in a Trap, by her Husband, who sold
her for ten Pounds, and sent her to Virginny."[50] Such actions were illegal, but kidnapping laws were only weakly enforced. Most kidnappers
were never prosecuted, and those who were often received minimal

punishment. For example, in 1680, a woman named Ann Servant was fined a mere thirteen shillings and sixpence for kidnapping and selling a young woman named Alice Flax. Similarly, in 1684, a couple was charged with kidnapping and selling a sixteen-year-old girl and received only a twelve-pence fine as punishment. In comparison, a horse thief would have been hanged.[51]

The kidnapped men and women were brought over to become indentured servants. However, in the early years of the colony there were a few attempts to kidnap women for wives. For example, in 1618, the colony's need for wives convinced Owen Evans, a messenger for the Privy Council, to kidnap single women and sell them to the female-scarce colony. Using a fake royal commission, Evans traveled to Somerset, England, and began rounding up women and forcing them onto ships. Hundreds of women fled in panic. According to contemporary reports, "forty [we]re said to have fled from one parish alone, and so successfully concealed themselves that their nearest friends did not know what had become of them."[52] Evan's plan did not succeed. Shortly after arriving in Somerset, his deception was revealed, and he was arrested and charged with treason. A few months later, a man named William Robinson, a chancery clerk, attempted to organize a similar kidnapping scam "to take up . . . yeoman's daughters or drive them . . . to serve His Maj for breeders in Virginia."[53] Like Evans, Robinson was caught and arrested for treason and then "hanged, drawn, and quartered."[54]

Evans and Robinson were punished because they had fraudulently claimed their actions had royal support. The fact that they had attempted to kidnap dozens of women was almost irrelevant. Kidnapping women was illegal, but the Crown had already demonstrated that under the right circumstances forced immigration would be permitted. Consequently, despite the prosecutions of Evans and Robinson, it is very likely that the Virginia Company could have requested and received permission to conscript female immigrants for marriage to the colonists. It is telling that the company never made such a request. Although the company accepted kidnapping as a means of acquiring laborers and servants, they appear to have considered the role of wife too important to be filled by unwilling and likely disreputable women. To achieve their vision of colonial wives, the company sought voluntary immigrants who came from good homes and families. However, the colony had acquired the reputation as "a misery, a death, a hell,"[55] and thus, most women were disinclined to immigrate. To change their minds, the company needed to offer these potential brides significant immigration incentives.

Many incentives were monetary. In addition to free passage, each woman was given a petticoat, a waistcoat, two pairs of stockings, a pair of garters, two smocks, a pair of gloves, a hat and bands, one round band, an apron, two pairs of shoes, a towel, two coifs, one "Croscloath," as well as worsted and yarn for stockings, six pairs of sheets, six canvas beds and bolsters, six rugs and six "course sead bedds" (hammocks).[56] They were also provided with food and shelter until they married.[57] Other benefits were less tangible. The company promised that the women would be married to freemen, not servants, that their husbands would be wealthy,[58] and that married households would be the first to receive servants. In addition, male colonists marrying the Jamestown brides were required to reimburse the company 120 (later 150) pounds of "good leaf tobacco" to cover the cost of the women's passage.[59] This requirement ensured that the potential husbands were wealthy, and it is the reason the women are sometimes referred to as "tobacco wives." This payment also guaranteed that the company would not lose money on the venture. Nevertheless, although the company clearly wished to recoup their outlays and even profit from the bridal program, the women were not sold. They were free to marry whomever they wished, even men too poor to reimburse the company.[60] In a letter to the Virginia governor, the company wrote that they wanted the women married to "honest and sufficient men, whose names will reach to present repayment." At the same time, the company also acknowledged that "if any of them shall unwarily or fondly bestow her self . . . uppon such as shall not be able to give present sattisfaction" they should be permitted to do so, and that chosen husbands should be "compelled to pay" only once they have the ability.[61] Clearly the company wanted reimbursement, but the Jamestown brides were not sold to the highest bidder.

The Jamestown brides were free to marry poor men, yet such unions were unlikely. Seventeenth-century marriages were primarily economic bargains. The subordinate legal status of women meant that pragmatic considerations defined their marital decisions. As historian Amanda Vickery has noted, during this period "the length of a man's rent roll remained the ultimate aphrodisiac."[62] Three hundred years earlier, the seventeenth-century Prior of Sennely-en-Sologne made a similar observation. He complained that his parishioners "get married out of financial interest rather than any other inclination" and that "[m]ost of them, when looking for a bride, only ask how many sheep."[63] In fact, at this time, economic considerations were so important that love could be viewed as an inconvenience. In 1690, Elizabeth Freke attempted to arrange the marriage of her son to the daughter of an earl, and she became greatly annoyed when he fell in love with the girl, because she believed it hurt her bargaining position. According to Freke, the girl's family "found my son so taken with the young lady that they would have made us their servants in being paymasters to the young couple. ... They found my son's inclination so far fixed towards this lady that they resolved to bring me to any terms." Freke nevertheless refused their terms and halted negotiations.[64]

The Jamestown bridal program benefited from the fact that seventeenth-century women frequently based their marital decisions on financial considerations. Most of the Jamestown brides came from modest backgrounds,[65] and their penury would have made marriage difficult. Many of the women would have needed to spend years in service before earning the funds necessary to establish a household.[66] In fact, a number of the brides were already working as servants when they signed up with the company. Marital immigration offered these women an alternative to years of servitude.[67] It also meant they could marry younger.[68] Although the average age of marriage for Englishwomen overall was twenty-six,[69] Jamestown brides averaged just twenty.[70] Whether these benefits outweighed the risks is a difficult question, yet in some instances even the increased risks associated with colonial life could turn out to be beneficial. For example, although the Chesapeake colonies were riddled with malaria, dysentery, and influenza,[71] the morbid upside was that most marriages were short and highly advantageous for surviving widows. In the southern colonies, the average marriage lasted barely fifteen years, and "the chances were only one in three that a marriage would last ten years."[72] If it was the woman who survived, generous property and inheritance laws could leave her significantly better off than her English counterpart.

Seventeenth-century England operated under the system of *feme covert*, or coverture, which means "covered woman." Coverture was the idea that upon marriage, a woman's independent legal identity gets subsumed or "covered" by her husband's.[73] Due to this doctrine, married women in England could not hold property in their own name, alter or dispose of property without their husband's consent (even if such property was their own inheritance), or make wills or appoint executors without their husband's agreement.[74] In the colonies, married women's rights were vastly different. In many of the colonies, particularly those with the greatest scarcity of women, married women were given property rights on par with those of their husbands. For example, in 1619, the members of the Virginia House of Burgesses specifically asked the Virginia Company to set aside parcels of land for both the male colonists and their wives.[75] They explained that "[i]n a newe plantation it is not knowen whether man or woman be the most necessary,"[76] and they wanted to ensure sufficient incentives to lure both types of colonists. A similar request was also made to set aside a parcel of land specifically for the Jamestown brides.[77] The land would have been known as "Maydes Town," but it was never distributed. Shortly after the request was submitted, Indians raided the colony and a substantial percentage of the colonists, including many of the Jamestown brides, were massacred.[78] Life in the Virginia colony was undeniably dangerous, yet the potential rewards, particularly for women, were substantial.

Land grants to female colonists and the fact that skilled female workers earned the same wages as their male counterparts are just a few examples of the greater gender equality in the early colonies.[79] In *Studies in the History of American Law*, historian Richard Morris describes the colonial period as a golden age for female independence when colonial women "were attaining a measure of individuality and independence in excess of that of their English sisters."[80] Morris even suggests that women enjoyed more freedom during the colonial period than they would in later centuries, when Victorian ideas about separate spheres increasingly relegated women to the home. This last claim is contentious,[81] but most historians agree that women in Maryland, Virginia, and South Carolina—the states with the fewest women—had greater access to economic and public roles than their English counterparts.[82]

Some colonial wives became prosperous by obtaining the status of *feme-sole trader*, which gave them the right to sue and be sued, conduct business, enter into contracts, sell real property, and wield the power of attorney.[83] However, the majority of colonial women who became wealthy did so through inheritance. Colonial widows typically inherited more than the one-third life estate required under English dower law.[84] If there were no children, most women inherited the whole estate outright, and even when there were children colonial husbands still tended to give all or a major part of the estate to their widows for life.[85] In contrast, English widows frequently received no more than their dower rights, and even when they did, their control over this additional property was often limited to their period of widowhood or until the children came of age.[86] There were a number of other ways colonial women obtained greater control over their wealth and property than Englishwomen. For example, colonial widows commonly served as executrixes of their late husband's estates,[87] and at least some women used this power to delay paying their husband's other heirs (often their own children) so that they could enjoy a greater portion of their husband's estate for longer.[88] Similarly, colonial widows often were the guardians of their minor children and were placed in control of their inheritance.[89] In England, guardians were almost always men.

Colonial inheritance practices and the high mortality rates left many colonial women quite wealthy.[90] In fact, in 1634, the Maryland legislature found the growing wealth of widows so concerning that they proposed a bill that would have required any "female inheriting land [to] marry (or remarry) within seven years of possession or forfeit her claim." Given the growing power and influence of colonial women, it is not surprising that the bill was defeated.[91] Many wealthy widows had no desire to remarry, but those who did had their choice of husbands.[92] In England, there were approximately nine males for every ten females.[93] In contrast, in Virginia, men outnumbered women six to one.[94] Not surprisingly, this gender disparity greatly influenced the role of women in the southern colonies. A 1666 advertisement for the South Carolina colony promised that "[i]f any Maid or single Woman have a desire to go over, they will think themselves in the Golden Age, when Men paid a Dowry for their Wives; for if they be but civil, and under 50 years of Age, some honest Man or other, will purchase them for their Wives."[95] A 1660s promotional pamphlet seeking female servants for the Maryland colonists also emphasized the benefits of the colony's gender disparity, noting that few women would need to complete their full period of indenture because men wishing to marry them would quickly buy out their tenure.[96] As these ads demonstrate, scarcity made colonial women valuable. At a time when women had few legal rights and were almost entirely dependent on men, colonial immigration increased their economic and social status. The breach of promise case brought against Cicely Jordan forcefully demonstrates this fact and shows the significant power wielded by colonial women, particularly with regard to marriage.[97]

In 1623, Cicely Jordan was living in the Virginia colony when her husband died unexpectedly. A few days after his death, she accepted the marriage proposal of Reverend Greville Pooley. However, in order to avoid the implications of impropriety surrounding an engagement arranged so soon after her husband's death, Jordan asked Pooley to keep their betrothal a secret. Pooley agreed, but then quickly broke his promise and began broadcasting their engagement about the colony.[98] Jordan was incensed, called off the engagement, and accepted the proposal of another suitor.[99] The jilted Pooley then sued Jordan for breach of promise.[100]

The evidence against Jordan was substantial. Pooley claimed that he and Jordan had entered into a marriage contract by using "such words or speech tending to a contract of marriage at one time as might entangle or breed scruples in their consciences."[101] He then produced a witness, Captain Madison, who testified that he heard Jordan agree to marry Pooley and heard Pooley speak the words of the marriage contract for himself and for Jordan.[102] In addition, two other witnesses also testified that they had heard Jordan state that Pooley "might have fared better had he not revealed [the engagement]."[103] Nevertheless, despite this persuasive evidence, the Virginia Council, the governing body that heard the case,[104] refused to issue a decision.[105] The council stated that it could not determine "so nice a difference,"[106] and referred the case to the Virginia Company in London.[107] Then, like the council, the company also declined to issue an official decision. Eventually, the case was delayed so long that Pooley was forced to withdraw his suit, and because there was no verdict in his favor, he was ordered to post a five-hundred-pound bond ensuring that he would never have any claim to Jordan or her property.[108]

Breach of promise cases arise when one party breaks off an engagement and the jilted party believes that he or she has been unfairly treated and harmed by the loss of the intended marriage.[109] In seventeenth-century England, it was rare for men to initiate these suits. Women filed the majority of them because they were typically the ones most injured by a failed engagement.[110] Nevertheless, in the Virginia colony, this situation was reversed. Pooley initiated the breach of promise suit because he was harmed by the lack of marriage; Jordan easily found another fiancé.

Pooley's evidence should have been more than enough to rule against Jordan. Under English law, it was well established that a present declaration of a future intent to be married was enough to form a binding contract.[111] It was also well established that jilted men could be entitled to significant damages.[112] For example, in the 1698 English case *Harrison v. Cage & Wife*,[113] the male plaintiff, Harrison, was awarded four hundred pounds after his fiancée had a change of heart. On appeal, the former fiancée argued that a man is not advanced by marriage and thus the damages were excessive. The court rejected this argument and reaffirmed long-standing precedent that men could be harmed by failed engagements.[114] In female-scarce Virginia, the harm of a broken engagement was undeniable and Pooley should have easily won his suit. Nevertheless, neither the Virginia Council nor the Virginia Company was willing to rule against Jordan. Instead, their inaction represented a tacit recognition of women's power in the colonial marriage market.[115]

After the Pooley case, the council passed a law expressing disapproval of Jordan's actions and indicating a strong desire to deter subsequent women from breaking their engagements.[116] The new law stated,

Whereas, to the great contempt of the majesty of God and ill example to others, certain women within this colony have, . . . contracted them[selves] to two several men at one time, whereby much trouble doth grow between parties, and the Governor and Council of State much disquieted. To prevent the like offense to others hereafter, it is by the Governor and Council ordered in Court that every minister give notice in his church, to his parishioners, that what man or woman soever shall use any words or speech tending to the contract of marriage, though not right and legal, yet so may entangle and breed struggle in their consciences, shall for the third offense undergo either corporal punishment, or other punishment by fine or otherwise according to the guilt of the persons so offending.[117]

Although the law was intended to serve as a stern rebuke to Jordan and women like her, its actual impact was minimal. The penalties did not apply until the "third offense," and even then the law stated only that the offender would "perhaps" be subject to corporal or other punishment.[118] The toothlessness of the law was demonstrated when, shortly after the Jordan case, another colonial woman, Eleanor Spragg, contracted herself to two men at one time,[119] and was simply forced to issue a single, public apology.[120] Following Spragg's offense, the law was revised again. The new version decreed that any person who entered a contract "of marriage to several persons, shall be whipped or fined according to the quality of the persons offending."[121] This change also had little practical effect.

In one telling example, Virginia colonist William Roscoe persuaded his fiancée Sarah Harrison to sign a written contract promising to marry him. Then, shortly thereafter, Harrison jilted Roscoe and married the Reverend James Blair. Although there was undeniable proof of an engagement, Harrison received no punishment.[122] Regardless of the actual written laws, colonial women like Harrison were often able to create their own marital rules. In fact, not only did Harrison jilt Roscoe without consequence, she was permitted to amend the traditional wedding vows during her 1687 wedding. According to witnesses, when the clergyman marrying them asked for her promise to obey, Harrison answered, "No obey." When the question was repeated, she replied "No obey" again. After the third refusal, the reverend acquiesced to her demands and performed the ceremony with no mention of the promise to obey.[123]

As the above examples demonstrate, colonial women had significantly greater power and control over their marital choices than did women in England. They lived in a community where they were valued and given access to wealth and power,[124] and by immigrating to the colonies, the Jamestown brides could take advantage of these benefits. Nevertheless, these women are often remembered as victims. In her 2008 book, *From Eve to Dawn*, feminist writer Marilyn French provides the following description of the Jamestown brides' arrival: "[T]he government decided to shanghai a hundred or so 'young and uncorrupt' girls, force them aboard a ship, and sell them as wives to Virginia men for the cost of their passage. Ninety girls were impressed in 1620, fifty more in 1621–22; all were soon married, but men clamored for more, insisting they needed women to wash their clothes and nurse them. Through terrorism and rape, the sex ratio became three men to every woman."[125] By describing the Jamestown brides as victims, French refuses to acknowledge the possibility that the women came willingly or that becoming a mail-order bride could be a rational or even wise decision.[126] Instead, she simply describes the Jamestown marriages as a form of prostitution and/or human trafficking.[127] French's inaccurate description confuses instances in which Englishwomen were kidnapped with the willing immigration of the Jamestown brides. However, despite this serious mistake, French is correct that marital immigration can become exploitative when governments fail to protect mail-order brides. A comparison between the experiences of two other sets of women, the French filles du roi and the Louisiana corrections girls, starkly highlights this fact. It also demonstrates that long after Jamestown, colonial governments continued to use mail-order marriage to help displace Indian people and acquire Indian lands.

2

The Filles du Roi

Between 1663 and 1673, nearly eight hundred Frenchwomen immigrated to New France as brides for the male colonists.[1] Known as the filles du roi, or "king's daughters," these women were recruited to help solve the colony's population problem.[2] The colony had spent years hoping to increase immigration, but most French perceived Canada as remote and dangerous and had no interest in immigrating.[3] Moreover, reports from the colony seemed to justify these fears. In 1627 the colony's governor described the colonists as living in constant terror of Indian attacks: "They are everywhere. They will stay hidden behind a stump for ten days, existing on nothing but a handful of corn, waiting to kill a man, or a woman. ... [T]he Iroquois are not content to burn the houses, they also burn the prisoners they take, and give them death only after torturing them continually in the most cruel manner they can devise."[4] Not surprisingly, few Frenchmen, let alone Frenchwomen, wanted to risk their lives in a poorly defended settlement surrounded by a dangerous enemy.[5] Consequently, by the mid-seventeenth century, more than half a century after the founding of Quebec, New France remained almost entirely male and was populated so sparsely that it resembled more an outpost than a colony.[6] Moreover, as the neighboring American colonies began to flourish, the slow growth in New France became particularly concerning.[7]

The problems inhibiting growth in New France resembled those the Virginia colony had experienced a generation earlier. A lack of marriageable women led most French colonists to view their time in the colony as temporary,[8] and nearly three-quarters returned to France within a few years.[9] This population loss was further compounded by the fact that many of the remaining colonists married native women and abandoned the colony to live with their wives' tribes.[10]

By the time the filles du roi arrived, desertion to the Indian tribes had become a significant problem. However, initially intermarriage had been encouraged as part of the French plan to assimilate the indigenous people. New France was founded with the expectation that significant numbers of Canadian Indians would convert to Christianity and become French citizens. The 1627 New France charter stated that "savages who will be led to the faith and to profess it will be considered natural Frenchmen, and ... will be able to come and live in France when they wish to, and there acquire property, with rights of inheritance and bequest, just as if they had been born Frenchmen, without being required to make any declaration or to become naturalized."[11] Prevailing ideology taught that Indian people were both culturally and religiously deficient, and colonial leaders presumed they would be eager to become French citizens. Intermarriage was therefore encouraged to increase the assimilation of native women.[12] In fact, the French government was so confident that large numbers of Indian women would convert to Christianity and become French that they even provided dowries for these prospective brides.[13] Nevertheless, assimilation proved much more difficult than anticipated, and the fund was never used.[14] According to Marie de l'Incarnation, the Ursuline Mother Superior charged with converting Indian women, "It [was] a very difficult thing, not to say impossible to Frenchify or civilize [Indian girls]. We have more experience in this than anyone else, and we have observed that out of a hundred who have passed through our hands we have scarcely civilized one."[15] French conversion efforts proved to be a failure, but even as missionaries struggled to convert natives, many colonists found the draw of Indian culture irresistible. Men abandoning the colony to live with their Indian wives eventually became so common that the term *ensauvagement* (meaning to become savage) was coined to describe the phenomenon.[16]

Deserting male colonists were drawn to the Indian way of life and the allure of Indian women. At the same time, many Indian women were equally eager to marry Frenchmen. Indian women married to colonists frequently served as intermediaries between the tribe and colony, and this enabled them to boost their prestige and authority within the tribe.[17] Intermarriage could also help women avoid traditional customs they might dislike such as wife swapping or sororal polygyny, the practice among certain tribes of a man marrying two or more sisters.[18] Most important, because women greatly outnumbered men in many tribes, intermarriage enabled those who would have otherwise remained single (and of low status) to become wives and mothers.[19]

Intermarriage benefited both parties, so it is not surprising that hundreds of male colonists and Indian women married. By 1679, Intendant Jacques Duchesneau estimated that between five and six hundred male colonists had deserted for Indian villages. One year later, this figure was estimated at eight hundred. By comparison, the entire population of New France at this time was fewer than ten thousand individuals.[20] The rate of intermarriage in New France was so high that one Canadian historian has even suggested that any Canadian "whose family arrived before the 1760s is probably part Aboriginal."[21]

Deserting colonists hampered the colony's growth, but even more worrisome to the colonial government was the betrayal this abandonment represented. Men choosing the Indian way of life were seen as traitors to the colonial enterprise. In some cases, this treason was literal. In 1556, a French-Indian relationship had almost destroyed the French colony in Brazil. According to New France chronicler Marc Lescarbot, a French interpreter in the Brazil colony had "married a Savage woman, [and led] the most filthy and Epicurean manner of life." Then, "in order to live after [his] desires," he conspired "to destroy the colony" by murdering its leaders.[22] In the end, it was only a co-conspirator's last minute change of heart that averted the murders.[23]

Similarly, in the seventeenth century, the English prevented Frenchmen from aiding the New France colony by exploiting the loyalty conflicts created by intermarriage. Many French colonists had married Iroquois women and were living with the Iroquois tribe in an area located along the border between the French and English colonies. However, the Iroquois and the English were military allies, and the English convinced the tribe's full-blooded members to forbid intermarried Frenchmen and their mixed-race children from interacting with or aiding the French colony. Specifically, English Colonel Thomas Dongan warned the Iroquois to closely monitor the Frenchmen and "take yt Care yt they goe not to Canida but that they shall live Close by your Castles or in yr Castles."[24] Intermarriage thus forced these men to choose between their country and their tribe.

Despite these examples, most intermarried Frenchmen were never driven to openly betray New France. Still, simply by abandoning the settlement, they committed an intolerable act of disloyalty. Their desertions were correctly understood as a rejection of both French civilization and Christianity, and as such they threatened to undermine the justification for the entire colonial enterprise. Like most colonizing powers, France rationalized colonization as a religious obligation. Citing Christ's command to "go throughout the world and preach the gospel to all creatures," the French began settling in North America and intermarriage was initially encouraged as a means "to expel idolatry, and to polish the barbarous ways of the Gentiles."[25] When it became clear that white/Indian relationships had the opposite effect, support for these marriages disappeared. In fact, Jesuit missionaries were some of the earliest and most vocal opponents of intermarriage.

In 1637, a group of Jesuit missionaries and Huron Indians met to discuss intermarriage between the male colonists and Huron women. The Hurons were highly enthusiastic about these unions and informed the Jesuits that the intermarried "French traders were proving to be quite good Hurons." When the Jesuits heard this, they were appalled. For them, the purpose of intermarriage was "to make [the Indians] like us, to give them the knowledge of the true God."[26] After this meeting, religious support for intermarriage disappeared.[27] Similarly, as colonial leaders began realizing that intermarriage was aiding the *ensauvagement* of the French colonists rather than the assimilation of the Indians, they also abandoned intermarriage efforts and began concentrating on ways to increase the immigration of single Frenchwomen.[28] The result was the filles du roi program.[29]

This program was premised on the belief that despite the high rates of intermarriage, most colonial men preferred the physical and cultural attributes of European women. Contemporary descriptions of Indian women were highly unflattering. Many accounts state that the animal grease they used to coat their hair and bodies, a combination of bear fat and skunk oil,[30] made them smell revolting. As one Jesuit priest noted, it made the Iroquois "smell to us like carrion."[31] Other descriptions disparaged the women's physical appearance. One particularly uncomplimentary description was provided by colonist Samuel Hearne with regard to Chipewyan women, whom he described "as destitute of real beauty as any nation I ever saw," adding that some were the "perfect antidotes to love and gallantry."[32] Given such descriptions, it is easy to see why the colonial leadership was confident they could reduce desertions by increasing the immigration of Frenchwomen to the colony. This was also the immigration plan favored by the king.

Colonial leaders supported the filles du roi plan, but they had initially hoped for a general increase in state-sponsored immigration. In 1666, three years after the first brides arrived, colonial leaders asked the king to send more immigrants of all kinds. He refused. Jean-Baptiste Colbert, the king's minister of finance, explained that "[i]t would not be prudent [for the king] to depopulate his Kingdom as would be necessary in order to populate Canada." Instead, Colbert assured the leaders that "the Country will become populated gradually, and, with the passing of a reasonable amount of time, will become quite considerable."[33] The French government recognized the colony's population difficulties but was not interested in sending large numbers of immigrants. Instead, it sought to increase the population of New France almost entirely through the "natural" means of childbirth, and this was the role of the filles du roi.

Given the importance of the filles du roi, it is not surprising that the French government was involved in nearly every aspect of their

Jean Talon, Bishop François de Laval, and several settlers welcome the king's daughters upon their arrival. Painting by Eleanor Fortescue-Brickdale. Wikimedia Commons.

journey.[34] In France, governmental authorities managed the recruitment and immigration of the women, and the king paid for their transport to the colony.[35] Upon arrival, the intendant greeted and settled the women, and when they married, the French government provided them with a dowry.[36] In addition, outlays for dowries and the program in general were substantial. Each bride received at least 50 livres,[37] many received 100, and at least two women were given 600.[38] Adding this sum to the cost of recruitment and transportation, historian Guillaume Aubert has estimated that the government spent between "12,570 livres and possibly more than 33,000 livres" on each filles du roi.[39] Altogether, he estimated the cost of recruitment and transportation between 1664 and 1669 to have been more than 410,000 livres.[40] Adjusted to today's rates, the "real price" of the project was about $6.4 million, but the "economic cost" of the project, measured as the project's relative share as a percentage of the output of the economy or GDP, was over $1 billion![41]

The purpose of the filles du roi program was to prevent desertions and increase the population of New France. Therefore, it is not surprising that significant funds were expended and that the women were selected with great care. The most important criteria for a filles du roi were youth (the majority were between the ages of twelve and twenty-five) and health.[42] In his first letter delineating the selection criteria for the filles du roi, Intendant Talon wrote that the women should be of "ages suitable for procreation, and most of all that they be very healthy."[43] After easily recruiting the first group of women for the program, Talon's requirements increased. Attractiveness was added to the list, and experience performing household chores was also requested.[44] In a letter to Colbert, Talon wrote, "All the king's daughters sent to New France last year are married, and almost all are pregnant or have had children, a testament to the fertility of this country. I strongly recommend that those who are destined for this country [next year] be in no way unattractive or have anything repugnant in their appearance, that they be healthy and strong, for the work of the country, or at least have some skill in household chores."[45]

Most of Talon's new requests were also easily met. Once again, the arriving brides were healthy and fertile.[46] In fact, studies indicate that this group of women, already picked for their perceived fertility, actually became more fertile once they settled in Canada.[47] One of the women, nineteen-year-old Catherine Paulo, married a farmer named Etienne Campeau and gave birth to fifteen children.[48] Another bride, twenty-nine-year-old Mathurine Thibault, married a recent widower and toolmaker and had six children.[49] However, more telling than the birthrate of any one woman is the fact that genetic studies of the modern French Canadian population indicate that the filles du roi and their husbands were responsible for two-thirds of the genetic makeup of over six million people.[50] Colbert's prediction proved prescient. Through marriage and childbirth these few hundred women became the foremothers of millions of French Canadians.[51]

The arrival of the French girls at Quebec. Watercolor by Charles William Jeffery. Wikimedia Commons.

Talon's request for pretty women also seems to have been fulfilled. According to legend, the renowned beauty of Quebec women derives from the fact that the boats carrying the king's daughters arrived in Quebec first. The Quebec men, who had the first chance to woo and marry the arriving women, chose the prettiest, whose exceptional beauty was then passed down to their descendants.[52] This story may be somewhat apocryphal (and women in Trois-Rivières and Montreal, both further up the river, undoubtedly object), but it is significant because the fact that the filles du roi were considered pretty indicates that their decision to immigrate was not an act of desperation. Under the harsh conditions of seventeenth-century France, sick or destitute women were rarely renowned for their beauty. These pretty women decided to immigrate because they viewed marital immigration as an opportunity rather than a last resort. This idea is also supported by the fact that Talon's third request, that the women come from the "country," was not achieved.

Talon correctly believed that women raised in the country would be better prepared for the harsh conditions of frontier life.[53] However, the opportunities offered by marital immigration were more attractive to city women.[54] Cities are more likely to have people looking to change their situation, and therefore, despite Talon's request for country girls, it is not surprising that the majority of the filles du roi came from urban locales.[55] Many of these women had lost their fathers or came from large families[56] and lacked the economic resources to secure good marriages.[57] Marital immigration alleviated this problem, and the French government's financial help actually put them in a privileged position compared to the average immigrant who arrived without any government assistance.[58] In addition, although most of the filles du roi came from modest backgrounds, a few were members of wealthy families, including some noblewomen. Despite their differences, the women all shared the belief that their best marital prospects lay in the New World.

That many of the filles du roi came from lower-class backgrounds was expected. However, even the program organizers were shocked by the number of noblewomen interested in immigrating. In a 1667 letter, Talon describes the recently arrived filles du roi: "They send us eighty-four girls from Dieppe and twenty-five from Rochelle; among them are fifteen or twenty of pretty good birth; several of them are really *demoiselles*, and tolerably well brought up."[59] A few years later, the number of noblewomen increased further and actually surpassed the quantity of available husbands. In 1669, Talon had asked Colbert to send three or four aristocratic girls for some of the single officers, and Colbert responded by sending fifteen. An annoyed Talon then testily informed Colbert that "[i]t is not expedient to send more *demoiselles*. I have had this year fifteen of them, instead of the four I asked for."[60]

The filles du roi program clearly appealed to both lower- and upper-class women, and even some married women took advantage of this opportunity. In Talon's letter to Colbert requesting young, pretty, and skilled women, he also asked for proof of marriageability, writing that it would be "good to have [the filles du roi] accompanied by a certificate from their Pastor or a local judge who can vouch for their being free and marriageable."[61] Some of the first group had husbands back in France, and Talon's request refers to the scandal that occurred when their marital status was revealed.[62] Talon had been greatly dismayed by this deception, but it actually reflects favorably on the program. At a time when divorce was unattainable and women had little access to money or property, marital immigration gave some the opportunity to leave unhappy marriages and begin again.[63]

These examples demonstrate that a wide range of women hoped to benefit from mail-order marriage. At the same time, most recognized that such marriages were risky. Marital immigration involved moving to a foreign land and marrying a stranger, and French property law, which deprived married women of their separate property, exacerbated these risks. Under the French legal system known as the Coutume de Paris, which was adopted by New France, "all of a married couple's assets, earnings, and debt were held jointly" but solely controlled by the husband.[64] The husband also had the exclusive right to dispose of any property his wife brought into the marriage. Consequently, although the filles du roi received dowries for marrying, they risked losing these funds, as well as any other property they brought with them, once they actually married.[65] In order to avoid this problem,[66] more than 82 percent of the women signed marital contracts ensuring they retained at least some of their separate property after marriage.[67]

Consider the contract between fille du roi Marie Grandin and colonist Jean Beaudet. This agreement guaranteed that Grandin would retain her dowry from the king and half of her other premarital property:

> The future husband [spouse] gives to his future wife [spouse] the sum of three hundred livres tournois to be taken first [before any debts of the marital community are paid] from their assets available at his death. With this in mind he mortgages [or guarantees] his assets [hypothèque

ses biens]. In addition, he takes [the future wife] as his spouse with all of her rights and all of the assets she presently possesses and those which she might obtain in the future through inheritance or otherwise. He also recognizes that his future spouse possesses three hundred livres tournois, which she adds to their legal possessions [*leurs avoirs*]. Of this sum, one hundred and fifty livres will belong to them in common and one hundred and fifty livres will always be the property of the future bride and of those who inherit from her, as will the fifty livres that the King gave to her to incite her to get married.[68]

The protections in the Grandin/Beaudet contract were fairly typical of filles du roi contracts. However, some arrangements were considerably more favorable to the potential bride. For example, before fille du roi Isabelle Hubert married colonist Louis Bolduc, she had him sign a contract containing a provision guaranteeing her five hundred livres worth of property in the event of separation.[69]

Hubert's contract provided significant protection against the uncertainties of marriage, but such an agreement would have been almost unheard of in France. According to Canadian economist Gillian Hamilton, in communities where potential brides and grooms share similar social and economic backgrounds, women are unlikely to receive contract terms more favorable than already existing property laws.[70] On the other hand, Hamilton notes that in communities where women were both scarce and valued, contracts protecting women's property rights are standard. According to Hamilton, "contracts [a]re anticipated in cases where women [a]re [considered] exceptional," which she defines as having "high outside value, especially if high relative to their husbands."[71] The fact that so many filles du roi signed marital contracts indicates that these women were highly valued and that because of their high value, they were able to protect themselves from some of the uncertainties inherent in marrying a stranger.

The filles du roi traveled halfway across the world to marry strangers. Nevertheless, by the time these couples said their vows, most of them were no longer strangers. When the filles du roi agreed to immigrate, they were promised the right to choose their partner and the right to refuse any suitor.[72] Therefore, although the male colonists were eager to marry, the women often took their time. In fact, they waited an average of five months before marrying.[73] Marie de l'Incarnation, the Ursuline nun who supervised many of the filles du roi courtships, portrayed the contrast between the eager male colonists and the more cautious women, writing that the men were so excited to woo the arriving women that "[n]o sooner ... have the vessels arrived than the young men go to get wives."[74] In contrast, she described the women as much more restrained. L'Incarnation noted approvingly that the women's first concern was whether the men had somewhere to live because they understood that "men who were not established suffered a great deal before they could lead a comfortable life."[75]

L'Incarnation's description shows that the filles du roi's marital decisions were based on practical concerns. Nevertheless, because the filles du roi had the opportunity to get to know their potential husbands, they actually had a greater chance of marrying for love than did most seventeenth-century Frenchwomen. In France, couples had limited opportunities to spend time together before a marriage. There were few public occasions to meet outside of church, and social events were infrequent. In fact, the first social "ball" was not even held until 1667.[76] In contrast, the filles du roi had so much time to get to know their potential spouse that many actually changed their minds. Among these women broken engagements were common, and some went through multiple fiancés before choosing a husband. For example, one woman, Catherine Gateau, first signed a marriage contract with Abraham Albert in October 1671. One month later she annulled her contract with Albert and signed one with Vivien Jean. She then annulled that one as well. However, two weeks later she changed her mind again, revalidated the marital contract with Jean, and finally married him. Another fille du roi, Catherine Le Roux, signed and then annulled one marital contract so that she could enter into a second contract with her former fiancé's brother. Overall, at least 10 percent of the filles du roi signed a marriage contract with a man other than their eventual spouse.[77]

The king had promised the filles du roi that they would not be forced into marriage. This provided them with the time and opportunity to change their minds. It also enabled some to refuse marriage altogether. Most filles du roi eventually married, but approximately 4 percent chose to remain single, and this is particularly significant given the fact that this was a right colonial men did not enjoy.[78] In 1668, Colbert wrote to Talon complaining about a group of men who had refused to marry and suggesting that "[t]hose [men] who may seem to have absolutely renounced marriage should be made to bear additional burdens, and be excluded from all honors; it would be well even to add some marks of infamy."[79] Talon agreed with Colbert and quickly issued an order stating that male colonists who did not marry after the arrival of the bride ships were forbidden from hunting, trading, or even entering the woods.[80] When men like Montreal bachelor Francois Lenoir violated this edict, they were presented with a choice. In Lenoir's case he was told to either marry after the next bride ships arrived or surrender one hundred fifty livres to the church of Montreal or the hospital.[81] Not surprisingly, Lenoir was married within the year.[82] However, Lenoir was not the only reluctant groom. Therefore, in addition to punishing single colonists, colonial leaders also began providing monetary incentives to encourage them to marry.

Initially, these marriage bonuses were offered only to specific men whom the colony hoped to retain. For example, between 1665 and 1668, the colony spent six thousand livres to encourage "four captains, three lieutenants, five ensigns, and a few minor officers to settle and marry."[83] In one case, Captain de la Mothe received sixteen hundred livres for marrying and settling in New France.[84] Then, in 1668, the French government began considering a more general policy of marital encouragement. In a letter to Talon, Colbert wrote, "I pray you ... to commend it to the consideration of the whole people, that their prosperity, their subsistence, and all that is dear to them, depend on a general resolution, never to be departed from, to marry youths at eighteen or nineteen years and girls at fourteen or fifteen; since abundance can never come to them except through the abundance of men."[85] Two years later, the king decreed that "all males who marry before the age of twenty, and all females before the age of sixteen, will receive twenty livres on their wedding day to be known as the 'King's gift.'"[86] The king also instituted rewards to encourage large families. Specifically, Canadians with ten living children were entitled to a pension of three hundred livres annually, those with twelve living children four hundred.[87]

The arrival of the filles du roi made these monetary marriage incentives possible, but this was not the only way the French government encouraged marriage. Long-standing rules and practices that could hinder marriage were ignored or relaxed during this period. For example, women who immigrated as indentured servants were often permitted to break their contracts in order to marry.[88] Similarly, widows were not punished for speedy remarriages. In fact, New France marriage records show that "four out of ten" widows remarried before the prescribed nine months,[89] and at least one remarried before her first husband was even buried.[90] In addition, it was common for widows to have sexual relations before remarrying, and many of these widows were visibly pregnant at their weddings.[91]

Even prostitution could be forgiven if the woman subsequently decided to marry and start a family. The infamous fille du roi Catherine Guichelin spent years as a prostitute and had multiple children out of wedlock. In France a woman like Guichelin would have been considered unmarriageable and likely imprisoned, but in New France she was simply forced to leave Quebec City.[92] Moreover, when she eventually tired of prostitution, she had little trouble finding a husband or being accepted as a respectable member of colonial society.

In France, widows who remarried too quickly or had sex during the mourning period would have risked *chivaree*, the French custom of humiliating and often physically harming or even killing couples who failed to follow approved social mores.[93] However, in the colony, female-directed punishments were rare. In fact, as misogyny became increasingly deadly in parts of Europe, New France stood out as a refuge for many persecuted women.[94]

In the seventeenth century, Europe was undergoing sweeping religious transformations, and many French Catholic women were drawn to the radical ideas of the Counter-Reformation and the possibility of a more active role in religious life.[95] Some of these women began establishing organizations devoted to practicing the contemplative life. Others started creating new lay associations to encourage female piety and charity. However, these attempts to gain religious autonomy resulted in a swift and deadly backlash. Many male religious authorities accused these women of demonic possession, and witch burnings and exorcisms became widespread. Religious women were also cloistered to limit their influence. Nevertheless, within this fearsome environment, New France became a sanctuary. In New France, religious women were welcomed, witch trials and exorcisms were nonexistent, cloistering was far less rigid and soon discarded,[96] and women's right to catechize, questioned in France until the late seventeenth century, was taken for granted as soon as missionary women appeared in the colony.[97] Moreover, although most of these religious women would never marry, the fact that they were eager to immigrate, were treated with respect, and were given power and influence undoubtedly influenced nonreligious women's perception of the colony.[98]

New France provided a female-friendly environment for women seeking greater marital control and personal independence. Unfortunately, this history was quickly forgotten, and by the early eighteenth century, descriptions of the filles du roi as loose women and sexual commodities began to proliferate.[99] In 1703, thirty years after the arrival of the last bride ships, the French writer La Hontan, who never saw the filles du roi, provided a description of their arrival:

> [S]hips were sent out freighted with girls of indifferent virtue, under the direction of a few pious old duennas, who divided them into three

classes. These vestals, were, so to speak, piled one on the other in three different halls, where the bridegrooms chose their brides as a butcher chooses his sheep out of the midst of the flock. There was wherewith to content the most fantastical in these three harems; for here were to be seen the tall and the short, the blond and the brown, the plump and the lean; everybody, in short, found a shoe to fit him.[100]

La Hontan's description is inaccurate. Great care was taken to ensure both the virtue of the filles du roi and their willingness to immigrate. A 1670 letter from Colbert to France's archbishop of Rouen, clearly states that the girls were to come voluntarily. He specifically directs the archbishop to seek "[i]n the parishes about Rouen … fifty or sixty girls [who] might be found who would be very glad to go to Canada and be married. I beg you to employ your credit and authority with the curés of thirty or forty of these parishes to try to find in each of them one or two girls disposed to go voluntarily for the sake of settlement in life."[101] Court records of the period also demonstrate that the filles du roi were neither prostitutes nor criminals. Out of more than seven hundred women, only five (a number that includes Catherine Guichelin) faced accusations of adultery, prostitution, or debauchery.[102]

La Hontan may have had little interest in promoting the true story of the filles du roi. In fact, he is well known for his fabulous fabrications. In his memoir chronicling his time in North America, La Hontan recounts his "discovery" of a river stretching from the Mississippi to the Pacific and describes traveling the crocodile-filled Ohio rivers. He also details his encounters with a tribe of bearded Indians living on islands in the Great Lakes who, according to La Hontan, rowed two hundred oared canoes, lived in buildings three stories tall, and followed a king who lived in a palace where he was attended to by hundreds of servants.[103] Given his history of embellishment, it is more than likely that La Hontan intentionally sensationalized the story of the filles du roi's arrival.

It is also possible that he confused these women with the filles de joie, Frenchwomen taken from Paris's overcrowded prisons and sent to a number of the French colonies, particularly the French islands of the Caribbean.[104] Many of these women were contemporaries of the filles du roi.[105] Confusing mail-order brides with prostitutes and other trafficked women has a long history, and even today a quick Google search reveals numerous sources that still refer to the filles du roi as prostitutes.[106] At the same time, there is a monumental difference between mail-order brides like the filles du roi and the prostitutes and other criminals who were routinely forced to immigrate to the American colonies against their will. The filles du roi immigrated voluntarily and were enticed and protected, and this is what made the program successful for both the women and the colony. In contrast, colonies that compelled female immigration experienced vastly different outcomes. An examination of female immigration to the Louisiana colony starkly demonstrates the dissimilarity between mail-order brides like the filles du roi and trafficked women like the Louisiana "corrections girls." This scrutiny also shows why mail-order marriage and female trafficking are so often perceived as interchangeable.

3

Corrections Girls and Casket Girls

The female immigration program in Louisiana was initially similar to those of the other early American colonies.[1] Like Virginia and New France, Louisiana had problems attracting colonists and suffered a severe gender imbalance. Louisiana first attempted to address this problem by encouraging intermarriage. However, as time went on and Frenchwomen were increasingly unwilling to move to the dangerous and disease-ridden colony, Louisiana turned to a policy of forced immigration. The conscription of female immigrants was disastrous for Louisiana, starkly highlighting the extreme difference between mail-order brides, women such as the filles du roi and the Jamestown wives who were protected and valued, and trafficked women.

The Louisiana colony, like New France a half century earlier, had first attempted to cope with the lack of female immigrants by encouraging intermarriage between male colonists and native women. In 1699, Pierre Le Moyne, Sieur d'Iberville, the founder of the Louisiana colony, requested and received permission from King Louis XIV "to allow the French who will settle in this country to marry Indian girls."[2] D'Iberville and the other early leaders of Louisiana believed intermarriage would help assimilate the local Indian tribes and stabilize the colony. However, it quickly became clear that these marriages were actually producing an opposite effect.[3] According to Commissary Jean-Baptiste du Bois Duclos, "successful" intermarriages occurred "not because [the wives] had become Frenchified, if one may use that term, but ... because those who have married them have themselves become almost Indian, residing among them and living in their manner, so that these Indian women have changed nothing or at least very little in their manner of living."[4] Colonial leaders began forbidding re-

Pierre LeMoyne d'Iberville. Wikimedia Commons.

lationships with Indian women, but such efforts proved mostly inef-
fective. With few Frenchwomen available, large numbers of colonial
men continued deserting in order to pursue relationships with native
women.[5]

One sympathetic Louisiana officer explained these desertions by
stating, "The sauvagesses are easy, the climate stimulating, and the
young men, for the most part Canadians, . . . are said to be very vigorous."[6] Another contemporary observer noted, "[T]he hunters and
backwoodsmen who are of strong and vigorous age and temperament
and who like the sex, not finding any who can hold them, are wanderers
among the Indian nations and satisfy their passions with the daughters of these Indians."[7] The effect of such desertions was staggering. By
1706, there were more than 110 desertions,[8] and the remaining colonists

numbered fewer than 200 individuals.[9] This tiny population could not care for itself and relied on help from neighboring Indian tribes, producing even more desertions.

During the winter months, many colonists, including entire garrisons, were forced to live among the Indian tribes in order to avoid starvation. Unsurprisingly, a fair number of these colonists developed close relationships with Indian women. In his memoir, colonist Andre Pénicaut described wintering in a local Indian village in 1706. He and his fellow colonists were warmly embraced by the entire tribe: "the men as well as the women and girls, all [were] delighted to see us come to stay with them." Pénicaut was housed with the chief's family and noted that he "received every possible favor," including the attentions of the chief's daughters. According to Pénicaut the "two daughters . . . were the most beautiful of all the savage girls in the district. The older one was twenty; she was called Oulchogonime, which in their language means the good daughter. The second was only eighteen, but was much taller than her older sister. She was named Ouilchil, which means the pretty spinner."[10] Close proximity led Pénicaut, as well as many other colonists, to develop romantic feelings for these beautiful women. In Pénicaut's account of that winter he refers to a kiss between the older daughter and a fellow colonist, stating, "I was not so sorry about this as I would have been if it had been the younger daughter kissing him." In the spring, Pénicaut and his fellow colonists were recalled to the colony, all of them "quite melancholy." According to Pénicaut, the only thing that "consoled [the men] for the loss of the favors of the girls" was the fact that they returned to the colony just as a new shipment of French wine arrived. Nevertheless, wine was insufficient to entice all the colonists back to Louisiana. Even after the recall, a significant number of colonists remained with their Indian hosts. Governor Bienville, who had assumed leadership after d'Iberville's death, vowed he would bring back all "the Frenchmen who are scattered among the Indians" and forbid them "to live there as libertines under the pretext that they have wives among them."[11] However, there was little Bienville could actually do to force the men back to the colony, and this became increasingly problematic as the surrounding English population continued to grow.[12]

Desertions to the Indian villages severely hampered the colony's growth and made it militarily vulnerable, but population concerns were not the only reason colonial leaders objected to white/Indian relationships. As it became increasingly clear that few Indian wives would assimilate and join the colony, racial fears started to infiltrate the discussion of interracial marriage. Opponents of intermarriage began arguing that Indian assimilation was impossible because the vices of Indian people were genetic and unchangeable. According to this view, intermarriage was dangerous and must be prevented because it mixed "good" blood with "bad" and degraded the former. Moreover, since this "bad blood" was considered more potent, the children of these mixed marriages would also be unsuitable additions to the colony.[13] Commissaire Duclos epitomized these racist concerns when he declared that interracial relationships must be prevented because of "the adulteration that such marriages will cause to the whiteness and purity of the children."[14] He then warned that without an influx of white women, "the colony [risked becoming] a colony of *mulastres* [people of mixed race]."[15]

Duclos recognized that colonial officials lacked the power to actually prevent white/Indian intermarriages, but he hoped that by increasing the number of Frenchwomen in the colony, the incidence of intermarriage could be drastically reduced. Other colonial leaders shared these beliefs. As a result, Louisiana's mail-order marriage program, initially intended to complement and even aid interracial marriages, was soon seen as the best means of preventing these marriages. Whiteness eventually became the most important marriage criterion, and as a result colonial leaders were increasingly willing to overlook almost everything else in their quest to increase the number of white women in the colony.

Initially, Louisiana's bridal recruitment was similar to that of New France. The Louisiana colony was established in 1699, and shortly thereafter d'Iberville made his first request for brides. In a letter to the French government, d'Iberville wrote, "If you want to make something of this country, it is absolutely necessary to send this year some families and a few girls ... who will be married off shortly after their arrival." D'Iberville repeated this request every year until 1704,[16] when King Louis XIV finally approved the plan, agreeing that it was not beneficial for his colonists to be alone.[17] The first brides sent to Louisiana resembled those who had preceded them in the colonies of Jamestown and New France. The women were chosen for their virtue and piety and with the hope that they would have many children and help increase the colonial population.[18] In a letter regarding the initial group of brides, Louis Phélypeaux de Pontchartrain, the chancellor of France, informed Bienville of the women's departure and of their good character. His letter also indicates that the immigration of French mail-order brides was initially intended to help assimilate Indian women and make them more suitable for intermarriage. He wrote,

His majesty sends by that ship [*Le Pelican*][19] 20 girls to be married to the Canadians and others who have begun habitations at Mobile in order that this colony can firmly establish itself. Each of these girls was raised in virtue and piety and knows how to work, which will render them useful in the colony by showing the Indian girls what they can do, for this there being no point in sending other than of virtue known and without reproach. His majesty entrusted the Bishop of Quebec to certify them, in order that they not be suspect of debauch. You will take care to establish them the best you can and to marry them to men capable of having them subsist with some degree of comfort.[20]

The "Pelican girls" arrived in 1704, and most were quickly married.[21] However, although the women were similar to those who had previously immigrated to Jamestown and New France, it quickly became clear that the Louisiana colony's commitment to these women was vastly different. Unlike these other colonial mail-order brides who came with some knowledge of the difficulties awaiting them, the Pelican girls were enticed with lies. In addition, while the filles du roi were well provided for when they reached New France, the struggling Louisiana colony could barely prevent them from starving.

In order to increase the number of women interested in immigrating, the French government had described Louisiana as a flourishing colony, flowing with milk and honey,[22] and teeming with well-established and successful men.[23] They were promised the colony was "well provisioned," and that they would be leaving Paris for a life of ease in Louisiana.[24] In fact, life in Louisiana was presented as a kind of prize, but the reality was nothing like this fictional utopia.[25]

Upon arrival, it became clear that the women would not be living the life of ease they had been promised.[26] Three of the women immediately died from disease, and the rest discovered they had arrived during one of the colony's "starving times."[27] In addition, despite the promise of rich husbands, only three of the women were "well married" and the rest had to accept inferior marriage prospects. Appalled by the government's deception, the women instigated a protest, known as the "petticoat insurrection."[28] They demanded the lives they had been promised, and some even boarded boats to force their way out of the colony.[29] However, when the French sea captains steadfastly refused them passage, it became clear the women were effectively prisoners.[30] The Pelican girls had been treated appallingly, yet, astoundingly, the colonial government viewed their complaints as frivolous.[31]

In a letter describing the women's protests, Bienville notes their unhappiness, but refuses to acknowledge the seriousness of their grievances. In fact, instead of recognizing their legitimate fury at the government's deception, he blames the insurrection on an aversion to corn: "The males in the colony begin through habit to be reconciled to corn as an article of nourishment; but the females who are mostly Parisians have for this kind of food a dogged aversion. Hence, they inveigh bitterly against his Grace, the Bishop of Quebec, who, they say, has enticed them away from home under the pretext of sending them to enjoy the milk and honey of the land of promise."[32] According to Louisiana legend, the women were eventually placated when Bienville had his housekeeper teach them Indian methods for cooking and spicing local dishes, supposedly the origin of creole cooking.[33] The story is charming, but it is doubtful the deceived women were appeased by cornbread and hominy. They likely simply resigned themselves to their fate.

After recognizing they were effectively trapped, most of the Pelican brides married quickly, but one woman, Francoise Marie Anne Boisrenaud, refused all offers of marriage.[34] The Pelican girls had been promised there would be no forced marriages, and Boisrenaud sought to enforce that promise. Her refusal exasperated Bienville, and he quickly wrote to Pontchartrain, asking if she could be "oblige[d] . . . to do like the others since there [were] several good suitors who [were] sighing for her."[35] Bienville's request was denied, but it foreshadowed the ensuing change in the Louisiana bridal program from one of nominal consent to one of outright kidnapping.[36]

Once word of the terrible conditions in the colony and the Pelican girls' unforgivable treatment made its way back to France, few additional Frenchwomen were willing to immigrate.[37] Nevertheless, the need for female immigrants remained as pressing as ever. Male colonists were continuing to desert the colony in droves, and the colony's birthrate was steadily declining.[38] At the same time, the formerly struggling English colonies were now flourishing and their rapid expansion presented a growing threat. By 1710, Commissaire Ordonnateur d'Artaguiette, the commandant of the struggling Mobile settlement, was begging the French government for a new shipment of female immigrants. According to d'Artaguiette, the "young men . . . need wives. I know only this one way to hold them."[39] Eventually d'Artaguiette's request was granted. In 1713, a group of twelve new mail-order brides were sent to the colony.

Incredibly, despite the colony's grave need of female colonists, these women were treated appallingly. Contemporary descriptions state the women were "extremely ugly" and "very poor having neither linen nor clothes nor beauty."[40] These accounts also claim that at least one of the women was seduced or possibly raped during the voyage to Louisiana, and that there were rumors that the captain had debauched all twelve.[41] Although the latter accusation was unquestionably false, it was enough to ruin the women's reputations and marriage prospects. As soon as the ship landed, the other passengers immediately began spreading rumors about the women and the government did nothing to quell this gossip. In fact, once it became clear that few colonists wanted to marry these poor, unattractive, and supposedly debauched women, they were essentially abandoned. Only three of them married, the rest were forsaken and left, according to Cadillac, "living in misery."[42]

For other potential mail-order brides, the treatment of the 1713 women was the last straw. The Louisiana colony offered its marital immigrants nothing but suffering and unhappiness. The living conditions in Louisiana were harsher than those of the New France, and instead of protecting female immigrants, the colonial government permitted them to be deceived, disrespected, and virtually imprisoned.[43] Consequently, it is little wonder that after 1713, even the most desperate single women could no longer be convinced to immigrate.[44] Louisiana's bridal program proved a failure. However, rather than changing tactics and promising new and stronger incentives for female immigrants, French officials shipped in thieves and prostitutes to serve as brides for the colonists.[45]

Supporters of Louisiana's revised immigration plan blamed the 1713 women's lack of marriage success on their absence of beauty. They did not believe the women's desperate circumstances or tarnished reputations were a factor.[46] Ordonnateur Duclos exemplified this view when he stated that, in the future, more "'attention should be directed toward the girls' figures than their virtues. The [colonists] are not very scrupulous about the girls' past conduct before they desire them, if [the colonists] had found some more attractive to their taste, they would have been able to marry them and get themselves established here which

Departure of the filles de joie from France. Etching by Pierre Dupin à la Watteau. Wikimedia Commons.

would increase the colony."[47] Duclos's view was accepted and shortly thereafter, female prisoners from the Paris penitentiaries began arriving in Louisiana.[48]

Involuntary immigration was common in the eighteenth century, and many countries experimented with the forced immigration of prisoners. England had sent thousands of unwilling men and women to the nearby Virginia colony, but the reaction to their arrival was mixed.[49] Many of the Virginia colonists objected to this policy, and in the late seventeenth century they succeeded in outlawing the practice.[50] During this period, France had also demonstrated contradictory feeling about the immigration of criminals. The king had sent thousands of convicts to help populate the French Antilles, but had prohibited compulsory immigration to New France and the Louisiana colony. In 1715,

King Louis XIV died and Philippe d'Orléans became regent. Shortly thereafter, France's previous aversion to forced immigration to Louisiana disappeared.[51]

Regent d'Orléans was known for his loose morals and constant debauchery, and perhaps it is not surprising that the colony's leaders were able to convince him to lift the ban on criminal immigration to the Louisiana colony. The pope had referred to d'Orléans as a "godless regent," and in his memoirs Sir Nathaniel Wraxall described d'Orléans as "undoubtedly one of the most immoral and profligate men whom we have beheld in modern ages." According to Wraxall, "The orgies of the 'Palais Royal' probably exceeded in depravity as well as in enormity everything of the same kind ever enacted in France. The incestuous fables of antiquity, and the unnatural amours of Cinyras and Myrrha, which we read with horror in Ovid, the revolting stories of Alexander VI and his daughter Lucretia Borgia, were universally believed to have been realised in the persons of the Duchess de Berri and the Abbess de Chelles with their own father [d'Orléans]."[52]

In 1717, d'Orléans repealed the ban on forced immigration and France began rounding up women from orphanages, poor houses, and penitentiaries and sending them to Louisiana as wives for the male colonists.[53] Many of these women had no intention of becoming colonial wives. The new "recruits" differed greatly from the colony's previous marital immigrants, and their arrival was anything but stabilizing. The majority had been taken from the Hôpital Général du Paris, which housed prostitutes and criminals as well as poor women and orphans.[54] Most were sickly and suffered from malnutrition, many were infected with venereal disease, and others were highly dangerous criminals.[55] One of the new arrivals had supposedly murdered fifteen people. However, in other instances, the arriving woman's only crime was having angered the wrong person. During this period, it was not uncommon for individuals to falsely denounce their enemies or neighbors, yet because female immigrants were so desperately needed, little effort was taken to verify these charges before shipping the accused off to the colony.[56]

Woman being released from Salpêtrière. Painting by Tony Robert-Fleury. Wikimedia Commons.

The compulsory immigration of Frenchwomen was unconscionable, but what happened to many of the women before they departed for Louisiana is equally horrific. Some were forcibly married to male prisoners bound for the colony, while others were chained and marched across France as a warning to other potential criminals. Hundreds died on these treks. In 1719, 150 female prisoners rioted to avoid the march and forced immigration to Louisiana. Six of them were shot, a dozen more were wounded, and the rest spent the winter starving, ill clothed, and housed in freezing conditions. In the spring, the survivors were shipped to the colony.[57] In total, approximately 7,000 women were deported to the colony, but most never made it. The majority died on the forced marches and perilous sea voyage. Only 1,300 actually arrived in the colony, of whom only 178 remained alive in 1721.[58]

The women who arrived in Louisiana after 1715 had been kidnapped and abused, and it is not surprising that large numbers refused to

Transport of inmates from Salpêtrière. Painting by Étienne Jeaurat. Wikimedia Commons.

marry. Many returned to France as soon as possible.[59] Others decided to remain in the colony and resume their previous criminal ways.[60] Prostitution quickly became rampant as these "correction girls," a term frequently used to describe the women sent from the Paris prisons, settled in the colony.[61] One of the largest shipments of correction girls occurred in 1721, when eighty-eight new "brides" arrived in Louisiana. Most had been inmates of La Salpêtrière, the infamous Paris prison, and their arrival was highly disruptive.[62] Regarding these women, Bienville wrote, "Since the 4th of March, nineteen of them have been married off. From those who came by the *Le Chameau* and *La Mutine*, ten have died. So that fifty-nine girls are still to be provided for. This will be difficult, as these girls were not well selected. . . . Whatever the vigilance exercised upon them, they could not be restrained."[63] As Bienville's letter indicates, Louisiana's experiment with forced immigration did not produce the abundance of marriageable women the colonial leaders had expected. Nevertheless, just when the problems of forced immigration looked like they would overwhelm the colony, a different group of female immigrants known as "the casket girls" supposedly arrived and helped save the colony.

The casket girls, or *filles à la cassette*, were the antithesis of the "correction girls." They are said to have been a group of modest young Frenchwomen so named because of the small chests in which they carried the linens, clothes, caps, chemises, stockings, and so on they had been given for their new life in the colony. Descriptions of the women portray them as beautiful and virtuous, as coming from nice, middle-class families and having excellent homemaking skills.[64] In addition,

Embarkment of the casket girls, or cassette girls, holding the small chests or cassettes in which they carried their clothes and personal belongings. The Historic New Orleans Collection, Acc. No. 1974.25.10.40.

the women are routinely described as highly sought-after but also vigilantly protected from disrepute.[65] Most accounts state they were permanently accompanied by three watchful nuns (sometimes the number is six), and a contingent of armed guards.[66] In addition, one well-known story about the casket girls states that the women were in such demand that a duel was nearly fought over the last one.[67] In short, these girls are typically depicted as an enhanced version of the filles du roi. They are the personification of female beauty and virtue, and, not surprisingly, nearly every prominent Louisiana family claims a casket girl as an ancestor.[68] Nevertheless, despite numerous descriptions of these women, there is no actual record of their arrival, and it is likely they never existed.[69]

The Louisiana casket girl legend may have originated from the colony's practice of providing free passage and a *trousseau* to women willing to accompany their husbands and fathers to the colony.[70] It is also possible that the story emerged from the handful of instances in which single women directly asked the colony to finance their immigration. Either way, this small number of immigrant wives and daughters, and even smaller number of single women, had little impact on the colonial population. They cannot be the legendary casket girls, yet the other female immigrants arriving during this period are even less likely candidates. Most of these women were neither beautiful nor virtuous, and in many instances their presence actually endangered the colony's survival. For example, contemporary descriptions of the duel that was almost fought over the last "casket girl" actually portray the woman as more "a guardsman" than "a girl" and hardly an innocent maiden.[71] Similarly, a 1725 account of the colony's female population provided by the Council of Louisiana depicts the colony as overrun with criminals and prostitutes,[72] and suggests "the necessity of purging the colony of . . . a number of women of bad life who are entirely lost."[73] In 1727, La Chaise, the French commissioner sent to check on the colony,[74] echoed the council's sentiments and bemoaned the large numbers of unmarried women "ruining the colony." La Chaise described these women as "useless" and claimed they "do nothing but cause disorder." Like the council, La Chaise also recommended returning these women to France.[75]

The women described by the council and La Chaise are clearly not "casket girls," and this may be why many descriptions of the casket girls state that they did not arrive until 1728.[76] However, historical records show only one ship with women, Ursuline nuns, arriving at that time.[77] It appears that the casket girls were merely a myth created by Louisianans who did not like the truth of their ancestry.[78] Still, this legend is significant because it provides an egregious example of the long-standing and frequent practice of conflating trafficked women and mail-order brides. Louisiana began with a real mail-order bride program, then turned it into a system to kidnap and traffic women, and then obscured this history with a fabricated story about mail-order brides. The actual history of Louisiana's female immigration program reveals that the correction girls were not mail-order brides and that the problems they endured resulted from the fact that Louisiana's "bridal program" was actually a governmental policy to exploit and kidnap female immigrants.

Comparing the bridal programs of New France and Virginia with that of Louisiana demonstrates that when bridal immigration is voluntary, protected, and incentivized, it benefits both the brides and the state. It also shows that when marital immigrants are not protected such immigration becomes exploitation, in the worst cases trafficking. Modern discussions of mail-order marriage tend to ignore these distinctions and view all mail-order brides as desperate or trafficked.[79] Laws enacted for the protection of mail-order brides also rely on this assumption.[80] Missing from these accounts, however, is the recognition that mail-order marriage can be both a sensible and a deliberate choice. The history of the early colonial mail-order brides shows that, when mail-order marriage is encouraged and protected, it provides a valuable opportunity for women to shape their own marital destinies.

Early mail-order bride programs benefited women and aided the process of colonization by helping to stabilize colonial populations and encourage growth. Then, once the colonial period ended, mail-order marriage largely disappeared. Over the next century, there was little need for large-scale mail-order bride programs. The American population was increasing naturally, and western expansion proceeded through incremental changes to the western border. However, once the pace of expansion increased, particularly after the 1849 gold rush, marital immigration reemerged. In America's western territories, mail-order brides were once again recruited to help cement transient populations and propel population growth and like their predecessors, frontier governments often provided female immigrants with substantial legal, monetary, and political incentives. Consequently, mail-order marriage once again became an attractive option for many eastern women.

4

Well Disposed toward the Ladies

Mail-Order Brides Go West

On February 2, 1849, Eliza Farnham published a newspaper advertisement seeking "intelligent, virtuous and efficient" women, "persons not under twenty-five years of age," to marry California's forty-niners. Interested applicants were asked to provide "satisfactory testimonials of education, character, capacity, etc." from clergymen or town authorities and to furnish $250 for their transport.[1]

Farnham's ad appeared shortly after the first reports of life in the gold rush mining camps began making their way back east. In these reports, the camps and mining towns were depicted as overflowing with wild men and teeming with lawlessness and debauchery.[2] The public found these reports troubling, but for Farnham, who had inherited property in California and was preparing to move there with her two young sons, such reports were particularly alarming. Nevertheless, rather than abandon her inheritance, Farnham decided to try to reform California's errant miners.

Long before Farnham suggested sending mail-order brides to California, she was already a well-known social reformer. In 1844, her lectures on abolition, women's rights, social philosophy, and penal reform led to her appointment as the matron of Sing Sing's women's prison. While at Sing Sing, Farnham earned praise for her sweeping prison reforms and gained literary prominence for the two books she published. The first was her biography, *Life in Prairie Land*, detailing the years she lived on the Illinois frontier. The second was her criminal treatise, *Rationale of Crime*, which argued against viewing criminals as evil.[3] Given her background in criminal and social reform, it is not surprising that when Farn-

Eliza Farnham's advertisement for her California Association of American Women. California Historical Society. Gift of Mrs. George Dunlap Lyman in memory of her husband, January 1951.

ham was faced with the prospect of moving to lawless and debauched California, she quickly proposed a plan for improvement. Farnham believed that California's problems stemmed from a lack of women and she hoped that marital immigration could reform the miners and make California hospitable for respectable families like her own.

California, like the earlier French and English colonies, was not devoid of women. Many native women lived throughout the territory. However, once the gold rush began, the sex ratios in California changed drastically. In 1849, there were at least three men for every woman. This ratio increased to nearly seven men per female by 1852 and was skewed even further if only white women were considered.[4] Such a dramatic gender imbalance should have led to a high number of white/Indian intermarriages, but unlike colonial settlers, the California miners rarely took Indian wives. Census records from the 1850s show few mixed marriages, and stories from the period convey a sense of both repugnance and fear regarding these relationships. One well-known story about the

Violence during the California gold rush. Library of Congress.

Eliza Farnham. Collection of New-York Historical Society.

dangers of white/Indian relationships involved a miner named Buck-skin Jack. After a disagreement, Jack killed the brother of his Indian consort. Shortly thereafter, the woman sought revenge and attempted to murder Jack in his sleep. After hearing of the attempt on his life, Jack's neighbors were so terrified that they ordered all the local "squaw men" to get rid of their Indian women. These men complied without protest.[5]

Though intermarriages were uncommon in California, the rape or forced concubinage of Indian women was widespread. In an article conveying the frequency of such assaults, the *Alta California* newspaper noted that where men could not "obtain a squaw by fair means, [they would] not hesitate to use foul." They would "drag off the squaw" and "knock down her friends" if they interfered. Hundreds of Indian women were forced to flee into the mountains "to avoid the violence of men who, under the influence of liquor, [would] not hesitate to do any deed." In fact, whole families were routinely driven from their "homes in the dead of winter by crowds of drunken men," intent on rape.[6]

The assaults on Indian women also increased other types of violence between Indians and white settlers. For example, when a white man named "Big Tom" kidnapped an Indian woman from the Nisenan tribe and refused to return her, the woman's tribe attacked and killed Tom. Tom was chopped into hundreds of little pieces, and the other whites in Big Tom's camp were also murdered.[7] In that case, the woman was rescued and able to rejoin her tribe, but many other Indian women died at the hands of their white assailants. Throughout the 1850s, thousands of

THE FREE TRAPPER'S INDIAN WIFE.

An Indian woman, named Umentecken, defending herself against a violent trapper. An illustration in Frances Fuller Victor's *Eleven Years in the Rocky Mountains*, a biography of mountain man Joe Meek.

Indian women were subjected to horrific assaults and deprivation, and when the 1860 census was published, it clearly reflected the fact that the female Indian population in parts of California had been decimated; in almost every age cohort for every county, Indian men substantially outnumbered Indian women.[8]

Eliza Farnham's mail-order marriage proposal was not intended to directly address the problem of Indian assaults, but it was related. Farnham recognized the dangers posed by large groups of young, transient males and believed that marriage and family life were the best solution for defusing this volatile situation. Her views on the reforming power of marriage were an outgrowth of her involvement in the domestic feminism movement.[9] Domestic feminism specifically advocated the restorative power of marriage and sought to achieve a more valued and powerful position for women by emphasizing women's ability to redeem society through their role as wives and mothers.[10] Adherents believed that social welfare work was simply an extension of motherhood and, as a result, sought to expand women's roles beyond the home and family.[11] For Farnham, marital immigration was a way to carry out the goals of domestic feminism. Women who went west to marry would be able to use their influence as wives and mothers to convince California's miners to abandon wickedness, embrace the role of moral citizens, and ultimately transform Californian society.

The ideas of the domestic feminism movement that motivated Farnham were well known, but they were also controversial. A decade after she published her mail-order bride ad, Farnham would attend the eighth annual Women's Rights Convention and provoke outrage when she presented a speech regarding the "superiority of women." Farnham's marriage plan contains hints of her radical views regarding the role of women, and it also skirted the line of respectability in other ways, particularly by making the potential brides come to the men. Only a few years earlier, in 1837, a number of papers expressed outrage when "[a]n impudent Yankee who has wandered into Indiana, and squatted down upon a piece of land" sent a letter to a friend asking him to "send one hundred girls" to join him and his fellow settlers out west. According to the papers, the man wanted one of the women for himself and promised to find husbands for the "other ninety and nine."[12] After hearing of the request, the *Burlington Free Press* issued the following scathing admonishment:

> Now this is one of the coolest pieces of impudence that we have seen for a long time. "Bring on your potatoes" said the laborer to the master, "and I will dig them for you." "Bring on your girls," says the Yankee hoosier, "and I will marry them." And this to the fastidious girls of New England and that
>   "Must be wooed,
>   And not unsought be won."
> But that is not all—he must, "the Sabaryte," have his first choice out of a hundred—and then will find husbands for the "poor rejected." Hard times and emigration may bring the New England girls to change some of their manners, but they have not come to that yet. They are not going to look out for customers at that distance, and say with the city advertiser, "orders from the country gratefully received."[13]

Given this reaction to the "Yankee hoosier," there was the real possibility that Farnham's plan would be similarly dismissed, and after it was announced, there were sporadic grumblings of unseemliness. For instance, the *Edgefield Advertiser* wrote, "We know not what notions others may have of female propriety; but to our taste and judgment there is something unfeminine in this enterprize, which attaches some degree of vulgarity to the fair sex."[14] On the whole, however, such criticisms were surprisingly rare. Instead, Farnham's proposal was greeted with widespread approval.[15] Supporters rallied behind her. Nineteenth-century luminaries such as the poet William Cullen Bryant, publisher Horace Greeley, and the Reverend Henry Ward Beecher all praised and encouraged her endeavor,[16] and the renowned novelist Catharine Maria Sedgwick wrote the following glowing endorsement:

> Mrs. Farnham, the celebrated matron of the Sing Sing prison, is going to Boston this week on an enterprise her circular will explain. She is, of all women ever created (within my knowledge of God's works), the fittest for the enterprise. She has nerves to explore alone the seven circles of Dante's Hell. She has physical strength and endurance, sound sense and philanthropy, earnestness, and a coolness that would say "I know!" if [an] angel were to tell her the secrets of the upper world. . . . I have promised her a letter to Mrs. Minot, who I know will be pleased to see so rare a specimen of womanhood, and who . . . will appreciate this singular woman.[17]

The project was also praised in numerous newspaper editorials. These papers described her mission as a "good one" and waxed eloquent about her "moral courage." The *New York Herald* wrote, "Her reward will be found in the blessings which her countrymen will invoke for her when the vessel in which the association is to sail shall have arrived in California with her precious cargo."[18] Similarly, the *New York Tribune* praised the expedition, writing that "[a] lady of this State, well known for her labors in many a philanthropic cause, is about forming a benevolent expedition to California, which cannot but prove of great public benefit, in the present unsettled condition of that region."[19] Not surprisingly, the strongest support came from the Californian papers. After receiving report of Farnham's plan, the *Alta California* wrote, "This is most gladdening intelligence of the day . . . Eliza Farnham and her girls are coming, and the dawning of brighter days for our golden land is even now perceptible. The day of regeneration is nigh at hand. . . . We shall . . . prepare ourselves to witness the great change which is shortly to follow, with feelings akin to hilarious joy."[20]

Part of the support for Farnham's proposal, particularly in western locations, was excitement over the prospect of increasing the female population. At the same time, this support also stemmed from the fact that although Farnham's motivations were radical, and the idea of western bridal immigration novel, large-scale female immigration programs

A LIVE WOMAN IN THE MINES.—See page 16.

A cartoon depicting female scarcity in California. Courtesy of the California History Room, California State Library, Sacramento.

were actually fairly common in the antebellum period and had proven highly beneficial.

These programs were first suggested in the 1830s. During this period, eastern textile factories had begun reducing wages and laying off female workers. In the town of Suffolk, Massachusetts, for instance, more than five hundred female mill workers were laid off, and the remaining workers saw their wages cut by 15 to 25 percent.[21] Hundreds of women started organizing and striking. In both 1834 and 1836, female mill workers instigated major strikes to protest wage cuts.[22] In the West, however, wages remained high and there were no similar protests.[23] As a result, reformers began to view migration as a solution to the East's labor problem.[24] Western states also approved of this plan and were eager to welcome female immigrants.[25]

Female laborers joined these expeditions in order to take advantage of the West's superior employment opportunities. They did not intentionally immigrate to marry, yet most eventually married local men. Consequently, the difference between these early female workers and later mail-order brides, many of whom also planned to work before marrying and settling down, was small and undoubtedly helped proposals like Farnham's win widespread approval. In addition, the seeming familiarity between the two programs also made them more appealing to the potential brides.

One of the earliest sponsored expeditions of female workers and teachers is described in an 1835 article from the *St. Louis Herald*. The article states,

> [A] company of "industrious, capable and intelligent" young women are about to start out from Northampton, Mass. for the valley of the West. They are ... needed as school teachers, to fill the various mechanical employments, which are the province of their sex, and above all, are needed as sweeteners of the toil and hardship of our young men, who now, in great numbers, are laboring in unblessed loneliness, over the vast domains of the West. These young women come out under the protection of a gentleman, and we do not hesitate, in the name of all that is pure and lovely, to promise them a hearty welcome from all classes of our fellow citizens.[26]

The *Herald* article does not provide the name of the "gentleman" escorting the female emigrants, but he was likely a member of one of the many philanthropic organizations created to finance and accompany women willing to move west. From the 1830s until the start of the Civil War, philanthropic female emigration societies were commonly proposed to remedy state gender imbalances and employment disparities. For example, in 1853, the *Windham County Democrat* published the following appeal for funds to start a female emigration society in Vermont:

> Not Good For Man To Be Alone: ... Why should there not ... be a female emigration fund established here, with a view to restore the so-

cial equilibrium that has been so fearfully disturbed by the flowing of our young men to the great El Dorado of the far west? How can they, whose sons and brothers, nephews and wards and neighbors have separated themselves from the social and domestic efficacies we have been considering—how can such turn their thoughts and charities to better account, than by making ways and means for repairing, in some degree, the perilous disproportion which has thus been created? Sending on those necessary elements of social health and prosperity, which by reason of their excess, are in danger of corrupting into evil here, and from the want of which there is in the nature of things certain to be a vast, manifold and hideous growth of evil there. We cannot persuade ourselves to think this is a matter that may be safely left to take care of itself.[27]

A few months later, the *Daily Dispatch* in Richmond, Virginia, published a similar appeal. In an article titled "Female Emigration," the paper wrote,

The New York papers frequently draw terrible pictures of distress among the poor female population of that city, some of whom perish from absolute want, and others are even tempted into crime by their extreme poverty. Now all this evil might be easily remedied by a proper direction of the run mad philanthropy of the North, and a little common sense on the part of the women themselves. . . . Let the Women's Rights Society of New York and the Kansas Emigration Society, instead of each persisting in a hopeless enterprise, combine their forces and their funds, and establish an association for promoting female emigration to Kansas or California. Whilst there is such an excess of females in the old communities, there is a great excess of male population in the extreme West. A double evil would be abated by such an association—the great want of Western society would be supplied, the increasing grievance of the New York society would be removed, and at the same time, by diminishing the excess of female population in New York, the condition of those who remain would be improved. Let them go to work, then, for an association of this kind, and raise funds to pay the passage out, of the poor needlewomen, provide them temporary assistance on their arrival, and facilities for placing themselves in useful positions.[28]

A description of a third organization, the recently established Women's Protective Emigration Society (WPES),[29] was provided by Horace Greeley in the *New-York Daily Tribune* on December 14, 1857. He wrote,

> This Society is just organized in this city by a number of ladies and gentlemen for the purpose of sending destitute young women and girls who are deprived of the means of obtaining their daily bread, to the Interior or the West, where they may find employment. . . . No rhetoric can exaggerate the awful condition of thousands—yes thousands—of respectable, industrious, virtuous girls in this metropolis whose wages are suddenly suspended, and who are left hopeless and helpless. It is estimated there are no less than 7,000 now ready to go West. . . . A woman may be defined to be a creature who receives half price for all she does, and pays full price for all she needs. . . . She earns as a child—she pays as a man. Besides, her sex, if not barbarous custom, cuts her off from the best rewarded callings. Her hands, feet and brain are clogged. . . . What, then, remains to be done? Simply individual action. Action prompt; action liberal, action abundant. There is no time to be lost.[30]

As the above examples demonstrate, female emigration was seen as a way to alleviate the labor unrest in the East and provide western states with female workers and eventually wives. Advocates believed such emigration was good for women, good for men, and good for society, but they did not limit their efforts to the migration of female wage earners.[31] Many of the most successful female emigration plans of the antebellum period involved the emigration of middle-class schoolteachers. Like wage-earning women, female schoolteachers also had limited employment opportunities in the East but were in high demand in the western states.[32] Consequently, throughout the 1840s, expeditions were organized to transport female school teachers to the "lawless" western territories so that they might provide a religious and civilizing influence.[33]

The most well known of these efforts to bring teachers west was a program organized by Vermont's governor, William Slade.[34] In the 1840s, Slade personally conducted hundreds of teachers, known as "Slade's girls," to Illinois, Wisconsin, and Iowa, and the program was considered an outstanding success. In 1855, the *Weekly Indiana State Sentinel* praised Slade's achievement: "Governor Slade has distributed his Yankee girls over the Union; and wherever one of them has taken up her abode, it has been better for society than the planting of a rosebush for a garden."[35] As the *Sentinel* recognized, the women who went west as teachers were deeply invested in their new homes and played an integral part in shaping these communities. One such "Slade girl," Harriet Bishop, became the first schoolteacher in Saint Paul. In a diary entry from 1848 Bishop conveyed her pride in her new home: "My how this town is growing. I counted the smoke of eighteen chimneys."[36]

Slade's girls and other female teachers came west for work, but it was assumed that most would eventually marry local men. In an 1855 article about the Oregon "Slade's girls," the editors of the *Oregon Times* noted that the women were "all married," including one who "married our late Governor Gaines, and another one, we believe, has been married *twice*." The editors further added that "[t]his is a great country for Yankee School-marms to thrive in" and wondered "if Ex-Governor Slade could not be induced to send us a 'few more of the same sort.'"[37] In a 1912 article for the *New England Magazine*, the Reverend James Hill also emphasized the program's marital success. He wrote, Slade's girls began by "teaching other people's children and ended by teaching their own."[38] He further added that the girls' contributions as wives were at least as important as those they made as teachers. Referring to an Iowa regiment that had fought bravely during the Civil War, Hill pointedly noted that the brave men who had "saved the day" were "most of them Slade's girls' boys."[39]

Farnham's emigration proposal was undoubtedly influenced by these earlier efforts and their success in bringing single women west. She believed that the lawlessness and immorality dominating the western territories was the direct result of the "the absence of woman,"[40] and that increasing the female population would be "one of the surest checks upon [California's] many ... evils."[41] Nevertheless, the difference between Farnham's plan and prior ones was that hers centered entirely on marriage. Previous female emigration advocates had viewed marriage as a desirable and likely consequence of female emigration, but Farnham was the first to specifically solicit eastern women for marriage to western men. Her mistake, however, was that, unlike earlier emigration plans, which had offered potential female emigrants significant benefits, her plan was concerned only with aiding men.

In her 1849 ad, Farnham wrote that she was looking for women willing to toil "beside the forty-niners, 'sympathizing with their successes, soothing their disappointments, [and] lightening their burdens.'" In addition, she specifically addressed her appeal to middle-class women because she believed they would be able to exert the most beneficial influence on Californian men. She implored these women to sacrifice their eastern comforts, their "seat of luxury by the fireside of an eastern home" and their memberships in "the resorts of the gay" in order to save western men from sin and debauchery.[42] Middle-class women were uninterested.

For most middle-class women, eastern comforts were already far from comfortable. For example, the relatively affluent Lydia Maria Child made the following tally of her year's housework: "360 dinners, 362 breakfasts, sitting room and kitchen swept and dusted 350 times, lamps filled 362 times, and the chamber and stairs swept and dusted 40 times."[43] Farnham's proposal simply offered these women a life of even greater drudgery as well as possible danger. Nevertheless, her proposal did appeal to working- and lower-class women. For these women, western emigration offered the possibility of a better life.

In the antebellum period, life for working-class women was extremely difficult. Low wages and scarce job opportunities were a constant problem, and rapid industrialization made performing even the most basic household chores extremely difficult.[44] For instance, most working-class homes were located next to the mills and factories and, as a result, were frequently coated in thick coal dust that required constant cleaning. In addition, even getting enough water for cleaning could be difficult. Due to the decisions of city planners and factory owners, working-class neighborhoods were typically the last to receive city services, so necessities such as running water and garbage pickup could be sporadic or nonexistent. In Pittsburgh, for example, women who wanted water for their home had to wake up as early as five o'clock to ensure they received water before it was diverted to the mills.[45] These hardships were significant, and many working-class women considered the "toil" described by Farnham to be more like a respite.

More than two hundred women, the majority of whom were working- and lower-class women, ultimately expressed interest in joining Farnham's Association of California Women. However, Farnham was not interested in bringing these types of women,[46] and her plan did not provide the financial assistance they would have needed to afford the trip.[47] In the end, only three women accompanied her on her journey to California, including one who left midjourney to marry the ship's steward, "a lazy, lying, worthless creature," according to Farnham.[48] Despite this disappointing result, Farnham's proposal, and the interest it garnered, revealed that eastern women were intrigued by the possibility of marital emigration.

Initially, the primary appeal of marital immigration was economic. For years, eastern women had watched men go west to "strike it rich," and many undoubtedly hoped to share in this wealth. Nevertheless, as time went on, the decision to immigrate was increasingly tied to women's desire for greater freedom and equality. By the 1840s, many American women were chafing under America's harsh coverture laws. In 1848, the Married Women's Property Act was passed, and shortly thereafter, the first Women's Rights Convention was held at Seneca Falls.[49] Consequently, by the time Farnham placed her ad, large numbers of American women were already actively seeking to reform marriage and increase their marital rights.[50] Western states quickly realized that eastern women's discontent with their legal and social position presented an unparalleled recruitment opportunity.

In the 1840s, western states began passing legal reforms intended to appeal to women dissatisfied with the slow pace of change in the East. Notably, in 1849, when California was creating its constitution, the delegates decided to forgo the common-law property regime and the long-standing doctrine of coverture and replaced it with the civil law tradition instead.[51] The new California constitution decreed that "[a]ll property, both real and personal, of the wife, owned or claimed by her before marriage and that acquired afterwards by gift, devise or descent, shall be her separate property."[52] This provision was a radical reform of the common-law tradition of coverture,[53] and it was done intentionally to spur female immigration. As delegate and bachelor Henry Halleck explained during the constitutional convention, "Having some hopes that I may be wedded ... I shall advocate this section in the Constitution, and I would call upon all the bachelors in this convention to vote for it. I do not think that we can offer a greater inducement for women of fortune to come to California. It is the very best provision to get us wives that we can introduce into the Constitution."[54] Halleck was not alone in thinking that a civil law regime benefitting women could incentivize immigration. When describing California's property laws to a friend, one early California lawyer boasted of "[t]he peculiar character of our laws here in regard to women," adding, "I presume there is no 'State in the Union' where the laws are so liberal, so just. ... So you see, we are particularly well disposed toward the ladies."[55]

California's adoption of civil property law reflected the general feeling among the Californian population that women were valuable and that any means of encouraging female immigration should be considered.[56] In one letter home, a California miner wrote, "if you were separated from *those dear little creatures* as I am, you would know how to appreciate their value … you would get *married immediately*."[57] A second miner expressed similar sentiments noting that "[i]t was only after leaving home … and removing to a sphere where she had a better opportunity of displaying her power, that I could estimate her real worth."[58] These changing attitudes about women's value also influenced how women viewed their own worth. In 1849, a woman named Dorothy Scraggs placed the following advertisement for a husband in the Marysville, California, newspaper:

A Husband Wanted

By a lady who can wash, cook, scour, sew, milk, spin, weave, hoe, (can't plow), cut wood, make fires, feed the pigs, raise chickens, rock the cradle, (gold-rocker, I thank you, Sir!), saw a plank, drive nails, etc. These are a few of the solid branches; now for the ornamental. "Long time ago" she went as far as syntax, read Murray's Geography and through two rules in Pike's Grammar. Could find 6 states on the Atlas. Could read, and you can see she can write. Can—no, *could*—paint roses, butterflies, ships, etc. Could once dance, can ride a horse, donkey, or oxen, besides a great many things too numerous to be named here. Oh, I hear you ask, could she scold? No, she can't you, you ____ ____ good for nothing____!

Now for her terms. Her age is none of your business. She is neither handsome nor a fright; yet an *old* man need *not* apply; nor any who have not a little more education than she has, and a great deal more gold, for there must be $20,000 settled on her before she will bind herself to perform all the above.[59]

Scraggs's advertisement demonstrates that she was well aware of her value as a woman in female-scarce California and California's new property regime ensured she would retain a share of this value. Under the laws of coverture, Scraggs would have lost her right to the $20,000 she was requesting when she married, but under California's new constitution it would remain her separate property.

California's liberal property laws protected married women by giving them control over their separate property. However, this was not the only way California law protected women from the uncertainties of marriage. California also instituted liberal divorce laws. In the early nineteenth century, divorce was rare and female-initiated divorce was virtually nonexistent. As a consequence, women were routinely stuck in unhappy or abusive marriages. In many states, it was actually a criminal act to help a wife leave her husband. In fact, it was not until 1864, in *Barnes v. Allen*, that a court first declared husbands had no cause of action against those who helped their wives leave them. In that case, Mr. Barnes's neighbor, Mr. Allen, had helped Mrs. Barnes leave her abusive husband. Mr. Barnes then sued Allen for "enticement," but the *Barnes* court rejected the suit, declaring that a wife is not "the chattel of the husband" and cannot be considered his "property."[60]

During this period, the law also gave husbands the right to recapture and, in some circumstances, confine a wife who attempted to leave.[61] The extent of the right to confine a wife was hotly contested, but most courts agreed a husband could require his wife to live with him and that he was entitled to monetary damages if she left without his permission.[62] In some cases, controlling husbands used this law to obtain a portion of their wives' separate property. For example in 1840, a young woman named Jane Swisshelm, left her marital home, against her husband's wishes, to care for her dying mother. After Jane's mother's death, her husband sued her estate (provided by her recently deceased mother) seeking compensation for the loss of her time and labor.[63] Shortly thereafter, Jane separated from her husband, but it took another twenty years before she succeeded in divorcing this cold and calculating man.

Feminist reformer Elizabeth Cady Stanton described the inability to divorce as the mark of a woman's slavery, and she stated there was "no other slavery so disastrous in its consequences on the race, or to individual respect, growth and development."[64] Consequently, the fact that California permitted divorce was a strong incentive for both single women as well as unhappily married women to immigrate.[65] In a gossipy letter to a friend back east, a San Francisco woman named Martha Hitchcock remarked on the practical effects of California's divorce laws. Hitchcock informed her friend that that she had recently run into "Col. Stevenson (of the NY regt)" (presumably a mutual acquaintance) who "married a very pretty woman, who got a divorce from one husband to marry him." A few lines later, Hitchcock apprised her friend of another recent transplant, "MRs. Bonner, who ran away from her husband with a MR. Plume, in Columbus," and "is living here with him, married of course."[66] From her letters, it is clear Hitchcock found the frequency of divorce in California somewhat scandalous, but many other Californian women happily acknowledged its advantages. Abby Mansur, another Californian woman, cheekily described the benefits of California's divorce laws: "I tell you that the women are in great demand in this country no matter whether they are married or not you need not think strange if you see me coming home with some good looking man some of these times with a pocket full of rocks ... it is all the go here for Ladys [sic] to leave there [sic] Husbands two out of three do it."[67]

The combination of easy divorce, strong property rights, and a booming economy made California highly attractive to female immigrants, and it did not take long before thousands of women had left the East Coast to settle in California.[68] In a letter dated April 14, 1850, San Francisco lawyer John McCracken wrote, "We find we are to enjoy at last, what we have so much needed, the sweet, the gentle, the saving influence of woman ... we have already arrivals of more than 2,000 women by sea, many more come across the country. I heard not long since of the arrival of an old Lady and her five daughters. They came in a wagon and seemed quite happy to think there were such chances to get well married."[69] The result of this influx of female immigrants was profound. According to the census, between 1850 and 1860, California's female population increased from 3 percent to 19 percent of the population, or more than 9,000 women.[70] Consequently, the sex ratio in California changed from 12.2 to 2.4 males per female in the general population, and parity among men and women under thirty.[71] Given this high rate of female immigration, additional attempts to bring groups of brides to California were quickly rendered unnecessary.[72] Nevertheless, in other parts of the West, natural immigration was still failing to produce the desired female population, so new mail-order bride expeditions were proposed, and unlike Farnham's mail-order bride plan, these efforts met with considerable success.

California's experience with female immigration had demonstrated that single women would move west if the incentives were right. Later mail-order bride expeditions drew on this experience and offered potential brides rewards large enough to offset the risks. Organizers of these later endeavors primarily targeted working-class women, recognizing that they had the most to gain from marital emigration and were the most likely to immigrate. One such expedition was organized by Archer, Thaddeus, and Samuel Benton to help find wives for the bachelors of Albany, Oregon.

In 1864, the town of Albany commissioned the Benton brothers to travel back east and convince single women to immigrate.[73] The town had determined that this was the only effective way to increase its female population, however, initially, Albany, like many other Oregon towns, had believed the availability of good jobs was all that was needed to spur female immigration. The *Puget's Sound Herald* expressed this view in an 1859 description of the state's numerous opportunities for women and urged women to immigrate: "How much better off they would be here, as the wives of wealthy and prospering farmers, mechanics, professional men and merchants, than they are in their present position. . . . Immediate employment can be obtained throughout the Territories at profitable wages, as milliners, dressmakers, school teachers, seamstresses, laundresses, housemaids, etc., etc. These pursuits are all seeking heads and hands to follow them here, at higher compensa-

tion than is obtained even in California."[74] The article acknowledged
the substantial expense of immigration, but expressed confidence that
money would not pose a serious hurdle: "[a]mong the female working
classes in the States there are some who have means sufficient to enable
them to come here, and we trust such will come, and leave their places
to those more needy." It predicted that "[s]ooner or later the tide of female emigration will set in. Of this there is no uncertainty" and ended
with the exhortation, "Don't be backward but come right along, all you
who want good husbands and comfortable homes, in the most beautiful country and finest climate of the world."[75]

The paper's optimism regarding the effect of monetary impediments
proved to be misplaced. The cost of immigration was a significant impediment, and few interested, single women had the financial resources
to respond to Oregon's immigration pleas. In 1860, an article from the
Cincinnati Daily Press noted, "The ninety-five bachelors of Steilacoom,
Oregon, are still 'disconsolate'—no girls there for wives in spite of their
appeal to female emigration."[76] Eventually, a number of Oregon's bachelor towns decided to finance their own bridal expeditions. The bachelors would pool their funds and dispatch one or two men back east to
recruit and accompany the single women back to Oregon.

In 1864, the Benton brothers arrived in Ellicott Mills, Maryland,
to begin their recruitment. Their choice of Ellicott Mills, a formerly
prosperous mill town that still boasted a substantial population, was
not haphazard. Before the Civil War, the town was briefly home to the
largest cotton mill in America but had fallen on hard times during the
war. Jobs were eliminated and wages, particularly those of women, were
cut significantly.[77] Many women increasingly found their job prospects
limited to domestic service.[78] Consequently, when the Benton brothers
printed up flyers advertising "Brides Wanted" and offering free passage
to the West, their offer garnered significant interest. Hundreds showed
up for the informational meeting and listened with rapt attention as Archer Benton described Oregon as "peaceful, tree-filled terrain, endless
blue skies, and a husband for every widow and spinster."[79]

The opportunities described by Benton were enticing, and many women accepted his offer. In her diary entry from the night of the information meeting, a young woman named Constance Ranney describes being dazzled by the promise of Oregon. She wrote, "Such a challenge was being presented . . . [and] it struck me. If I don't do this I will spend my entire working life as a servant for the rich here."[80] Further on in her diary entry, Ranney noted an additional benefit of immigration, social equality. She wrote that many of the girls signing up were from good families, "the kind of families that would never have me in their parlors because I am a servant." She recognized that such distinctions would not matter in Oregon. "In Oregon, we will all be the same," wrote Ranney, "just women looking for husbands. None of us any better than the other." Women like Ranney found the promise of social and financial mobility a powerful motivation; by the time the Benton brothers left Maryland, more than one hundred women had decided to accompany them back to Oregon.[81]

The arrival of large numbers of single women in the Oregon Territory helped remedy an immigration problem the federal government had been grappling with for decades. Under the Treaty of 1818, the United States and Britain had agreed to a joint occupancy of the Oregon Territory. Then, in the 1840s, American settlers flooded into the territory and demanded independence from British rule. Britain reluctantly ceded the territory, but American control remained tenuous, and without significant population growth, British re-annexation continued to pose a threat. In order to eliminate this risk, the federal government needed to increase the population. A number of immigration incentives were implemented but achieved only limited success, particularly with regard to the immigration of single women. Moreover, even after the British threat receded, slow population growth meant the prospect of statehood remained elusive.

The Oregon Territory had easily attracted single male immigrants who flocked to the territory seeking work as miners, loggers, and trappers. However, without viable marriage prospects, most remained transient. The extent of the problem is clearly demonstrated in a study on Roseburg, Oregon, which looked at the 1860 census and found that "only one-third of single men stayed for more than five years, but about two-thirds of married men did."[82] Consequently, when in 1843 family groups started to immigrate to certain parts of the territory, particularly the fertile Willamette River Valley, the government immediately proposed legislation to further encourage this type of family immigration.[83] The proposed bill would have granted 640 acres of land to each white male inhabitant of Oregon Territory (an area that includes the present-day states of Oregon, Washington, and Idaho and parts of Wyoming), plus another 160 if he was married and another 160 for each child.[84] The 1843 bill did not pass, but seven years later, Congress successfully enacted the Donation Land Act, unequivocally demonstrating the government's desire to increase the number of family groups settling in the territory.

Under the Donation Land Act, married couples were permitted to claim twice the land available to single men (320 acres vs. 160).[85] In addition, in order to make immigration particularly attractive to women, the act dispensed with the normal rules of coverture and guaranteed that half the claimed land would become the separate estate of the wife.[86] In a letter to Congress before the passage of the act, Oregon delegate Samuel R. Thurston expressed strong support for this separate property provision specifically because he believed it made female immigration more likely: "[E]migrating to Oregon from the States, places the female beyond the reach of her kindred and former friends and it is certainly no more than right to place some little means of protection in her own hands. But the object is to produce a population, and this provision is an encouragement of the women to peril the dangers and hardships of the journey."[87]

The Donation Land Act successfully induced families to move to the fertile farmlands within the Oregon Territory. However, because the act was geared toward wives, rather than single women, it did little to reduce the gender imbalance in the majority of the territory. As a result, increasing numbers of male settlers began forming relationships with local Indian women. These relationships were considered racially objectionable, but the larger concern was that they would hamper the territory's statehood ambitions. Before a territory could be admitted as a state, it needed to show it was "civilized," and many of the territory's leaders feared that high rates of intermarriage signaled the opposite.[88] Nevertheless, with few white women in the territory, there was little they could do to prevent male settlers from marrying native women.[89]

In 1855, the Oregon territorial government passed a law voiding solemnized marriages between whites and all other racial groups, but this ban was more symbolic than effective and did little to prevent interracial relationships. In fact, the territory continued to recognize white/Indian marriages as a valid form of common-law marriage for another decade.[90] Without a large influx of white women, true interracial marriage bans were unrealistic.

In 1862, in an effort to increase the immigration of single women, Congress passed a second land act, known as the Homestead Act. This act was the first law to give single women the right to claim land in the West. It stated that any "person," who was either the "head of a family or who ha[d] arrived at the age of twenty-one years," could obtain a homestead if he or she lived on and farmed the property for five years.[91] As a result, single, divorced, or widowed women became eligible to receive 160 acres of their own land.[92] However, although free land was a powerful immigration incentive, as was the equality of opportunity represented, homesteading was extremely difficult, and few single women were actually in a position to take advantage. Even experienced farm families faced numerous hardships and setbacks as they attempted to "prove their claims." Not surprisingly, most of the single female homesteaders filed their claims next to a fiancé, parent, or brother in order to have help, both physically and financially, in claiming their homestead.[93] Only a handful of women were able to homestead entirely on their own. Consequently, the primary beneficiaries

Wyoming settler Richard "Beaver Dick" Leigh with his Indian wife and children. Courtesy of the Wyoming State Archives, Department of State Parks and Cultural Resources.

of the act were engaged couples and Oregon families with unmarried daughters; it did little to bring new women to the territory.

For most single, eastern women, homesteading was simply not a viable option. However, when bridal recruiters like the Benton brothers offered to finance their travel and accompany them west, many women were finally able to realistically consider immigrating. Then, as the number of white women in the territory increased, interracial marriage bans became realistic. Many of the settlers' Indian wives were replaced with the arriving white women and interracial marriage bans began to be enforced. The case *In re Estate of Wilbur* is one such example. The *Wilbur* case was brought by an Indian woman named Kitty Wilbur to challenge her deceased husband's white wife's inheritance claim. Kitty was John Wilbur's first wife. The two were married in 1867 or 1868 according to Indian custom and had three children together. Then, in 1876 Wilbur abandoned Kitty to marry a mail-order bride named Sarah

In the bow, Qunhulahl, a masked man impersonating the Thunderbird, dances as others row to the shore of the bride's village. Library of Congress.

Wilcox. After Wilbur died, Kitty sued for recognition as Wilbur's only lawful wife. However, rather than recognizing the validity of Kitty and Wilbur's marriage, the court published a sexualized account of their relationship, treating Kitty more as a prostitute than a wife. In the opinion, the court referred to Kitty as "the dusky maiden of the forest" and the "sable enchantress" and dubbed her husband the "amorous swain." In similarly florid prose, it described how Wilbur was smitten when he "heard her sweetly guttural accents in the sighing of the floating mist" and how he was captivated by "her voluptuous form." The court then took substantial pains to portray their marriage as a financial transaction. It provided an extensive description of Kitty's "bride price," describing the sixty dollars Wilbur gave Kitty's father as "the highest sum on record paid for a wife" and claimed that under Indian custom, a bride could be returned and a husband could "receive back his canoe, or blankets or whatever the bride price consisted of." Given this depiction of their relationship, it is not surprising the court held that the Wilburs were never validly married.[94] The court found Kitty was entitled to nothing,[95] and concluded its opinion stating that "[t]hey lived together, and had children born to them, and that was all."[96]

Kitty married John Wilbur at a time when few white women resided in the Oregon Territory. However, by the time Sarah Wilcox immigrated, the female population had increased substantially. Bridal recruiters like the Benton brothers brought hundreds of single women to the territory. However, the most famous bridal recruiter was a man named Asa Mercer. In 1864, the same year the Benton brothers undertook their recruitment efforts, Mercer began recruiting women for his Seattle mail-order bride expedition. Like the Bentons, Mercer targeted women from declining eastern industrial towns, but he barely mentioned marriage in his recruitment speeches. Instead, Mercer focused exclusively on the middle-class employment prospects available to women in Seattle and the high value afforded women's skills and abilities. He recognized that economic considerations were the primary motivation for many women contemplating mail-order marriage. Flora Engle, one of the women who accompanied Mercer on his second mail-order bride voyage, noted this recruitment tactic, stating "every appeal was to the pocket."[97] He enticed women with descriptions of "sparsely settled towns along the water's edge" where "small fortunes might be made."[98]

Mercer's first expedition was not particularly successful, as only eleven women accompanied him back to Seattle. Even so, the town's gratitude was immense. In fact, his efforts to increase female immigration were so appreciated that they served as the primary basis for his election to public office.[99] One week after arriving back in Seattle, the *Seattle Gazette* issued the following endorsement: "The thanks of the whole community, and of the bachelors in particular, are due Mr. Mercer for his efforts in encouraging this much-needed kind of immigration. Mr. Mercer is the Union candidate for joint councilman for King

Asa Mercer. University of Washington Libraries, Digital Collection, Portraits Collection UW3388.

and Kitsap counties, and all bachelors, old and young, may, on election day, have an opportunity of expressing through the ballot box, their appreciation of his devotedness to the cause of the Union, matrimonial as well as national."[100] In the end, support for Mercer was so strong "he was unanimously elected to the upper house of the Territorial Legislative Assembly."[101] Shortly thereafter, he was appointed president of the new Territorial University at Seattle.[102]

Given this response, it is not surprising that soon after returning home, Mercer quickly began planning a second and much larger expedition.[103] To finance this second voyage, he had interested men pay three hundred dollars and sign a document in which he promised "to bring a suitable wife, of good moral character and reputation from the East to Seattle on or before September 1865, for each of the parties whose signatures are hereunto attached, they first paying me or my agent the sum of three hundred dollars, with which to pay the passage of such ladies and to compensate me for my trouble."[104] Hundreds of men "signed up for a wife," and after receiving the funds Mercer traveled back east and once again began recruiting women from declining mill towns.[105]

Mercer's second trip was extremely successful. More than one hundred women agreed to accompany him back to Seattle. In fact, his immigration plan sparked so much national interest that the *New York Times* dispatched journalist Roger Conant to accompany the brides and provide an account of the voyage and their reception in Seattle. Conant's articles are lively and colorful and clearly demonstrate that despite the wife-buying "contracts," the women were very much in control. Like many colonial mail-order brides, the majority of the Mercer brides did not marry immediately, and those who did were the ones who had the most to gain from quick marriages. For example, Conant wrote that the first woman to accept an offer of marriage was a widow with three young sons, the youngest of whom was a particular troublemaker. The child had caused so much mischief on the journey that Conant wrote he had nearly wrung the boy's neck "at least a dozen times during the voyage."[106] For this boy's harried single mother, a quick marriage was desirable. According to Conant, the woman was introduced to "an old back woodsman" at three in the afternoon, was proposed to at six, and accepted at nine.[107]

Conant's accounts of other speedy marriages also reveal women getting the better end of the bargain. For example, he described two additional rapid marriages that also involved much older women. The first of these marriages was between a "lady ... over 40 years of age," and "[a] frisky youth who was over powered with her charms." The second involved a "Mrs. Horton," for whom "70 years have already sighed their gentle breezes over her head."[108] Regarding the latter, Conant wrote,

Mercer Belles cartoon. *Harper's Weekly*, February 3, 1866, 80.

With one foot in the grave, and the other placed on the altar, she will probably pass the remainder of her days on earth, singing that good old song:

> "I am a gay and happy wife,
> For I've married a festive cuss;
> And I can recline for the rest of my life
> In his arms without any fuss."[109]

These women benefited from marrying quickly, but many of the other Mercer girls were not interested in hasty marriages and rejected their eager beaus. After one such rebuff, the spurned suitor forlornly asked the woman why she had immigrated if she "didn't come out to get married." The woman replied, "To make pants, coats and vests ... for such fellows as you."[110] As her answer demonstrates, many of the Mercer girls viewed marital immigration as a way to increase their economic as well as their marital prospects. The majority of the Mercer girls planned to marry, but they did not need to. They had the skills to support themselves and even profit as they waited until they were ready. The women were in control, just as they had hoped they would be. As their statements demonstrate, the Mercer girls left their homes and families and traveled thousands of miles in order to gain greater command and independence over their economic, social, and political destinies.[111]

Given such desires, it is not surprising that a number of the Mercer brides came from families noted for their reform ideas. In fact, one of the women, Mehitable Haskell Elder, was the niece of Hitty Haskell, a famous Massachusetts suffragist and abolitionist. Once in Oregon, Elder continued working for women's suffrage and was one of the primary organizers of the 1871 Women's Rights Convention in Olympia. She also helped raise the necessary funds to sponsor Susan B. Anthony as the territory's delegate to the National Woman Suffrage Association Convention.[112] Similarly, another of the Mercer girls, Lizzie Ordway, became one of the founders of Seattle's women's suffrage movement and one of the first women elected in the territory.[113] Marital immigration provided women like Elder and Ordway an opportunity to improve both their own lives and advance the cause of women in general. However, these benefits were not limited to American mail-order brides. A few miles north, in the Canadian west, a group of British mail-order brides were experiencing similar benefits.

In the 1850s, the Canadian territory of British Columbia was thinly populated and consisted primarily of female-scarce logging and mining towns. As in the Oregon Territory, population growth in British Columbia was slow. However, the territory had the additional problem of potential annexation. In the 1840s, British Columbia had lost control of a significant portion of its land after large numbers of American settlers had flooded into the Washington territory, and claimed it for the United States. By the 1850s, a similar pattern appeared to be repeating itself in other areas of British Columbia. Moreover, despite the pleas of the territorial government, Britain had done very little to halt the growing influx of American settlers.[114] As Americans flooded into these lands, it appeared increasingly likely that the rest of British Columbia would soon become American territory. Then, in 1858, gold was discovered, changing everything.

James Douglas, chief factor of the Columbia Department at Fort Victoria and governor of Vancouver Island, recognized the political opportunity presented by the discovery of gold. In a cunning effort to force the British government to finally attend to the struggling territory, the governor decided to create a gold rush. Instead of concealing the find, Douglas shipped the gold to San Francisco for smelting. As he had anticipated, the news spread rapidly. Within weeks, tens of thousands of American miners poured into British Columbia, seeking gold and annexation. A popular song among the American miners had the following lyrics:

> Soon our banner will be streaming,
> Soon the eagle will be screaming,
> And the lion—see it cowers,
> Hurrah boys, the river's ours.[115]

As thousands of Americans streamed into Canada, Britain was finally forced to focus on the status of British Columbia and even then, it was almost too late. In the fall of 1858, a group of American miners led by Ned McGowan decided to annex part of British Columbia. According to McGowan, "We had arranged a plan, in case of a

Oregon Question cartoon. Library of Congress.

collision with the [British] troops, to take Fort Yale and then go down the river and capture Fort Hope. ... This would, we supposed, bring on the fight and put an end to the long agony and public clamor—through the press of the country—that our boundary line must be 'fifty-four forty or fight.'"[116] Luckily for Britain, the Royal Engineers arrived in the territory in the nick of time and were able to thwart McGowan's annexation plan. Shortly thereafter, Britain enacted the British Columbia Act of 1858.[117]

This act established the official colony of British Columbia and declared that it was to be a "second England."[118] It also announced that all immigrants must accept British sovereignty. Nevertheless, in order to make this condition more palatable to the American miners and hopefully entice them to stay, the act promised that those who accepted this condition would receive free land: "Foreigners, as such, are not entitled to grants of waste land of the Crown in British Colonies. But it is the strong desire of Her Majesty's Government to attract to this territory all peaceful settlers, without regard to nation. Naturalization should, therefore, be granted to all who desire it . . . and with naturalization the right of acquiring Crown land should follow."[119] As the text makes clear, the act was an attempt to capitalize on the opportunity presented by the gold rush. British Columbia needed settlers, and the gold rush had brought thousands of miners to the territory. The difficulty was that most of these potential immigrants were transient Americans who the government feared would disappear once their mining claims had been exhausted. Therefore, the British government offered the newly arrived miners free land hoping that this would incentivize them to accept British sovereignty and permanently settle in the territory.[120]

In many ways, the plan was solid, but there was one significant problem: few women resided in the colony, and without women, most of the American miners were unwilling to stay.[121] In addition, the lack of marriageable women was also causing Canadians to abandon the colony. Colonial minister Matthew Macfie, who wrote a book describing life in early British Columbia, specifically noted this problem. According to Macfie, there were "many well-disposed single [Canadian] men prospering in the various trades and professions, who are anxious to adopt this country as their home. But the scope for selecting wives is so limited that they feel compelled to go to California in search of their interesting object, and not unfrequently are they tempted to remain on American soil—their industry as producers and expenditure as consumers being lost to the colonies."[122] Other British Columbians echoed Macfie's observations regarding the dangers of female scarcity and the need for female immigration. For example, an editorial in Victoria's *Times* lamented, "There is probably no country where the paucity of women . . . is so injuriously felt. . . . Oh! if 50 or 100 should arrive from England every month . . . what a blessing it would be to us and the colony at large." The same author also predicted that "[w]ithout [women] the men will never settle in the country."[123] Editors of another Victoria newspaper, the *Colonist*, repeated these sentiments. They stated it was imperative that the "[g]overnment or someone else provides wives for our young men," and warned that without women, "the society here and throughout these colonies will prove *shiftless* for a long time."[124]

In response to such pleas, Alexander Grant Dallas, chief factor of the Hudson Bay Company, which governed Vancouver Island, and son-in-law to Governor Douglas, printed the following advertisement in the *London Times* on January 1, 1862:

> Permit me to draw attention to a crying evil—the want of women. I believe there is not one to every hundred men at the mines; without them the male population will never settle this country and innumerable evils are the consequence. A large number of the weaker sex could obtain wages, with the certainty of marriage in the background.
>
> The miner is not very particular—plain, fat and fifty even would not be objected to, while good looking girls would be the nuggets and prized accordingly. An immigration of such character would be a great boon to the colony as I am sure it would be to many under-paid and over-worked women who drag out a weary existence in the dismal streets and alleys of the metropolis.[125]

Dallas's ad may have sparked interest among the "under-paid and over-worked" women who read it, but without financial assistance, few such women would have been able to make the journey. As previous marriage migration programs had demonstrated, free passage was essential. The problem was that the territorial government did not have the money to finance marital immigration programs. Moreover, although there were plenty of wealthy Britons with the money to sponsor such emigration, they were not particularly concerned with the love lives of backwoods miners. This apathy disappeared, however, particularly among religious Britons, when they learned that, instead of remaining single, lonely Canadian men were entering into relationships with native women. Ultimately, it was the threat of intermarriage that spurred the creation of mail-order bride expeditions to British Columbia.

In 1858, Canadian minister Reverend R. C. Lundin Brown wrote a letter to the bishop of Oxford, Samuel Wilberforce, seeking support for female emigration to the colony.[126] Brown's letter emphasized the proliferation of interracial relationships throughout the colony and warned that such marriages would "ruin Religion and morals in this fine country."[127] In order to avert this danger, Brown suggested the immediate immigration of white women. The colonists were eager to marry white women if they were available: "Dozens of men have told me they would gladly marry if they could. I was speaking one evening on the subject of the dearth of females, and mentioned my intention of writing to beg that a plan of emigration be set on foot; whereupon one member of the company immediately exclaimed, 'Then sir, I pre-empt a wife'; another, and another, and all round the circle of those listening to me earnestly exclaimed the same."[128]

Other Canadian ministers, such as Macfie and Bishop George Hills, had also been quite vocal in voicing their objections to interracial marriages. In Macfie's book, *Vancouver Island and British Columbia: Their History, Resources, and Prospects,* he railed against the "[h]undreds of dissolute white men ... liv[ing] in open concubinage with these [native women] wretched creatures."[129] Similarly, Hills's diary also contained numerous references and condemnations of the interracial "immorality" he encountered throughout the Canadian West. Referring to the gold rush town of Douglas, Hills wrote, "almost every man in Douglas lives with an Indian woman" and described a particularly scandalous example in which the local magistrate and constable were both competing for the affections of the same Indian woman. According to Hills, this love triangle occurred after the magistrate sent the constable on a long-distance errand and, while he was gone, convinced the woman to come live with him. When the constable returned, he tried to woo her back, but he was unsuccessful and "eventually gave up."[130]

Reports like those of Hills, Brown, and Macfie were effective. Shortly after receiving Brown's letter, Wilberforce helped found the Columbia Emigration Society (CES). The goal of the organization was

A fur trapper and his Indian bride. Watercolor by Alfred
Jacob Miller.

to prevent interracial marriage and protect the colony from "all the evils
of heathendom."[131] The group believed that by financing the immigration of white women to British Columbia,[132] they could decrease the
rate of mixed marriages,[133] while simultaneously encouraging British
Columbian "men to become permanent colonists."[134] They expected
that the arrival of substantial numbers of white women would reduce
the need for intermarriage and make it possible to deny recognition to
intermarriages performed according to native custom. They were correct. According to historian Cynthia Comacchio, "the arrival of white

women effectively ended the long-standing practice of intermarriage according to the 'custom of the country,' as white men began to leave their Aboriginal families for new unions with white women."[135] The case of William Connolly demonstrates the effectiveness of this plan.

Connolly was the chief factor of the North West Company. In 1830, he retired from the company, left his Cree wife of nearly thirty years, and moved to Montreal to marry his cousin.[136] In 1867, Connolly's Indian children sued his estate and won their inheritance claim based on Connolly having been validly married to their mother.[137] The judge ruled that their union was considered valid both because they "had been married according to the customs and usages" of the Cree people and "because the consent of both parties, the essential element of 'civilized' marriage, had been proved by twenty-eight years of repute, public acknowledgement, and cohabitation as man and wife."

When the *Connolly* case was decided, the practice of marriage according to the "custom of the country" was still relatively common, but within a generation, these marriages were declared invalid. In 1886, the Canadian court overturned the Connolly decision and ruled that the court would not accept that the "cohabitation of a civilized man and a savage woman, even for a long period of time, gives rise to the presumption that they consented to be married in our sense of marriage."[138]

The purpose of Wilberforce's CES was to "save" British Columbia by sponsoring female immigration and preventing intermarriages.[139] However, as Eliza Farnham's failed mail-order bride effort had demonstrated, saving men is not a particularly compelling incentive for potential female immigrants. In the nineteenth century, immigration, particularly transatlantic immigration, was risky and uncertain. Most prospective mail-order brides needed more than a belief in racial hierarchies to induce them to emigrate. Both the Benton and Mercer voyages were successful because they offered eastern women a feasible alternative to a life of limited opportunities and increased marginalization. In the end, it was these factors, not religious zeal or racial bigotry, that spurred British women's immigration as well.

At the time CES was founded, England was panicking over its "surplus" woman problem. Throughout the 1850s, the number of unmarried women in England had increased significantly, and by 1862 it was estimated that there were half a million more single women than men. According to William Rathbone Greg, author of the infamous treatise *Why Are Women Redundant?*, this disparity was a crisis of unparalleled proportion: "[T]here is an enormous and increasing number of single women in the nation, a number quite disproportionate and quite abnormal; a number which, positively and relatively, is indicative of an unwholesome social state, and is both productive and prognostic of much wretchedness and wrong."[140] After describing this pressing problem, Greg concluded that the only solution was massive female emigration.

The idea of the "surplus woman" was insulting and degrading, but it forced English feminists to seriously consider the role of women in English society. In the end, they also concluded that emigration was the solution. For these female leaders, emigration was an appropriate response to a society where women were undervalued in general and where single, educated women, in particular, were seen as a burden. As the English feminist Bessie Parkes stated, "Seeing, as I do daily, how great is the comparative delicacy both in brain and in the bodily frames of women of the middle and upper class, of the bad effect on them of long hours of sedentary toil, the more anxious I become to see the immense surplus of the sex in England lightened by judicious, well conducted, and morally guarded emigration to our colonies, where the disproportion is equally enormous, and where they are wanted in every social capacity."[141] Feminist Maria Rye echoed these sentiments and this led her to establish the Female Middle Class Emigration Society (FMCES). The purpose of FMCES was to help women overcome the barriers to middle-class employment through marital immigration. Unlike Greg, Rye did not see employment and marriage as opposites. In fact, she saw marriage and immigration as two sides of the same coin. Rye believed that where women had good employment prospects, they also had good marriage prospects. Consequently, she advised her recruiters to "[t]each your protégés to emigrate; send them where the men want wives, the mothers want governesses, where the shopkeepers, the schools, and the sick will thoroughly appreciate your exertions, and heartily welcome your women."[142] The surplus women debate had highlighted the widespread antagonism directed at single women in England, particularly educated women, and these protests convinced many women that their best opportunities lay in the colonies.[143] Consequently, although the motivations of FMCES were quite different from the racist concerns of CES, their overall goal was the same and the groups decided to join forces.[144] Together, they sponsored two successful mail-order bride voyages to British Columbia.

The first group of British mail-order brides arrived on the *Tynemouth* in 1862, the second on the *Robert Lowe* a year later. The arrivals garnered immense excitement. The day was declared a holiday. Stores closed and everyone came to the docks, dressed in their best clothes, eager to watch the scores of lonely miners try to woo the new arrivals. One savvy shopkeeper even placed signs, stating, "The girls have arrived! Now is your chance to get a fine suit of clothes to make a respectable appearance."[145] As the women disembarked, they were immediately inundated with offers of marriage. In many cases, the miners' wooing tactics were crude. The richer miners would simply hold up gold nuggets and propose as the women walked by.[146] In one case, a particularly eager man grabbed the arm of one of the women as she disembarked and proposed while placing two thousand dollars in her hand.[147] After staring at the fortune she had just been handed, the woman accepted, and the crowd went wild. The couple married shortly thereafter, but the ultimate outcome of this union is unclear.[148] Although there are descriptions of a beautiful wedding, there are also reports that the groom became so intoxicated after the ceremony that the bride changed her mind. Apparently, the next day the groom was spotted searching for his bride "as he had not seen her since supper."[149]

Despite this notable exception, quick weddings were once again rare. Most of the women did not rush into marriage, and at least half wouldn't even consider marriage until after they had had the chance to take advantage of Victoria's high wages and good working conditions.[150] The Victoria Female Emigration Committee noted that when the arriving women were interviewed, the common response was that they wanted to work and would frequently tell the committee members, "I don't care where I goes, or what I does, so long as I gets plenty of money."[151] In a letter to her family, one of the recent arrivals wrote, "I got a situation and a very happy one. Mrs. ___ is such a gentle, kind lady and three such good, well behaved children. I have £74 a year in wages."[152] This wage was more than double what the average domestic could expect to earn in England,[153] and one of the results of such high wages was that the women had no need to marry quickly or even at all. Although most eventually did marry, a few entrepreneurial women stayed single and used their earnings to establish a business. For example, one of the Tynemouth women, Florence Wilson, was initially employed as a governess. However, she soon realized she could be much more successful in business, so she began working for a local family, sewing clothes. A few months later, she opened a stationery shop and shortly thereafter went north to the center of the gold rush, where she opened a library and became British Columbia's first librarian.[154] Wilson also founded an acting troupe, purchased multiple mining claims, became proprietor of Florence Co. mining, and even established her own saloon.[155]

As in America, immigration also provided many Canadian mail-order brides with the opportunity to surmount class barriers.[156] The majority of these women began their life in Canada as servants or governesses, but, unlike back in England, these roles were usually temporary and many went on to become prominent members of Victoria society.[157] One woman, Emma Lazenby Spencer, came to Victoria as an unemployed mill worker. She then took a job as one of Victoria's first Sunday school teachers, married a local bookstore owner, opened a dry goods store with him, and, eventually, became one of the richest women in Victoria. Spencer then used her money to help establish a refuge for poor and "fallen" women, founded the first maternity ward, and served as president of Victoria's Women's Christian Temperance Movement.[158]

The experiences of Canadian mail-order brides were similar to those of their American counterparts. In both cases, the complex forces of feminism, imperialism, capitalism, and racism created a situation in which divergent interests aligned to produce support for a variety of large-scale marital immigration programs. Each of these programs led to the immigration of hundreds of mail-order brides and benefited these women through increased financial, legal, and social opportunities. However, the period of political and financial support for each of these programs was relatively brief. By the second half of the century, interracial marriage and annexation were no longer considered significant threats and the government's interest in mail-order marriage began to wane. At the same time, improved communication and transportation meant that individuals could now arrange their own mail-order marriages. Large portions of the American West were still predominantly male, and these men increasingly turned to marital advertisements as a way to achieve marriage. By the end of the century, thousands of couples had used matrimonial ads to enter into mail-order marriages, but support for these marriages disappeared once growing numbers of foreign women began using mail-order marriage to immigrate to the United States.

PART II

Mail-Order Marriage Acquires a Bad Reputation

5

Advertising for Love

The Rise of Matrimonial Advertisements

Early American mail-order marriages were supported and even celebrated, but they were also relatively rare. Then, after the Civil War, mail-order marriage became widespread. There were a number of reasons for this change, but one of the most important was the increasing use of matrimonial advertisements. Matrimonial ads benefited American men and women by giving them the ability to create their own mail-order marriages. These ads provided mail-order participants with more information about their potential spouse and more control over the terms of their future marriage. This change made mail-order marriage more attractive to a greater number of women, but the use of these ads also altered the perception of mail-order marriage.[1] Unlike government-sponsored mail-order marriages, which had been closely monitored and imbued with a sense of nationalistic purpose, the mail-order marriages created through matrimonial ads were highly individualistic and mostly unsupervised. In addition, by the time matrimonial ads began to appear in American newspapers, the practice had already become widespread in Britain where these ads were often employed by men and women seeking to subvert parental and governmental authority. This history affected how Americans viewed matrimonial ads and left them suspicious of the marriages these ads generated. Consequently, in order to understand the changing perception of mail-order marriage in post–Civil War America, it is important to first examine the history of British matrimonial advertising.

The first British matrimonial advertisements began as a joke. In 1660, a London periodical called the *Mercurius Fumigosus* printed a fake advertisement purporting to be from a "worthy, plump, fresh, free and willing Widdow" who sought a man "to labour in her Corporation." The ad instructed all those interested to "come to this pure piece of iniquity" and promised that the man who presents "the true picture of his Tool," would unquestionably "find favour."[2] A few years later, another periodical, *Poor Robin's Intelligence*, printed a similar ad. This ad purported to be from a "Worcestershire Gentlewoman" with a "face just of the complexion of a Garden-walk new gravel'd" who sought a husband "professing the Ingenious mystery of 'Chimney-scouring.'"[3] These two ads were lewd jokes, but in 1695 the first legitimate matrimonial advertisements appeared.[4]

The ads were printed in a pamphlet titled *A Collection for Improvement of Husbandry and Trade* and were printed alongside ads for an Arabian stallion, a secondhand bed, and a cobbler's apprentice.[5] The first of these ads described a thirty-year-old man with a "Very Good Estate" who was searching for "some Good Young Gentlewoman that has a Fortune of £3,000 or thereabouts."[6] The second advertised "A Young Man about 25 Years of Age, in a very good Trade, and whose Father will make him worth £1000," who "would willingly embrace a suitable Match." He further added that "[h]e has been brought up a Dissenter, with his Parents, and is a sober Man."[7]

The ads were intended to cause a sensation. The pamphlet's publisher, John Houghton, believed that given the long history of comical matrimonial ads, the first serious ads would garner considerable interest and, hopefully, profit.[8] Consequently, rather than burying the ads in small print in the middle of the pamphlet, he specifically called attention to them by printing them in a larger and bolder font than the surrounding news articles.[9] At the same time, he also wanted these ads to be taken seriously, so he captioned them with the statement that although he expected the advertisements to be greeted with ridicule initially, he hoped that after "the Nine Days Wonder and Laughter (usually attending new things) are over ... such Advertisements may prove useful."[10] Houghton got his wish. Matrimonial advertising was an immediate success. By 1710, all fifty-three of London's major newspapers contained matrimonial advertisements.[11]

The rise of the matrimonial ad was directly related to the rapid urbanization of England. From the mid-sixteenth century to the end of the seventeenth, London was transformed from a city of eighty thousand inhabitants into a metropolis of more than half a million people.[12] Thousands of men and women flowed into the city from the countryside to take advantage of new job opportunities.[13] Urban employment gave both men and women significant independence from parental control. However, for women, these new jobs also gave them the means to furnish their own dowries and, correspondingly, the freedom to make their own marital choices. As the popular period newspaper, the *Athenian Mercury*,[14] noted, this financial independence meant that a woman "could largely disregard parental advice" since she was "almost as much at her own dispose as a widow."[15]

Growing financial independence enabled young men and women to embrace growing Enlightenment ideals. Enlightenment thinkers championed the value of choice in social relationships, and they specifically defined love as the most important criterion to be considered when choosing a spouse.[16] The *Athenian Mercury* responded to these changing ideas about marriage by offering women advice on the qualities they should look for in a spouse. According to British historian Helen Berry, this was "a fairly radical position to take, since it recognized that women had a degree of autonomy in certain matters which was anomalous to their generally subordinate status in society."[17] However, this acceptance of female autonomy was rarely emulated. Instead, the more common response to the rising demand for marital choice was to forbid it. In defiance, significant numbers of young men and women began arranging their own marriages, resulting in a parental panic and the introduction of legal reforms intended to reassert parental control.[18]

The first of these changes was the decision to finally and definitively void marriage broker contracts. Marriage broker contracts were a well-established method used by young men and women to arrange marriage without parental assistance or approval. These contracts had long been treated with concern, but they had never been forbidden. In fact, certain courts had gone out of their way to enforce these contracts. For example, in the 1598 case of *Blandford v. Andrews,* a hopeful suitor named Blandford promised to pay a man named Andrews eighty pounds if Andrews would arrange his marriage to Bridget Palmer by the Feast of St. Bartholomew. Andrews agreed. However, before Andrews could speak with Bridget at the Feast, Blandford found Bridget, called her a whore, and promised that if he married her, he would tie her to a post. Unsurprisingly, when Andrews subsequently approached Bridget with the marriage proposal, she refused and Andrews made no further attempts to create the match. Blandford then sued Andrews. Shockingly, the court ruled for Blandford, stating that Andrews should have tried harder, but by late seventeenth century, judicial attitudes had changed.[19]

In two court cases, *Drury v. Hooke* and *Hall and Keene v. Potter,* marriage broker contracts were finally and conclusively declared void.[20] *Drury v. Hooke* was decided in 1686 and concerned a marriage between a young man and woman, arranged by a marriage broker without the consent of the woman's parents. The young man desired the marriage because he believed the woman was wealthy. However, after marrying, the husband learned the woman's fortune was less than he anticipated, and he refused to pay the broker fee.[21] The marriage broker then sued the husband to enforce the contract, but the court held the entire contract invalid.[22] The *Drury* court described marriage broker contracts as abominable and equated them to "a sort of kidnapping." The chancellor held that "such bonds are of very ill Consequence" and "not to be countenanced." He further added that these contracts were particularly disturbing in instances where the parties had living parents.[23]

The facts of *Drury* exemplified everything that was wrong with marriage broker contracts. The case involved a greedy man using a marriage broker to enrich himself while potentially harming a young girl and her family. Consequently, although the *Drury* case seemed to declare all broker contracts void, the fact that it involved a financially disadvantageous marriage left open the possibility that the court's ruling applied only to dishonest contracts. This possibility was then eliminated in 1696 in *Hall and Keene v. Potter*,[24] which clearly held that all marriage broker contracts, even advantageous ones, undermined parental control and were void.[25]

The *Hall and Keene* case arose out of a contract entered into by Thomas Thinne and his marriage broker, Mrs. Potter. Thinne promised Mrs. Potter one thousand pounds if she could arrange his marriage to Lady Ogle, "a widow of great fortune and honor, being the daughter and heir of Josceline Percy, the last Earl of Northumberland." Mrs. Potter successfully arranged the marriage, but Thinne died before it could take place. After Thinne's death, Potter sued Thinne's executors, Hall and Keene, for payment and they refused, arguing that all marital broker contracts are void because "contracts for procuring of marriages are of dangerous consequence, and tend to the ruin of families."[26] The court agreed. Although the court acknowledged that Potter had made a good match,[27] it was the court's fear of the bad match that prompted its decision.[28] The court was haunted by the specter of the emotional young woman, convinced by the greedy matchmaker to marry beneath her and ruin her noble family. The court believed this potential harm was so great that it outweighed any possible benefits that could result from a particular contract. Consequently, the court ruled that marriages should be facilitated only through the help of friends and family and declared all marriage broker contracts, regardless of their merits, void.[29]

The fear of emotional young women entering into bad marriages and ruining themselves or their families also led to the outlawing of "clandestine marriage." In the seventeenth and eighteenth centuries, men and women who wanted to arrange their own marriages and avoid parental control increasingly turned to clandestine marriage.[30] These were performed by a member of the clergy, but without public notice or a public ceremony, and were valid regardless of parental objection.[31]

Understandably, clandestine marriages were viewed as a threat to parental control and there were growing attempts to outlaw them. One of the first proposals was a 1685 bill focusing on the possibility of clandestine marriage between a noble child and a menial servant. The bill was addressed to "minors having or expecting considerable estates, real or personal." It noted with panic that such minors "are daily subject to be inveighed or forced away from their fathers or guardians" and it sought to eliminate this danger by outlawing clandestine marriages.[32]

The 1685 bill failed to pass, but a decade later, the rise of a new form of clandestine marriage, known as the Fleet marriage (in reference to the famous debtors prison where they were performed), eventually created the support needed to outlaw the practice. Fleet marriages originated as a way to avoid the 1694 marriage tax.[33] In order to collect this tax, clergy were required to keep a record of all marriages they performed. However, certain clergymen, specifically incarcerated ministers, fell outside the scope of the 1694 statute and could not be forced to register marriages or help collect the marriage taxes.[34] These ministers had no property or parishes, so the law was powerless to punish them. They could not be removed from office for they had no congregation; they could not be locked up because they were already imprisoned; and they could not be fined for they had already been incarcerated for lack of money.[35] As a result, the business of these irregular marriages took off.[36]

The majority of participants liked Fleet marriages because they were tax-free and thus cheaper than regular marriages. However, they also presented an attractive option for those wishing to keep their unions private or even secret. Many upper-class couples and some nobility began to seek the services of the Fleet parsons, resulting in a tremendous backlash.[37] Parents from these social groups were livid when they realized their children were using Fleet marriages to wed without their consent. London's growing middle class also began to fear these marriages because they viewed them as a threat to their newly acquired social standing.[38] Consequently, the next proposal to outlaw clandestine marriage was broader and no longer focused exclusively on the

Caricature of a Fleet marriage. Wikimedia Commons.

children of nobility. In fact, the 1736 proposal to outlaw clandestine marriages originated in the House of Commons and referred to the "many Persons under Age, who are intitled [sic] to considerable Fortunes, are frequently married without the Consent of their Parents or Guardians." The 1736 proposal sought to ameliorate this problem by permitting parents to void any minor marriages entered into without parental consent.[39] This second proposed ban also failed to pass, but in 1753, Parliament finally outlawed clandestine marriage. The ban was known as Lord Hardwicke's Act.[40]

Lord Hardwicke's Act ended the practice of clandestine marriages and secured parental power over marriage by changing the requirements necessary to create a legal marriage. Under the act, a legal marriage required banns or a license, a solemn public celebration in an Anglican church or chapel, and two or more witnesses. It also required all clergy to keep detailed records of every marriage performed.[41] The recording requirement was in response to the fact that clandestine marriage records were often falsified and phony oaths were common. This meant a spouse, generally a wife, had no evidence upon which to rely if her husband subsequently abandoned her.[42] In addition, the act voided all marriages contracted by minors without parental consent and decreed that any clergy who performed clandestine marriages would be punished with exile to the colonies for fourteen years.[43] Last, it stated that the punishment for falsifying records was death.[44]

Hardwicke's Act eliminated the practice of clandestine marriage, but did not stem the desire of single men and women to control their marriage choices. Thousands of young couples began eloping to Scotland, particularly the border town of Gretna Green, where they could still marry without parental consent.[45] In addition, increasing numbers of young men and women began turning to matrimonial advertisements as a new means of skirting parental control. For women in particular, matrimonial advertisements provided a way to counterbalance the appalling disrespect for female marital decisions enshrined in Hardwicke's Act.

Supporters of the act had promoted it by convincing members of Parliament that women were irrational and their choices could not be trusted. John Sayer, one of the act's strongest advocates, argued it was necessary because the passion of women was like that of a "high mettled colt, which if at first well broke affords his master many delightful rides: but for want of this is all his life long unruly, vicious, and dangerous."[46] Sayer's views on female autonomy were common among the supporters of the act, and even opponents expressed little concern for women. The majority of men who opposed the act were simply worried that it would permit rich men to hoard their daughters.[47] For example, one of the principal opponents was Robert Nugent, a man who had made his fortune by marrying rich women.[48] In fact, Nugent had gained such a reputation for his advantageous marriages that Earl Robert Walpole coined the term to "Nugentize," which means to marry up.[49] According to Nugent, the problem with Hardwicke's Act was not that it would infringe on women's autonomy, but that it would enable the wealthy to "secure all the rich heiresses in the kingdom to those of their own body."[50] Charles Townshend, another opponent of the act, echoed these sentiments. He also likened women to property and worried about the unfairness of hoarding this property. Townshend compared women in clandestine marriages to "goods entered without clearance from the proper civil officer" but argued that women should nevertheless be allowed to marry poorer men because such marriages benefited the public by dispersing wealth.[51]

Hardwicke's Act epitomized the idea that women were chattel and should have little say in their marital destinies. However, eighteenth-century Englishwomen were increasingly rejecting this view. By the late 1700s, women like Mary Wollstonecraft were speaking out against the subordination of women. In Wollstonecraft's 1792 treatise, *A Vindication of the Rights of Woman*, she wrote that men should "treat [women] like rational creatures, instead of flattering their *fascinating* graces, and viewing them as if they were in a childhood, unable to stand alone." She further added that her purpose in writing the book was "to persuade women to endeavor to acquire strength, both of mind and body, and to convince them that the soft phrases, susceptibility of heart, delicacy of sentiment, and refinement of taste, are almost synonymous with epithets of weakness."[52]

Wollstonecraft's words resonated with the many eighteenth-century women who sought greater equality, particularly in their marital relationships,[53] but this desire for equality was made more difficult by women's growing marital disadvantage. Since the mid-seventeenth century, the amount needed for aristocratic women to secure a marriage had doubled,[54] and a decline in real wages had also made it harder for lower- and middle-class women to amass the dowries they needed to find a husband.[55] Despite the growing references to the value of love, the majority of eighteenth-century marriages were still based on monetary considerations. In fact, the importance of money was arguably increasing. Marriage announcements from this period routinely describe the fortunes of the brides (but rarely the husbands) either by listing an explicit monetary amount or with words such "as 'large,' 'ample,' 'considerable' or 'handsome.'" The announcement of Gilbert Burton's marriage was typical. It stated that "Gilbert Burton, Esq; eldest son to George Burton, Esq; was married to ... Miss Craddock, only daughter to Mr. Craddock, late an eminent goldsmith in Lombard Street, a beautiful young lady with a fortune of £10,000." The growing mercenary nature of eighteenth-century marriage is further exemplified by the 1742 publication *A Master Key to the Rich Ladies Treasury: The Widower and Bachelor's Directory*, which provided the names, addresses, and fortunes of four hundred wealthy women, including a number of whom were in their seventies and eighties.[56]

Added to these monetary difficulties was the fact that, in urban areas, single men were relatively scarce. Rural to urban migration was primarily female, and a significantly greater number of marriageable women than men lived in cities. This gender disparity was then further compounded by war (England was engaged in the War of the League of Augsburg) and colonial emigration, both of which had dramatically reduced the number of single men in England.[57] Moreover, large numbers of the remaining single men were uninterested in marriage. In cities like London, unmarried men were able to live comfortable lives as bachelors and many found this option highly attractive. By 1695, there were areas in London where these single men accounted for more than 20 percent of the population.[58]

The above factors greatly reduced many women's marital opportunities, and this, combined with a desire for greater marital autonomy, set the stage for an explosion in matrimonial advertising and the rise of female-authored ads.[59] The first matrimonial advertisements were all written by men, but, in the years after Hardwicke's Act, women began authoring matrimonial advertisements. These ads provided women with many of the same benefits as earlier colonial marriage expeditions. They helped women increase their marital value, expand their number of suitors, and improve their economic and social circumstances. At the same time, they also provided women with a number of advantages over earlier mail-order bride programs. Specifically, they gave mail-order brides significantly more control over their future marriages.

Early mail-order brides had little knowledge of the type of men they were agreeing to marry. They were also unable to request certain qualities in their future husbands or even negotiate the terms of their marriages. The rise of matrimonial advertisements improved this situation. Matrimonial advertisements and matrimonial correspondence provided potential mail-order brides with important information regarding the men they were agreeing to marry and gave women substantially more control over the circumstances of their marriages.

The first female-authored ad was published in the *Aris Gazette* in 1761. The ad was written by two friends and stated,

> To the men of Sense, Wanted, for two young Ladies, whose persons are
>   Amiable, straight and free
>   From natural or chance Deformity,—Pomfret two agreeable Partners
> for Life, Men of Integrity and Worth, between the age of 24 and 30, if in
> Trade will be most agreeable. They are Ladies about the same Age, with
> very handsome Fortunes and whose Characters bear the strictest
> Enquiry.[60]

The ad's request for men of "integrity and worth" between twenty-four and thirty and in trade followed the format established by the numerous male-written matrimonial ads. However, the female authors also took the unusual step of including a quote from John Pomfret's poem, "To His Friend Inclined to Marry." Pomfret's poem lists various things a man should look for in a woman, and eventually concludes with the Enlightenment idea that love is the most important criterion.[61] By including the Pomfret quote, the ad's authors indicate that they are seeking not only a love match but also, like the poem's male author, to define their marriage criteria.[62]

The demands in the 1761 ad are subtle, but as female-authored ads became more common, the authors of these ads became increasingly willing to dictate their marital desires. For example, in 1787, the *Times* printed the following highly specific ad from a woman seeking a husband. According to the writer, her future husband was someone who

> [m]ust never drink above two bottles of claret, or one of port at a sitting, and that but three times week. His education must be liberal, his address captivating. In company he must pay a constant attention to his spouse, and not ogle, or intrigue, by squints and looks, with pert misses, who constantly give men encouragement by made-up leers, and manufactured sight. He must love and cherish the women [*sic*] only he has promised to do so in the sight of heaven. He must never get up after twelve or rise before nine o'clock: in a word, he must be the very man he ought to be.[63]

Many of this writer's demands are unreasonable. However, her unreasonableness is intriguing. At a time when wives were supposed to be meek and docile, this author rejected that stereotype and used matrimonial advertising to help arrange a different kind of union. Consequently, regardless of whether this particular woman was able to find a husband who met her numerous requirements, her ad shows how women could use matrimonial ads to find men open to more unconventional marital arrangements.[64] Not surprisingly, the feminist potential of these ads did not go unnoticed.

In Sarah Gardner's 1777 play, *The Matrimonial Advertisement, or a Bold Stroke for a Husband*, she explicitly presents matrimonial ads as a means of improving women's lives by giving them greater control over their marital prospects. The play centers on a rich and powerful widow and her search for a husband. When the widow was young, she was forced to marry a man of her parents' choosing. Now that she is older and independent, she is determined to marry for love and, in order to arrange this love match, the widow places a matrimonial ad: "Any Gentleman, well born, well educated, well principled, of sound morals

and unblemished character, charitable enough to take a young agree-
able Widow with a plentiful fortune; and who is very desirous of enjoy-
ing the supreme felicities of the married state with such a partner: let
him address a line to the Widow Windfall, at Madame l'Bronze ... at
the Lamb in Love Lane."[65] Gardner presents the widow's decision to
advertise as empowering, but she is also aware that it is controversial,
and she has one of the widow's suitors provide the following defense
of female matrimonial advertisers. The suitor states, "And why not? ...
when a lady swerves from the general rule and makes the first advances
she is deemed indelicate. Fy! 'tis illiberal! An untainted mind is above
all prejudice."[66]

Interestingly, the widow's defender is actually a false suitor, a man interested only in her fortune, but this makes the impact of his statement
even more forceful. The widow, with her "untainted mind," is above reproach and achieves happiness through her ad. It is only the false suitor,
with his devious motives, who is harmed by his involvement in marital
advertising. When he attempts to convince the widow of his affections,
she easily recognizes that he is solely interested in her fortune. Therefore, instead of falling for his deception, she quickly rejects his suit and
leaves him "confounded with shame" for being the "first of [his] family, that has been outwitted by a woman."[67] In this way, Gardner's play
dismisses the common criticism that matrimonial ads harm women's
reputations or increase their likelihood of deception. Instead, the play
shows how such ads were used by intelligent women to initiate courtships and increase their marital choices.[68]

By the time Gardner's play was produced, matrimonial advertising
in England had become pervasive. By 1777, it was so widely used that
one young lady was able to complain "the mode of advertising is become too general" (this did not stop her from placing her own ad).[69] In
America, however, matrimonial advertising was much slower to catch
on. The first American matrimonial ads were all jokes; only decades
later did serious ads begin to be published.

One of the earliest joke matrimonials was an ad written in 1722 by Benjamin Franklin and published in the *New England Courant*. Franklin's ad stated,

> Advertisement.
> Several Journeymen Gentlemen (some Foreigners, and others of our Own Growth), never sully'd with Business, and fit for Town or Country Diversion, are willing to dispose of themselves in Marriage, as follows, viz.: Some to old Virgins, who, by long Industry have laid up £500, or proved themselves capable of maintaining a husband in a genteel and commendable Idleness. Some to old or young Widows, who have Estates of their first husband's getting, to dispose of at their second husband's pleasure. And some to young Ladies, under age, who have their Fortunes in their own Hands, and are willing to maintain a pretty, genteel Man, rather than be without him.
>
> N.B. The above Gentlemen may be spoke with almost any hour in the day at the Tick-Tavern, in Prodigal Square, and will proceed to Courtship as soon as their Mistresses shall pay their Tavern Score.[70]

A few months later, the paper ran another Franklin penned ad further mocking the supposed mercenary nature of matrimonial advertisements. The ad read,

> Any young Gentlewoman (Virgin or Widow) that is minded to dispose of her self in Marriage to a well accomplish'd young Widower, and has five or six hundred Pounds to secure to him by Deed of Gift, she may repair to the Sign of the Glass-Lanthorn in Steeple-Square, to find all the encouragement she can reasonably desire.[71]

As these joke ads demonstrate, American colonists were familiar enough with the form and purpose of matrimonial advertisements to make fun of them, but demographic differences between the two countries made matrimonial advertisements far less useful in colonial America.

Unlike England, America was primarily rural, with no comparable cities and limited migration. Moreover, in the small country towns and villages where most Americans lived, marriage was a necessity and being "picky" or remaining single was not an option.[72] In fact, being single was outlawed in many colonial towns. For example, one Connecticut town law forbade "any young unmarried man to keep house," and another required all single persons to live with their families.[73]

Many colonial towns also imposed significant penalties on adult children who attempted to leave home. For example, one Connecticut town "taxed 'lone-men' twenty shillings a week 'for the selfish luxury of solitary living.'"[74] Similarly, a Massachusetts town discouraged bachelors by requiring that "every unmarried man in the township shall kill six blackbirds, or three crows, while he remains single."[75] In Hartford, Connecticut, a bachelor tax was imposed on both the single man and any who aided his unmarried state by renting him lodgings.[76] Specifically, the Hartford law stated that "'Bourders, Sojourners, and Young persons' are required to 'attend to the Worship of God' in the families where they live and 'to be subject to the domestick Government of the same,' or else forfeit five shillings for every breach of the law."[77] A few single men were able to circumvent such prohibitions, but it was extremely difficult. When two Connecticut bachelors sought to share a home in violation of one of these ordinances, they had to bring their case to court and receive a special dispensation from the town authorities before their request was granted. Even then, the authorities made them promise to "carry themselves soberly and ... not entertain idle persons to the evil expense of time by day or night."[78]

Given the difficulties faced by those attempting to remain single, it is not surprising that marriage in colonial America was nearly universal and that parental control over children and their marital decisions was much stronger than in England.[79] In addition to prohibitions on leaving home, parental control was cemented through numerous statutes requiring parental consent for marriage. In 1632, Virginia enacted the first parental consent statute, but it was soon followed by many others.[80] In 1637, the Plymouth Colony prohibited "'any motion of marriage to any man's daughter or mayde servant' without having 'first obtayned leaue' of the parents or master."[81] Ten years later, Massachusetts law declared that "whereas God hath committed the care and power into the hands of parents for the disposing their Children in Marriage, so that it is against rule, to seek to draw away the affections of young maidens under pretence of purpose of marriage, before their parents have given way and allowance in that respect."[82] A New Haven, Connecticut law from this period was even more explicit. It forbade marriage without parental consent and also provided numerous examples of the ways a wily suitor could attempt to violate this requirement including "speech, writing, message, company-keeping, unnecessary familiarity, disorderly night meetings, sinful dalliance, gifts, or any other way, directly or indirectly."[83]

Most of the colonial parental consent laws preceded Hardwicke's Act by decades.[84] In addition, unlike Hardwicke's Act, which applied only to children under twenty-one, American consent laws rarely included an age limit.[85] The purpose of these laws was to aggressively cement parental control. Legal records demonstrate that colonial courts were not hesitant to aid parents in this goal. For instance, in 1648, a court ordered Thomas Dunn to abstain from visiting Martha Knott of Sandwich, Massachusetts; in 1652, Jonathan Coventry was indicted for asking Katherine Bradbury to marry him; in 1658, a Massachusetts court ordered Paul Wilson to pay a ten-pound fine for soliciting the deacon's daughter against her father's will; and in 1660, Arthur Howland was fined five pounds for wooing Plymouth governor Thomas Prence's daughter without permission, a transgression that he committed again seven years later and was again fined.[86] This deference to parental control began to recede in the eighteenth century, but it likely contributed to the delay in American matrimonial advertisings.

When the first American matrimonial advertisement was finally published in 1759, it is not surprising that the author specifically requested a woman unconstrained by parental authority. The ad appeared in the *Boston Evening Post* on February 23, 1759:

> To the Ladies. Any young Lady between the Age of Eighteen and twenty three of a Midling Stature; brown Hair, regular Features and a Lively Brisk Eye: Of Good Morals & not Tinctured with anything that may Sully so Distinguishable a Form possessed of 3 or 400£ entirely her own Disposal and where there will be no necessity of going Through the tiresome Talk of addressing Parents or Guardians for their consent: Such a one by leaving a Line directed for A. W. at the British Coffee House in King Street appointing where an Interview may be had will meet with a Person who flatters himself he shall not be thought Disagreeable by any Lady answering the above description. N.B. Profound Secrecy will be observ'd. No Trifling Answers will be regarded.[87]

Whether this ad culminated in marriage is unknown. What is clear, however, is that it did not portend an explosion in matrimonial advertising. Unlike in Britain, where matrimonial ads had experienced almost immediate popularity, in America, another century passed before this mode of courtship became widespread. In the interim, matrimonial advertisements grew steadily but were far from common and were treated primarily as the province of fools and cheats.

Antebellum newspapers would gleefully and ominously recount stories of people caught in marital scams. For instance, in 1852, the *New York Daily Times* ran a particularly humiliating story about a matrimonial hoax carried out by a group of bored English stockbrokers from Leeds. According to the *Times*, the men came up with the idea for the trick after reading a sappy matrimonial ad and deciding it would be amusing to answer it.[88] Writing as a young and beautiful woman named "Miss Bailey," the men began a correspondence with the ad's author. After a short time, they invited the man to meet "Miss Bailey,"

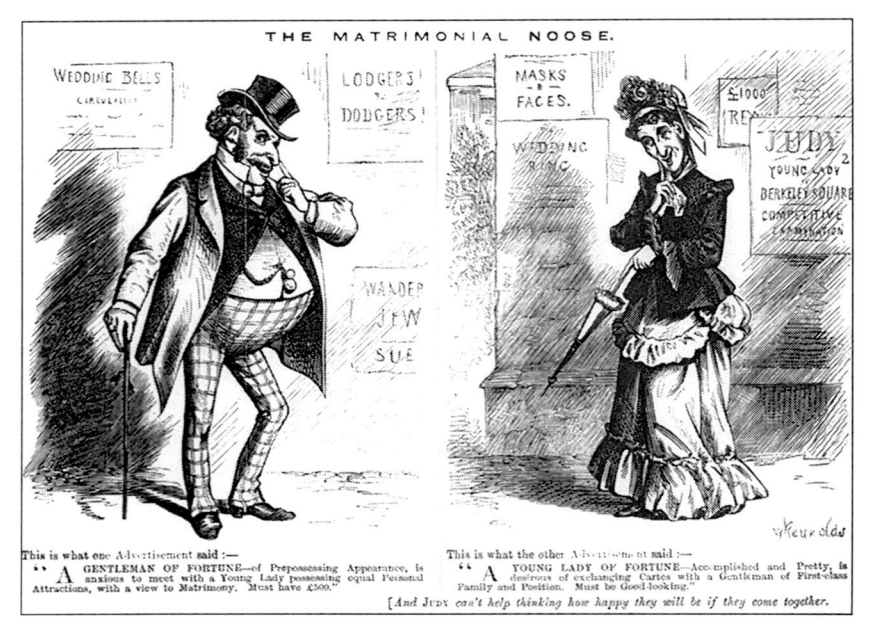

Misleading matrimonial advertisement. A History of Working-Class Marriage, http://workingclassmarriage.gla.ac.uk/tag/personal-ads/.

who would be one of the stockbrokers dressed in drag. The advertiser agreed and, according to the article, "was smitten at first sight." The love-struck man proceeded to declare his affections and propose marriage, "especially when it was made known that the proprietor of this graceful form had £1,500 in her own right." At this point, one hundred of Miss Bailey's collaborators rushed into the room, surrounded the poor suitor, informed him that he had been duped, and took turns reading out loud his entire correspondence. Then, when the oration was complete, the room cheered for Miss Bailey, who stood, dressed as a man, and "acknowledged the compliment." The article ends with a description of the mortified man's departure and the words "he has not since been heard of."[89]

A few years after the Leeds story, the *Times* published another, more menacing article, emphasizing the dangers of matrimonial advertisements. The article involved a man named Charles Chester and chronicled his numerous matrimonial swindles. The article, which was probably fictional, appeared in 1856 under the headline "Romantic Rascality: A Lion among the Ladies" and was clearly a response to the growing popularity of matrimonial ads. Chester is described as a handsome charmer and scoundrel, who abandoned a wife and child in Louisiana and then moved to the Northeast, where he ingratiated himself into New York high society and managed to dupe a number of rich widows into marrying him. Then, because the number of women he could meet this way was limited, he turned to matrimonial advertisements, through which he made "the acquaintance of many foolish women." According to the article, "Many he deceived . . . by advertising for a wife under various names. . . . He first gained the confidence of these ladies, won their affections, proposed to all of them and was by all accepted."[90] The article then explains that Chester's scam was eventually discovered when three of the would-be brides were having their wedding gowns tailored by the same dressmaker, at the same time, and began chatting to each other about their respective fiancés. After a brief discussion, the women realized they were all engaged to the same man.[91] Two of the women fainted, and the article mentions that cologne and cold water were required to arouse them. The piece ends by stating that "[a]t length, fearful, perhaps, of the storm that he had raised, or from some other [reason], the scoundrel accepted an appointment of surgeon on the Isthmus and prepared to start for that place."[92]

A few days after publishing the Chester article, the *Times'* editors claimed to have received numerous additional letters from women who had also been scammed by Chester. The editors declared that given the large number of women being deceived by Chester and presumably others like him, it was their obligation to issue a warning regarding matrimonial advertisements:

> We are in the receipt of a number of letters from ladies, in various parts of the country, who have been to a greater or less extent the victims of

[Chester's] intrigues, begging that their names may not be made public, in connection with the letters they have written. They need not feel the slightest alarm on this score. But we hope they will learn a lesson from their experience, in this instance, which will be of service to them hereafter. They should understand that the matrimonial advertisements, which abound in some of our City papers, are, in nine cases out of ten, merely the tricks of profligate scoundrels, who seek, in this way, to open an acquaintance for the prosecution of their libertine purposes. . . . We are aware that very many young ladies answer these advertisements "for the fun of the thing," and without any serious intention:—but it is very dangerous sport, and may end in compromising their characters to an extent they do not dream of at the onset.

We trust the revelations of this case will check the somewhat active business that has been done for some months past in the line of advertising for wives.[93]

The entire Chester saga appears to have been created as an elaborate warning to women not to engage in matrimonial advertising. However, the *Times* did not limit its concern to women. Shortly after publishing the Chester story, the paper ran another story, also likely fictional, clearly intended to dissuade men from placing matrimonial advertisements. It involved a man named Charley Baker who would amuse himself by answering matrimonial advertisements as a woman named Sallie Baker, a wealthy young woman living with her controlling brother.[94] After receiving a reply to his ad, Baker would suggest the suitor (referred to as a Softie) call on "Sallie" the next day at nine o'clock in the morning. When the man rang the door and asked to see Sallie, Baker would pretend to be Sallie's brother and inform the suitor he did not wish for his sister to receive calls from strangers and then slam the door in the man's face. When the suitor rang again an hour later as instructed in Sallie's letter, Baker would greet him with a cowhide and beat the "rascal who would lead his sister astray." The article ended by noting approvingly that in this manner Baker had used up six rawhides and "taught sense to a score or two of Softies."[95]

Although the Baker and Chester stories are almost certainly fictional, they convey the very real disapproval of matrimonial advertising increasingly common in antebellum America. The majority of Americans viewed them as unnecessary and risky, and those who fell victim to matrimonial scams were perceived as deserving of the resulting deception. The *New York Tribune's* response to a letter from a victim of a matrimonial scam exemplifies this view. The man wrote,

> *To the Editor of the N. Y. Tribune.*
>
> Sir: An old hag in Philadelphia gets her living by occasionally advertising in your paper as a *"prepossessing"* and *"confiding young lady in want of a husband."* From those green enough to reply, she manages, by various *artful pretenses,* to extract from $5 to $10, and then drops the correspondence and goes in for another haul. You ought to expose her. New York, April 14, 1858, A Victim[96]

The *New York Tribune* printed the letter and was willing to aid in the "old hag's" exposure, yet the editors' reply shows they felt very little pity for "A Victim."[97] They responded,

> We do not mean to take the part of swindlers; but we can't help believing that "A Victim" has been served just right—as many victims had been before him, and many more will be after him. For how came he to respond to this "prepossessing" and "confiding young lady"? Was he really in want of a wife? If he were, are the prepossessing young ladies within the sphere of his acquaintance so invincibly averse to matrimony that he can make no impression on the obdurate heart of even one among them? If so, we must believe his experience an uncommon one. But no—those who really desire to make or improve the acquaintance of young ladies with a view to marriage, are under no necessity

of either advertising or responding to advertisements. This is not the mode in which any young woman who desires and deserves a worthy life-partner is at all likely to seek one or ought to do so. Probably nineteen of every twenty matrimonial advertisements are decoys, put forth by libertines or "hags" to lure victims into their toils; and those who respond to them are usually quite as bad as their authors.[98]

The *Tribune*'s statements regarding the ease of entering marriage may have been true for the majority of Americans, but not for all. For the unconventional, radical, or just different, matrimonial advertisements offered an unparalleled means of meeting like-minded individuals. Therefore it is not surprising that some of the earliest publications to solicit matrimonial ads were non-mainstream periodicals. For example, in 1845, the *Water-Cure Journal*, which was popular with the small but growing vegetarianism movement, began seeking matrimonial ads in order help its readers find compatible marriage partners. Most of the authors of these advertisements had radical views on health and social policy issues, and many were affiliated with the women's rights movement or abolition. For example, in an 1855 issue, a woman named Annie published the following: "No. 53—I am thirty-one years of age, large, healthy, good looking, good hearted, a practical vegetarian and hydropath, wear the Bloomer when I choose. As for musical talents, believe I could sing to my own BABIES. Should make a loving wife. Should prefer a farmer or mechanic. Not over-particular. He must be a Water Cure and Vegetarian. ANNIE."[99] By stating she wears bloomers, Annie was indicating her affinity with the women's rights movement. Bloomers were pants worn under short skirts that were developed as an alternative to the restrictive female fashions of the time. They were originally created for health reasons, but because of the freedom of movement they provided, they were quickly adopted by the women's rights movement and became a symbol of reform in the 1850s.

In the same issue, a woman named Gertrude placed an equally radical ad:

No. 64—Am 28 years of age, neither handsome or a "singing angel"; but understand the music of the pudding-slice. Am in no hurry about marrying; but think I should like to find my partner as soon as 31. Am 5 feet 4 inches in height, and must be mated phrenologically and spiritually, or not at all. Should wish one who could do without tea, coffee, pork, beef, mutton, and feather-beds; a practical anti-slavery man, anti-tobacco, and I care not if anti-razor—in short, one who acts upon principle rather than policy. Age anywhere between my own and 40. GERTRUDE.[100]

As these examples demonstrate, some antebellum women began using matrimonial ads to dictate the terms of their marriage and seek alternatives to the repressive gender roles and beliefs of the period. Nevertheless, while such uses may have empowered individual women, they also fostered a backlash against matrimonial advertisements. Women who responded to or placed matrimonial ads were seen as unfeminine, improper, or worse. Such views are readily apparent in the mock advertisement and reply printed in an 1843 issue of the *Jeffersonian Republican*. The exchange began with seven ads supposedly from "seven gentlemen," all who expressed a desire to find a wife. Immediately following these ads was the reply of a woman named Maria Lovewell, who epitomized every negative stereotype about the kind of women that answered matrimonial advertisements.

Lovewell begins her response by noting that that she is "handsome; as to temper, that is yet to try," but she cheekily adds, "but all young ladies are good-tempered till married."[101] Lovewell then proceeds to critique the advertisements of each of the seven men. The first is too rich, and she fears it will "make him giddy and foolish"; the second is too handsome and thus must be "vain"; the third is an officer in the Navy, which means he lacks "moral virtue"; four and five are in dry goods, which makes them "bankrupts"; number six "has nothing but prospects . . . that may never be realized"; and seven is actually quite appealing, but she rejects him because she is not convinced he will be

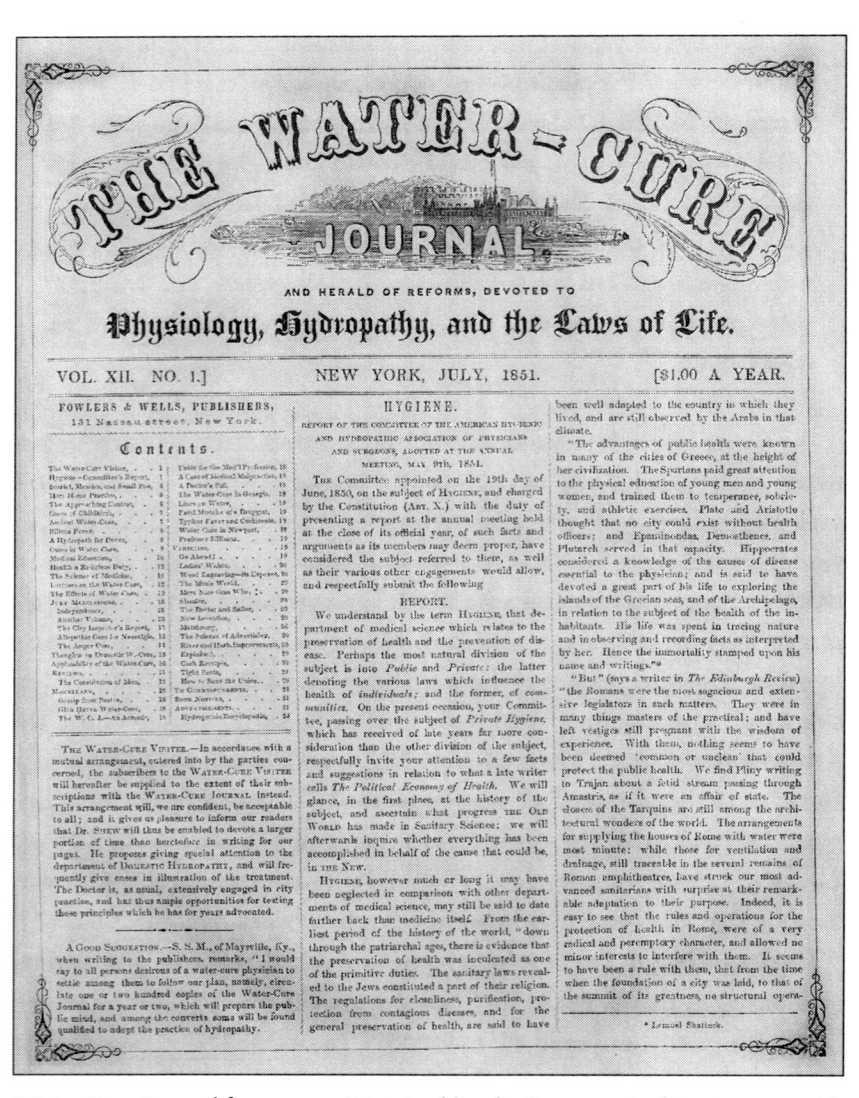

Water-Cure Journal front page. Digitized by the Internet Archive in 2012 with funding from Open Knowledge Commons and Harvard Medical School.

able to give lectures or speeches without looking at his notes.[102] Finally, after ridiculously rejecting all the men, she concludes with the following feminist declaration:

> I want a husband, but I suppose ladies have as much right of choice as gentlemen. The man I want, must not be disagreeable in person, use no tobacco or snuff, drink no rum or ardent spirits, well educated, accustomed to good company, a lover of his wife and children, if he should have any, ambitious to improve in knowledge and usefulness, a keeper at home, and anything but a dandy. He must read his Bible, and love to go to church.
>
> These are my views, if any of your seven gentlemen come up to this standard—I need say no more.[103]

Lovewell's request may seem reasonable by today's standards, but at the time it demonstrated that only difficult and demanding women placed matrimonial advertisements. It warned potential male advertisers that instead of finding a loving and obedient wife, they were much more likely to encounter an irrational shrew, brazenly dictating her marriage terms.

The Lovewell article implied that any woman who would dare make such demands is neither respectable nor feminine and other social critics echoed these beliefs. For example, Fanny Fern, the famous antebellum women's columnist, described female matrimonial advertisers as crass and shameful: "A woman must first have ignored the sweetest attributes of womanhood, have overstepped the last barrier of self-respect, who would parley with a stranger on such a topic. . . . No, never let woman be the wooer, save as the flowers woo, with their sweetness—save as the summer wind woos—silently unfolding the rose's heart."[104]

These views regarding female propriety were widespread and undoubtedly kept many women from placing or responding to matrimonial advertisements. This was unfortunate because matrimonial advertising frequently benefited women and provided the means of exerting greater control over their marriages. Regardless, as long as matrimonial advertising was seen as unnecessary, this form of introduction was viewed with suspicion and distaste. The eruption of the Civil War then changed these views. Suddenly, it was no longer unseemly for a woman to correspond with a stranger. Moreover, given the war's decimation of the male population, it was also no longer considered unnecessary. This growing support for matrimonial correspondence helped usher in the "golden age" of the American mail-order bride, yet the long-established connection between matrimonial advertising and impropriety, radicalism, and disrepute never entirely disappeared. Pioneer mail-order brides were encouraged and protected, but fears surrounding this form of courtship were always lurking. Consequently, when the demographic need for mail-order brides out West decreased, the distrust of mail-order marriage returned stronger than ever and ultimately eclipsed the once widespread recognition of mail-order marriage's benefits.

6

Wanted—Correspondence

In the years after the Civil War, America experienced an explosion in mail-order marriage. Tens of thousands of women became mail-order brides and used this form of marriage to improve their marital prospects and pursue the greater freedoms available in the American West. However, although the advantages these marital immigrants received were real, the support for mail-order marriage was superficial and fleeting. Once western states achieved their demographic objectives they had little interest in continuing to promote mail-order marriage and quickly stopped extolling its benefits and began emphasizing its dangers. Meanwhile, eastern support for mail-order marriages had always been tenuous, and without the West's population concerns, these states saw little reason to promote mail-order marriages. Consequently, even during the height of mail-order marriage's popularity, the views regarding these marriages were decidedly mixed, demonstrating that mail-order marriages are most supported when they provide national benefits in addition to individual ones.

The rise of nineteenth-century mail-order marriages began during the Civil War as matrimonial correspondence was reconceived as a patriotic duty. Prior to the war, it was considered unwise and improper for respectable women to correspond with unknown men, but after war erupted, women were encouraged to write to strangers. At first, most women wrote only to soldiers they knew, but this meant men received war correspondence only if they had mothers, sisters, wives, or female friends. Those soldiers without these relationships, young, bored, scared, and lonely, also craved feminine letters from the home front. As a result, some soldiers began placing "Wanted: Correspondence" ads in newspapers and requesting responses from "'fair and patriotic' dam-

Envelope addressed by Lou Pearl Riggen. Courtesy of Ohio University Press, Athens, OH.

sels," and popular periodicals started encouraging women to answer these requests.[1] Women were advised it was their patriotic duty to ensure that all soldiers, known and unknown, received correspondence. One of the most forceful of these exhortations was an *Atlantic Monthly* article titled "A Call to My Country Women."

This treatise was written by Gail Hamilton, a noted essayist and fierce advocate for women's rights. In the article, Hamilton describes letter writing as the most important contribution women could make to the war effort.[2] She implores her female readers to forgo other war work, such as sewing (for "stitching does not crush rebellion"), and seize their pens with "passionate purpose." Hamilton instructs them to channel their "soul of fire" into letters for the front lines.[3] Appeals like Hamilton's were effective, and American women eagerly embraced this patriotic view of correspondence. One young letter writer, a woman named Lou Riggen, demonstrates this nationalistic ardor in her letter to Lieutenant E. L. Lybarger, a man she had never met, in which she states that she would happily do nothing but war correspondence if she could "by this means contribute one mite toward the closing of this insatiable war."[4]

Greenwood Glen:

Jany 23d 1884.

Lieutenant Gilbarger.

      Excuse this empty
letter. I have not the slightest doubt,
that it will be so excessively timid,
so utterly overcome with its own insig-
nificance, that it will occupy just
about a month in reaching its desti-
nation. I know the poor innocent
paper will tremble and flutter at
your righteous indignation, because it
is not the bearer of that photograph
instead of useless apologies,— which
articles I always did despise.
I think I hear you say: "Pshaw! the
girl does not intend to redeem her
promise;" then you will enter into
quite a logical disquisition, as follows;

Letter from Lou Pearl Riggen. Courtesy of Ohio University Press,
Athens, OH.

Riggen's patriotic sentiments were undoubtedly genuine. At the same time, her letters reveal that war correspondence differed very little from the previously maligned matrimonial correspondence. In the following letter to Lybarger, it is clear that Riggen's patriotic ardor is closely intertwined with her romantic aspirations. Riggen begins her letter unsure if Lybarger has survived a previous battle. As a result, she initially focuses on the glory and sacrifice of war:

> I scarcely know how to commence writing to you, before I received your last letter you were probably included in the list of "killed, wounded or missing," of the last battle; the sad tale which follows either victory or defeat. I sincerely hope not however. I hope you are not among those unreturning braves whose deaths, thought glorious, and in a glorious cause "make countless thousands mourn" that among those left to rally once again round the flag is my pleasant correspondent—not I hope selfishly for the sake of that correspondence so pleasant, but for the sake of his mother, and sisters if he has any, for the sake of the Country waiting to be rescued by valiant arms and stout hearts from ignoble slavery.

A few lines later, however, the stiff and ceremonial tone of the letter disappears:

> You flatter me exceedingly. "Counterhopper! loafer!" O, O how could I help laughing at the funny idea? What a pleasant impression my letters must have made. I never had a very flattering opinion of my letter writing ability until the reception of your last. If you judge from my letters that I belong to one of the aforementioned classes how can you be "very well pleased?"
>
> You certainly do not expect my photograph though I have a decided curiosity (the heritage of the world in general) to see your photo.[5]

In this latter part of the letter, Riggen is clearly attempting to capitalize on the romantic possibilities offered by war correspondence.[6]

Unfortunately for Riggen, this particular soldier did not desire a romantic relationship. The two corresponded for years, but when the war ended, Lybarger married his cousin and left Riggen brokenhearted. Nevertheless, many other soldiers did form romantic relationships with their female correspondents, and wanted-correspondence ads were frequently explicit about the possibility of love and marriage within the context of patriotism. Consider the following:

> A Frenchman, an officer in the Army of the Potomac, aged twenty-eight, of unexceptionable character, without lady acquaintances, wishes to open a correspondence with some young lady with a view to matrimony. No carte de visite nor money required. All he asks is amiability. Address Captain Louis Allard, Sixty-second regiment, N.Y.S.V., Washington, D.C., or elsewhere.[7]

> A young soldier, having served in the Army of the Potomac since it was first organized, and now in camp near Falmouth, desires to open a correspondence with a young lady of intelligence, with a view to matrimony on his return home. No trifling. Address C.H. De Arty, Second United States Infantry, Gen. Sykes' division, Army of the Potomac, Va.[8]

Both these ads explicitly refer to the possibility of marriage, but they also make numerous references to the bravery and commitment of the ads' authors.

Allard states that he was in the N.Y.S.V., a volunteer regiment. This means he was not drafted, but chose to fight for the Union. Similarly, De Arty wrote that he had been with the Army of the Potomac since it was first organized, which signified he had been a Unionist since the beginning of the war and had reenlisted after his first commission was completed (originally, soldiers signed up for only ninety days).[9] In addition, the fact that both men are part of the Army of the Potomac is particularly significant. This was a division well known for its bravery and, at the time these ads were placed, had just suffered particularly devastating casualties. Therefore, it is likely that the reference to the men's division, prominently placed in the first line of both ads, was specifically included to elicit feelings of patriotic sympathy. In fact, allusions to death and danger were common in wanted-correspondence ads, and many soldiers included morbid lines like "with a view for matrimony if the fortunes of the war should prove."[10] Consequently, by noting their division, both Allard and De Arty were able to emphasize the very real dangers they were facing and present their matrimonial ad as something akin to a soldier's dying wish.

Ads like those of Allard and De Arty were highly effective at transforming matrimonial correspondence from a foolish or improper action into a patriotic one. Thousands of women responded to such ads. However, it was actually the end of the war that had the greatest impact on matrimonial correspondence.[11] By the time the Civil War concluded, an entire generation of young men had been killed, and with their deaths, tens of thousands of women faced the prospect of never marrying. Suddenly, matrimonial advertisements could no longer be dismissed as unnecessary. War had altered the marital landscape, and many women began to view matrimonial advertisements as their last chance for marriage.[12]

Western states quickly recognized that the tragedy of war presented an unparalleled immigration opportunity. After the war, most western states continued to suffer from a shortage of women, so many state legislatures began offering eastern women compelling and unprecedented incentives to immigrate. These acts were a continuation of the prewar policy of incentivizing female immigration through legal benefits. In 1849, California had enacted property protections for married women. Similar laws were then passed in Kansas in 1855,[13] Oregon in 1857, and Nevada in 1864.[14] In all three of these states, the explicit purpose of these female-friendly laws was to increase female immigration. Shortly after the Kansas law was enacted, an article in the *Anti-Slavery Bugle* (an Ohio newspaper) described the law as an "Invitation to Female Emigrants." The paper also predicted it would be highly effective warning

1901 L-R: Bill Daucks, Frank Geduhn, Esli Apgar, Harvey Dimon Apgar

A group of Montana men advertising for wives. Glacier National Park, "Land-owner News 2009," http://www.nps.gov/glac/learn/management/upload/Landowner_news_09.pdf.

that "[u]nless the older States are willing to risk the loss of the flower of their female population, we see nothing left for them but to imitate the example of Kansas."[15]

Once the Civil War ended, these immigration incentives increased. In 1869, the year the transcontinental railroad was completed and western emigration became substantially easier, Wyoming became the first state to pass female suffrage,[16] and the state also enacted laws forbidding sex discrimination in the hiring of teachers and passed a resolution giving women the right to attend legislative sessions.[17] They made these changes specifically to entice women to come. As the Wyoming legislators explained, the "territory desperately needed immigrants,

An all-male dance in Lubbock, Texas. *Stag Dance at Lubbock.* Erwin E. Smith (1886–1947). Copyright © Erwin E. Smith Foundation, Erwin E. Smith Collection of the Library of Congress on Deposit at the Amon Carter Museum of American Art, Fort Worth, TX. Courtesy of Texas State Library and Archives Commission.

particularly the feminine variety."[18] Similarly, in an 1872 article titled "The Woman Movement in Wyoming," Edward M. Lee explains that these legislators were swayed not by public sentiment, but by the belief that female equality would act as a "first class advertisement" for the comparatively unknown territory.[19]

Contemporary Wyoming newspapers echoed these beliefs. For example, after suffrage passed, one Cheyenne newspaper enthusiastically wrote, "We now expect at once quite an immigration of ladies to Wyoming. We say to them all, come on. There is room for a great many here yet."[20] One hopeful Wyomingite even placed his own ad in the *Revolution*, a suffrage newspaper. He wrote, "there is probably no state in the Union, where women have more freedom and are less deprived of their rights," and he encouraged "the girls to come to this higher plain of Human Rights."[21]

Not surprisingly, women's rights advocates quickly recognized the political opportunity presented by female scarcity and began advocating women's suffrage as a way to increase female immigration. For example, in a speech before the Washington territorial legislature, suffrage advocate Susan B. Anthony promised that female suffrage would be followed by "the most gratifying of results—the immigration of a large number of good women to the Territory."[22] Similarly, Henry B. Blackwell, editor of the *Woman's Journal*, spoke before the Montana constitutional convention, assuring territorial legislators that giving women the right to vote would result in the "immigration of a large number of good women to the territory."[23]

These advocacy efforts were effective, and many western states soon followed Wyoming's lead. Women gained the franchise in Utah in 1870, Washington in 1883, Montana in 1887, Colorado in 1893,[24] and Idaho in 1896.[25] By 1915, women had suffrage in every western state save Texas and New Mexico. In contrast, not a single eastern state had granted the right to women.

Mail-order marriage helped many mail-order brides achieve greater political rights, but for African American mail-order brides in particular, the rights they gained through marital immigration could be even more substantial. Not only did mail-order marriage give many of these women the right to vote, it also gave them a way to escape the South and its crushing racial restrictions. Consequently, although African American brides were never as numerous as their white counterparts, their experience with this type of marriage was similar. Both groups used mail-order marriage as a means to change their circumstances and better their lives. For example, African American mail-order bride Emily Brinson met her husband, Thomas Detter, a Nevada miner and prominent advocate for African American civil rights, through a matrimonial advertisement and married him in June 1876 in a sumptuous ceremony that transcended racial prejudices. The *Eureka Sentinel* published a description of their wedding, stating it was "attended by nearly all of the colored folks in town, besides some twenty-five or thirty white people, including some of our most prominent citizens and their wives."[26]

A significant number of African American mail-order brides also came West due to the immigration efforts of the Busy Bee Club, a group, founded in 1885 by six African American women, seeking to increase female immigration to Tucson, Arizona. In order to attract these female immigrants, the club placed matrimonial advertisements in numerous eastern papers and then supplied interested women with one-way tickets paid for by the town's bachelors.[27]

Mail-order marriage enabled African American as well as white women to leave unfortunate circumstances and move to places where they would have greater freedom and acceptance. A study by law professor Lawrence Friedman confirms that the ability or inability of women to move could literally have life-changing consequences.[28] Friedman examined the rates of infanticide in Britain, the eastern United States, and the American West and discovered that while the rates in Britain and the eastern United States were significant, bordering on epidemic,[29] the tragedy was nearly nonexistent in the west.[30] This difference led Friedman to conclude that infanticide is a crime of immobility, something women do when they have no other options and cannot leave. In places like the American West, where women had greater mobility and the chance to "drop old identities and conceal their *lack* of a marriage," infanticide disappeared.[31] Thus, Friedman's work shows how mail-order marriage, which increased female mobility, could also be potentially life-saving. This enhanced mobility helped in other, less drastic, ways as well.

In order to undertake the uncertainties of marital immigration, mail-order brides needed to be bold and self-sufficient. Consequently, western states seeking mail-order brides began praising these "unfeminine" traits and applauding women who did not conform to the rigid gender roles of the period. Nineteenth-century western papers were full of stories admiring the independence and fortitude of mail-order brides.[32] For example, in 1887, the *Daily Yellowstone Journal* published a story about a mail-order bride who arrived in Miles City, Montana, two weeks before her groom expected her. When he did not appear, she spent two days making "inquiries concerning the recreant lover." Then, after failing to obtain any information about him, she traveled to Helena to find a job. Shortly thereafter, the would-be groom arrived in Miles City, discovered his mistake, and rushed off to Helena to find his bride. He located her, and they were quickly married.[33] In this particular story, the couple was reunited, but not all missing grooms turned up. That same year, the *Chicago News* published an article about a mail-order bride from New York who arrived in the Dakota Territory to find that her prospective groom had deserted her and the territory. Despite this setback, this resourceful woman was unfazed and, within four days of arrival, had received "12 proposals of marriage" and was busy "trying to pick out the man she likes best."[34]

In addition to stories about the occasional jilted bride, western newspapers also published numerous articles about women rejecting their intended fiancés. Given the gender imbalance in the West, most potential grooms were eager to marry their intended brides, but the women were often more hesitant and many unapologetically rejected would-be grooms who failed to meet their expectations. For example, in 1890, the *Virginia City Enterprise* (a Nevada newspaper) ran an article titled "The Young Man Failed to Suit." The article described a matrimonial correspondence between an eastern woman and a Nevada man who had become acquainted through a matrimonial advertisement. After the two became engaged, the woman traveled to Nevada intending to marry the man, but after meeting him in person, she decided that she was "not pleased with his appearance, and refuse[d] to perform her part of the contract." Nevertheless, she was pleased with Nevada and, the paper, noted "she is still here."[35] An 1874 article from the *Western Advance* (an Oregon newspaper) described a similar rejection. In this case, the matrimonial correspondence occurred between an eastern woman and a Nebraskan man. According to the paper, the two began writing after the woman answered the man's matrimonial advertisement, and shortly thereafter they became engaged. The woman then traveled to Omaha to meet her new fiancé, but "when she reached that famous city ... she was disappointed with his personal appearance and refused point blank to permit the tying of the nuptial knot."[36]

Both articles depict mail-order brides firmly in control of their marital decisions, and female-authored matrimonial advertisements further demonstrate how mail-order marriage helped women take a more active role in the courtship process. These ads allowed women to specify what qualities they were looking for in a spouse. It is clear that many female advertisers reveled in the liberating aspects of this courtship medium and the ability it gave them to express their desires honestly. For example, in 1910, a woman placed the following ad in a Missouri paper:

> Attractive woman, not a day over thirty, would be pleased to correspond with eligible man. Not absolutely necessary that he should be young. Would prefer one with property, but one with a good paying position would be satisfactory. The young lady is of medium height, has brown hair and gray eyes, not fat, although, most decidedly, she is not skinny. Her friends say she is a fine looking woman. Object matrimony. Reason for this advertisement, the young woman lives in a little dinky town, where the best catches are the boys behind the counters in the dry goods and clothing stores, and every one of them is spoken for by the time he is out of his short pants.[37]

A similarly direct ad was placed in a Calgary newspaper in 1916 by a group of women:

> We have looked over the eligibles here, but find most of them standing in front of the bar or out autoing with somebody's else wife. We don't call them men. What we want is a real man with real brains and

real honor; a man who would like a good, clean wife and a good clean home and honor them both. . . . Now, if some good bachelor with plenty of backbone, brains and brawn; who keeps himself scrubbed and brushes his teeth; who pays enough attention to his fingernails to keep them from going into mourning for past decency, wants a home and a "homey" wife, and thinks he can stand a little scolding once in a while to give spice to life, we shall be mighty glad to hear from him and all about him.[38]

Female-authored ads gave women more control over the marital process, which changed the way men approached mail-order marriage. Consider the following ad placed by an Arkansas farmer in 1855: "Any Gal that's got a bed, a coffee pot, and a skillit; knows how to cut out britches, can make a huntin' shirt, and knows how to take care of children, can have my services until death parts both of us."[39] This advertisement is solely a list of things the farmer wants his future wife to do or provide for him, which likely did not appeal to many women. However, female-placed ads showed men how they could make themselves more attractive matrimonial candidates. For example, the following letter was written in response to a female-authored matrimonial advertisement:

In inclose my photograf with My Full Description. It shows the features as nachel as can bee only it is to Dark; I am very lite Complexion, Gray eyes, Orbon hair, 6-foot high, waight 190 Lbs, inclined to be hump shouldered; A Muskler Man and a widower 28 years old with A Commen Schol Equations, but hav Got Anof to Atten to Enny Businness, I am Strictly Morrel. Don't Use Tobacco Nor Whiskey . . . I hav Only One Thing to Offer, And it is Neither Lands Nar Gold. But a Strong Arm and a True Hart and will lay Down My Life for the Rite Girl and Be Happy, for I am tired of living Alone. The girl that Steels my Hart and takes my name for the Remainder of My Lif I will make Happy, for I am hunting a Girl that I can idleise and Make a Angle of.[40]

Unlike the Arkansas farmer who lists the qualities he desired in a wife, the above respondent provides a list of the qualities that would make him a good husband. Not surprisingly, matrimonial advertisements particularly appealed to women who wanted more equal relationships. In fact, an 1890 study by criminologist Arthur MacDonald specifically found that the desire for greater equality motivated the majority of female matrimonial respondents.

For his study, MacDonald placed a fake matrimonial advertisement in a variety of New York City newspapers and then conducted interviews with the respondents to discover why they replied. One woman explained that her interest came from the fact that matrimonial correspondence permitted her "to break through conventionalities."[41] A second respondent echoed this sentiment: "[I am] tired of the society act, and fancy I'd like just a tiny bit of bohemianism."[42] Other interviewees were even more explicit in linking matrimonial correspondence with a desire for independence and especially equality. For example, "Miss D" explained that she answered matrimonial ads because "[I a]m *very* independent, and I have views of my own which some people do not approve of."[43] When asked to give an example of these ideas, Miss D responded with a forceful condemnation of the marriage double standard, stating that the traditional marriage arrangement was unfair in that it expected women to be "perfectly pure" while allowing men to be "the most awful rakes that ever existed."[44] According to Miss D, either women should be granted more liberty or men should also have to meet the same standards of sexual purity. Another respondent, "Miss I," expressed similar sentiments: "[I]n regard to women ... society has imposed such a system of reserve upon them, that it is not always easy for them to throw off. If they were as free and natural as men, they would be misunderstood and misinterpreted in ninety-nine cases out of a hundred."[45]

MacDonald's study revealed that women used matrimonial advertising in order to pursue the type of freedoms and equality they felt were unavailable in the traditional marriage arrangement. Such desires are admirable. However, MacDonald found them scandalous and believed they bordered on moral depravity. His views were not uncommon, particularly in the East, where matrimonial ads were never able to fully disassociate themselves from the trace of disrepute.

The late nineteenth century was the height of the separate spheres ideology, when respectable women were expected to be passive and weak. Matrimonial correspondence, particularly female-authored ads, challenged these assumptions. Therefore, it is not surprising that in eastern cities critics often leveled the most damning accusations they could at these ads, that they were solicitations for sex. For example, in an 1862 editorial in the *New York Times*, the author railed against the *New York Herald*'s matrimonial column stating, "The 'Personal' and 'Matrimonial' columns of the *Herald* grow more shameless and loathsome every day, teeming with undisguised proposals for prostitution, which certainly come within the spirit of even the most lenient repressive statutes of all civilized countries."[46] Similarly, in 1869 Junius Browne published *The Great Metropolis, a Mirror of New York* and described the city's marriage brokers (go-betweens who often placed ads for customers) as "growing less matrimonial and more and more mercenary agents for assignation."[47]

In addition, eastern papers continued to ridicule matrimonial advertisers by publishing stories detailing elaborate matrimonial hoaxes. For example, in 1876, the *New York Times* and a number of other American papers ran an article titled "An Amusing Matrimonial Hoax," about a Glasgow merchant who placed a matrimonial advertisement answered by a group of young men posing as an eligible young lady. According to the article, the advertiser was invited to have dinner with the supposed young lady and her father. After dinner, the "father" pulled off his disguise and revealed the trick. The embarrassed man then tried to leave, but the door was locked; when he attempted to open it, he pulled a string and was doused in flour. He then put on his hat, found it filled with paraffin oil, and was hit with a bag of sulfur flour. Finally, when the man was permitted to open the door and leave the building, he was bombarded with soot and rotten eggs.[48] A year later, the *New York Times* ran a similar hoax story involving a lonely grocer who answered a matrimonial advertisement from a woman named "Agnes." However, instead of taking him for tea at her aunt's house, the woman delivered him to a group of young men who tied him up, covered him in treacle (a substance like molasses), and left him bound to a hedge.[49]

Eastern papers further attempted to discourage matrimonial advertising by publishing sensational stories about the dangers of mail-order marriage, including a handful of cases involving murder. One of the most notorious and horrific examples of mail-order murder was the case of Johann Otto Hoch, a nineteenth-century serial killer known as the Chicago Bluebeard. Hoch found his victims through matrimonial advertisements and murdered as many as fifty women in the 1890s. Eventually, Hoch became careless and was apprehended.

Hoch met his last victim, Marie Walcker, through an ad he placed in the *Abend Post*, a German evening newspaper published in Chicago: "Matrimonial—Widow, without children; the end of the thirties; German; own home; wishes acquaintance of a lady; object, matrimony."[50] The ad attracted the attention of Walcker, a forty-five-year-old divorcee who made her living by washing, house cleaning, and other general work. She also owned a small candy shop. After seeing Hoch's ad, she sent him the following reply: "Dear Sir: In answer to your honorable advertisement, I hereby inform you that I am a lady standing alone. I am 45 years of age. I have a small business, also a few hundred dollars—a little fortune—a few hundred dollars. If you are in earnest, I tell you I shall be. I may be spoken or seen any time during the day. Address No. 12 Willow Street. Marie Walcker."[51] The two arranged a meeting and Hoch proposed. On the morning of the marriage, Walcker sold her store for seventy-five dollars, which she gave to Hoch. She also gave him eighty dollars in cash and access to her bank account. Less than one week later, Walcker became ill. She was described as very pale with sores around her mouth. A few days later her symptoms worsened, and she began having severe pain in her stomach and became incontinent.

Hoch called for the doctor and then wrote to his wife's sister, Amelia Fischer, informing her that Walcker was very sick. Fischer immediately rushed to visit Walcker, whom she described as pale and yellow, experiencing frequent vomiting, restlessness, and nervousness, and suffering from horrible stomach pain and a violent thirst. Walcker died a few days later. The same day as his wife's death, Hoch proposed to Fischer, and amazingly she accepted. Fortunately, Walcker's other sister was not so easily charmed. She thought Walcker's death was suspicious, and alerted police to the possible poisoning. When Walcker's body was exhumed and autopsied, arsenic poisoning was confirmed.

Matrimonial advertisements gave Hoch a simple way to meet potential victims and the anonymity to reinvent himself over and over again. At least two other serial killers used similar methods to find victims, highlighting the potential dangers of mail-order marriage.[52] However, these horrific murders were extremely rare. The most common crimes related to mail-order marriages were theft, fraud, and seduction, but even these were decreasing as states instituted substantial legal reforms to protect single women from being harmed during the premarital period. Consequently, despite the growing emphasis on the danger of mail-order marriage, they actually became less risky as the century progressed.

On June 6, 1902, the *Iola Register* printed an article titled "Insane from Courting," describing "Edna Smith, a pretty 17-year-old girl of Lincoln, Nebraska" who was taken to the hospital after "suffering dementia and hysteria." Smith "appealed to a policeman for aid, saying she was alone and penniless. To the police matron she confessed having corresponded with several men she met through a matrimonial agency." After making this confession, Smith then "broke down, her mind gave away, and the doctors have been unable to calm her."[53] The article implies that Smith was seduced and then abandoned by one of her matrimonial correspondents, seemingly demonstrating the danger of matrimonial correspondence. However, although matrimonial advertisements may have contributed to Smith's seduction, they were not the main cause. Seduction was a growing problem in the post–Civil War period, due to rapid modernization and changes in the way courtships were conducted, and it was certainly not a problem confined solely or even primarily to mail-order marriage.

Monitoring courtship had traditionally been the role of the family and local community, but by the late nineteenth century, parental control had decreased significantly and rapid urbanization had further weakened traditional community ties.[54] Families and communities could no longer effectively police their children's premarital relationships, so the state assumed this role.[55] Specifically, in order to protect single women, courts and legislators began expanding marital rights into the "premarital" period and transforming the formerly weak torts of seduction and breach of promise to marry into strong causes of action with significant and severe penalties.

The tort of seduction was well established by the beginning of the nineteenth century. It was defined as the act of "seducing and having illicit connection with an unmarried female of previous chaste character" under a "promise of marriage."[56] However, the legal "victim" of seduction was the "woman's father, guardian or master."[57] Seduced women were not protected. In fact, the law viewed such women as equally responsible for their seduction, and arguments that a woman had only consented because the seducer had promised marriage were typically considered irrelevant.[58]

The difficulties caused by this male-centered definition of seduction are readily apparent and were poignantly demonstrated in a seduction suit from 1804. A woman named Rebecca Frost attempted to sue her former lover for seduction after he promised to marry her but abandoned her alone and pregnant. Frost demonstrated that she had been of "previously chaste character" before she met George Marshall and provided multiple witnesses who testified that Marshall had declared his intention to marry her. In fact, Marshall had even secured permission from Frost's family. Nevertheless, despite this evidence, South Carolina Judge Joseph Brevard denied Frost's claim. According to Brevard, any other ruling would allow a woman "to take advantage of her own frailty and turpitude; and might have a tendency to encourage lewdness."[59]

In 1843, Chief Justice John Bannister Gibson of the Pennsylvania Supreme Court issued a similar ruling in another seduction case. Like Brevard, Gibson blamed the woman for her seduction and found the seducer's promises of marriage irrelevant. According to Gibson, "Every girl who is silly enough to surrender her citadel of virtue to her lover, on the credit of general professions of love, is silly enough to believe that she is going to be married out of hand; and it must not be forgotten that professions are not promises."[60]

For judges like Brevard and Gibson, women "foolish" enough to be seduced deserved what they got. However, by the mid-nineteenth century, these harsh attitudes were changing. Courts were increasingly concerned with protecting women from seduction and offering them substantial compensation when seduction did occur. For example, in the 1850 New York seduction case *Wells v. Padgett*, the court awarded damages to the female plaintiff and explained its decision by stating, "[T]he female and seducer do not stand on equal grounds. She is the weaker party and the victim of his acts, and the seduction has been practiced upon her under the false color of a promise of marriage, which he never intended to perform."[61] *Wells* was one of the first decisions to treat seduced women as victims. However, other courts quickly adopted this reasoning. As a result, women were increasingly able to bring seduction suits, paving the way for its criminalization.

Originally, the fact that seduction was solely a tort meant that perpetrators could be forced to pay monetary damages for the harms they caused but could not be charged with a crime. But as the nineteenth century progressed, there was a growing movement to criminalize seduction. In 1840, the New York state legislature received twenty thousand petitions seeking its criminalization,[62] and thousands of similar petitions were presented to the Massachusetts legislature in 1845.[63] These petitions were effective. By 1850 both New York and Massachusetts had enacted statutes criminalizing seduction and other states followed soon after. By the end of the century, more than forty-one U.S. jurisdictions had enacted criminal seduction statutes. Seducers now faced serious repercussions for their actions: not only thousands of dollars in fines but also decades in prison.[64] Consequently, although matrimonial advertisements may have made it easier to find potential seduction victims, growing legal penalties dramatically reduced the attractiveness of seduction.

The changes in seduction law were accompanied by legal changes regarding breach of promise actions. Initially, breach of promise suits focused solely on the economics of the broken marriage contract, limiting the amounts victims could receive. However, as the century advanced, judges began allowing punitive and exemplary damages.[65] This meant that jilted lovers could be compensated for both the actual economic loss that resulted from the aborted courtship and the emotional suffering and social stigma they had experienced. In his *Introduction to American Law*, nineteenth-century Ohio lawyer Timothy Walker wrote that these changes to breach of promise compensation meant "very heavy damages are often received in such suits,"[66] a drastic understatement. Due to these legal changes, successful breach of promise plaintiffs began receiving awards similar to what they would have received as a divorcing spouse. It became common for plaintiffs to be given a share of both the breaching party's current assets and a claim to future income. In addition, they were also often "awarded damages for the emotional anguish, and humiliation," and for any harm to future marriage prospects.[67]

A third legal change that protected nineteenth-century women from potential marriage fraud was the increased recognition of common-law marriages: those that have not been solemnized before an officiant, such as a judge or priest, yet nevertheless conform to a pattern of behavior that forms a legal marriage. Common-law marriages have a long history in the United States, but they were often controversial, and in the early part of the nineteenth century the legality of these marriages was hotly contested. Then, in 1877, the Supreme Court decided *Meister v. Moore* and decisively upheld the legality of common-law marriage.[68] By 1890, most states permitted the practice.

Like the changes to seduction and breach of promise actions, the expanded recognition of common-law marriage helped to protect women against marital fraud and exploitation.[69] Common-law marriage reframed a nonmarital relationship as marital and gave the participants the associated protections. Women in common-law marriages no longer had to rely on the promise of their intended husbands to legalize it. Instead, if they lived in a marriage-like relationship, and their husband treated them as a wife, they would be considered married. The legality of common-law marriage also meant that women in these relationships no longer had to worry that their partner's death or desertion could leave them in legal limbo. If they had been living together and behaving as man and wife, they were considered common-law married and the woman was protected.

These legal changes reflected a transformation in the way women in nonmarital relationships were perceived. By extending marriage-like protections to these nonmarital relationships, the law converted the potentially subversive courtship process into something wholesome and deserving of protection.[70] As Judge Sutherland stated in his treatise on damages, "It is the policy of the law to encourage matrimony," and breach of promise suits reflect the fact that "society has an interest in contracts of matrimony both before and after they are consummated."[71]

Changes to the law regarding seduction, breach of promise, and common-law marriage protected all women, but they were particularly valuable for those considering mail-order marriage. These reforms meant potential mail-order brides were no longer at the mercy of their fiancés' promises. Instead, they could insist on having their common-law marriages recognized, could sue their former paramours for significant damages if they turned out to be liars or frauds, and could initiate criminal proceedings if they were the victims of seduction. Most important, however, contemporary accounts demonstrate that many mail-order brides were aware of these legal protections and willing to use them. For example, when a widow named Catharine Duggan was defrauded and abandoned by a man she met through a matrimonial ad, she did not hesitate to sue her former paramour for breach of promise to marry.

Duggan met Charles Le Roy in the spring of 1884 after Le Roy, who lived in New England, placed an ad in a New York paper advertising for a wife. The ad stated "a gentleman of 32, good-looking and smart, with $5,000, desired the acquaintance of a lady of means, one that wanted a good husband." Duggan replied and the two began a correspondence. In his letters to Duggan, Le Roy presented himself as earnest and trustworthy. He wrote that he did not drink or chew tobacco and wanted to marry quickly. He also wrote that he was looking for a good and honest wife and that he "didn't care if she was not handsome."[72] After corresponding for a short time, the two arranged a meeting and became engaged. Shortly thereafter, Le Roy informed Duggan that he had become ensnared in a bad business deal concerning some horses and needed a loan to settle the debt before they could marry. Duggan loaned him the money, but within days Le Roy disappeared. Then, after realizing Le Roy had no plans to return, Duggan sued him for breach of promise.[73]

A similar story led to the case of *Kaufman v. Fye*, also a breach of marriage case.[74] However, unlike Le Roy, who simply wanted Duggan's money, W. P. Kaufman had a more amorous theft in mind. In 1894, Kaufman, who was forty years old and already married, began a matrimonial correspondence with a twenty-one-year-old seamstress from Chicago named Birdie Fye. The two corresponded for a short time, and shortly thereafter Kaufman proposed. Kaufman then convinced Fye to visit him. Although Kaufman had promised in his letters to treat Fye "as a sister," as soon as Fye arrived he attempted to turn the relationship physical. In fact, the court records note that on one occasion Kaufman caught Fye by the ankle with such ardor that it required her to strike him "violently" and "[knock] the fire out of his eyes like electric car wheels." After being repeatedly rebuffed, Kaufman broke off their engagement. Fye then sued him for breach of promise and won.[75]

In a third example, *People v. Adams*,[76] the would-be groom was more successful in his seduction. John Adams and Rosa Renz met through a matrimonial advertisement. After a short correspondence, they became engaged and Adams suggested that Renz travel to Cincinnati to meet him and get married. Renz agreed. She arrived on a Saturday and wanted to wed immediately, but Adams informed her that marriage licenses could not be obtained on the weekend and that they would have to wait until Monday. That Monday Adams offered another excuse and suggested they travel to Cleveland to be married. On the trip, Adams attempted to pass Renz off as his wife and share a hotel room, but she objected and they stayed in separate rooms. In Cleveland, Adams made further excuses for delaying the wedding, and he then suggested they travel to Detroit. In Detroit, Adams once again tried to register Renz as his wife, but she refused, saying they would not share a room until they were man and wife. Adams then left to get the marriage license and returned a short time later with three papers for her to sign. After Renz signed them, Adams told her they were married. They then proceeded to live together as man and wife, but Renz soon suspected she had been tricked and contacted a detective.[77] Adams was eventually arrested and convicted of seduction. In addition, the court noted that had Adams been single (he was already married when these events took place), the court would have found his actions satisfied the requirements for common-law marriage.[78]

Women like Renz, Fye, and Duggan, in answering matrimonial advertisements, took risks that did not pan out. Nevertheless, these cases demonstrate that the legal changes regarding breach of promise and seduction as well as the recognition of common-law marriage all helped reduce the dangers associated with matrimonial advertisements. These protections also contributed to the proliferation of mail-order marriage. By the end of the nineteenth century, mail-order marriage was widespread and dozens of newspapers, consisting solely of matrimonial advertisements, had been created to help facilitate these marriages. The most well-known matrimonial newspaper was the *Matrimonial*

News, which was printed in two cities for more than thirty years and claimed to have assisted in the creation of more than twenty-six hundred marriages.[79] There were numerous other similar papers, including *Heart and Hand, Wedding Bells, Cupid's Messenger, New York Cupid*, and *Standard Correspondence Club*.[80] However, despite the extensive use of matrimonial advertisements, the clear benefits, and the significant protections for female participants, mail-order marriage was never fully accepted by the American public. Papers continued to publish numerous stories about the dangers of this form of courtship,[81] and victims of matrimonial fraud continued to be berated for their "foolishness."[82] In 1907, one Saint Louis judge even stated that he regretted there was no law to "punish the victims of matrimonial advertisements."[83] Consequently, by the early twentieth century, it was clear that despite the numerous benefits of mail-order marriage, these unions had acquired a decidedly mixed reputation. These misgivings then transformed into outright hostility once the primary practitioners of mail-order marriage changed from white Americans to foreign women of color.

7

Marriage at the Border

Mail-order marriage became widespread in the late nineteenth century, and thousands of American women traveled west as mail-order brides. However, public opinion regarding these marriages was mixed. Western states needed female immigrants and frequently praised and encouraged mail-order marriage. At the same time, these marriages were also criticized as foolish and risky. But as the racial demographics of the brides changed, the conflicted view of mail-order marriage disappeared. The new impression, at least with regard to foreign mail-order marriages, was one of unequivocal hostility.

Foreign mail-order marriages undermined nineteenth-century U.S. immigration policies enacted to keep out racially, economically, and socially "undesirable" immigrants. These laws barred most single women from immigrating to the United States, but marriage to an American citizen or permanent resident allowed foreign women to circumvent these restrictions. Consequently, mail-order marriage became an attractive option for foreign women seeking to immigrate. At the same time, this loophole also angered many white Americans. Opponents of foreign mail-order brides increasingly viewed these women as scheming and opportunistic, criticisms that were particularly pronounced with regard to Asian brides.

The first significant Asian immigration to the United States began in 1849 after the gold rush boosted demand for laborers, miners, and railroad workers. Thousands of men left China to fill these positions. The majority of these men planned to return to China, but some settled in America. As the need for cheap labor decreased, those who remained were increasingly viewed as unwelcome competition for employment and white Americans began demanding immigration restrictions to prevent the arrival of additional Chinese immigrants.

In 1870, Congress responded to these concerns by barring the ability of Chinese immigrants to naturalize; the only Chinese now eligible for citizenship were the American-born children of Chinese immigrants. Five years later, Congress attempted to limit the number of American-born Chinese by banning the immigration of Chinese prostitutes and then labeling nearly all Chinese female immigrants as prostitutes. Last, in 1882 Congress passed the Chinese Exclusion Act, effectively ending Chinese immigration and with it the marriage hopes of thousands of Chinese men already admitted.[1]

The Chinese Exclusion Act barred all laborers, both male and female, from entering the United States and decreed that women immigrating to marry Chinese laborers would be evaluated in the same immigration category as their intended husbands. Consequently, because most Chinese immigrants were laborers, this new law meant they could no longer seek wives from China.[2] In addition, state antimiscegenation laws prevented Chinese men from marrying anyone other than an Asian woman. Therefore, given the scarcity of Asian women in the United States and the inability of additional Chinese women to immigrate, the Chinese Exclusion Act prevented the majority of Chinese immigrants from marrying and having families.[3]

The Chinese Exclusion Act ended Chinese immigration to the United States, but it did not block the immigration of other Asian immigrants. In fact, just as most Chinese immigration was ending, Japanese immigration was exploding. The Japanese government had barred its citizens from emigrating to the United States, but in 1885, the ban was lifted and thousands of immigrants left Japan, eager to escape widespread political turmoil and economic hardship.[4] In 1884, the year before the immigration ban was lifted, one-seventh of Japan's rice land was foreclosed and the countryside was filled with riots. In addition, urban conditions were almost as bad: low wages, appalling working conditions, and a nascent labor movement ruthlessly suppressed by the

A cartoon depicting America's anti-Chinese sentiment. Library of Congress.

government.[5] A young Japanese factory worker provided the following description of factory life: "From morning, while it was still dark, we worked in the lamplit factory till ten at night. After work, we hardly had the strength to stand on our feet. When we worked late into the night, they occasionally gave us a yam. We then had to do our washing, fix our hair, and so on. By then it would be eleven o'clock. There was no heat even in the winter, and so we had to sleep huddled together."[6]

Immigration offered an alternative to grueling and dangerous factory work. In addition, wages in America were as much as twenty-five times higher than those in Japan and were also available to women.[7] Once emigration was permitted, many Japanese men and women seized the opportunity to leave Japan, but as their numbers in America began to rise, U.S. anti-Japanese sentiment also increased. By the turn of the twentieth century, a ban on Japanese immigration appeared inevitable. Consequently, in 1907 the Japanese government decided to institute a self-imposed limit on Japanese emigration to avoid the embarrassment of a ban. This decision was known as the Gentlemen's Agreement. The 1907 agreement curtailed most Japanese immigration to the United States, but unlike the Chinese Exclusion Act, it still permitted the immigration of the wives and children of the Japanese men already in the United States. It was this crucial difference that led to the rise of "picture brides."

Like the Chinese men who had preceded them, the majority of nineteenth-century Japanese immigrants were male, so they had difficulty finding suitable wives. In order to marry, many of these men were forced to return to their homeland. However, the trip back to Japan was costly, and returning men risked being subject to Japan's military draft. In addition, U.S. restrictions on Japanese immigration meant that reentry could be problematic or even impossible. To avoid these difficulties, many Japanese men seeking to marry began turning to mail-order marriage, to "picture brides."[8]

Picture-bride marriages were typically arranged through the help of mutual friends or the family of the potential bride and groom. The couple would be put into contact and then exchange photos and cor-

Japanese picture brides arriving in the United States. Nichi Bei, http://www.
nichibei.org/wp-content/uploads/2014/12/PictureBrides.jpg.

respondence. If they decided to marry, most of the men would wed by
proxy, which meant that the groom would have another man represent
him at a marriage ceremony in Japan, where such marriages were legal.
After this proxy marriage, the new bride was granted a passport and
permitted to immigrate to America.[9]

Because most picture marriages were facilitated through mutual
friends and family members, these unions were similar to traditional
arranged marriages.[10] Nevertheless, there were a number of significant differences that clearly establish these relationships as mail-order
marriages. First, like most late nineteenth-century mail-order brides,
Japanese picture brides traveled thousands of miles to marry strangers. In addition, like the thousands of American mail-order brides who
preceded them, the majority of picture brides actively chose marital
immigration, and they did so for similar reasons.[11] Many picture brides
were poor women from traditional farming villages, looking to escape

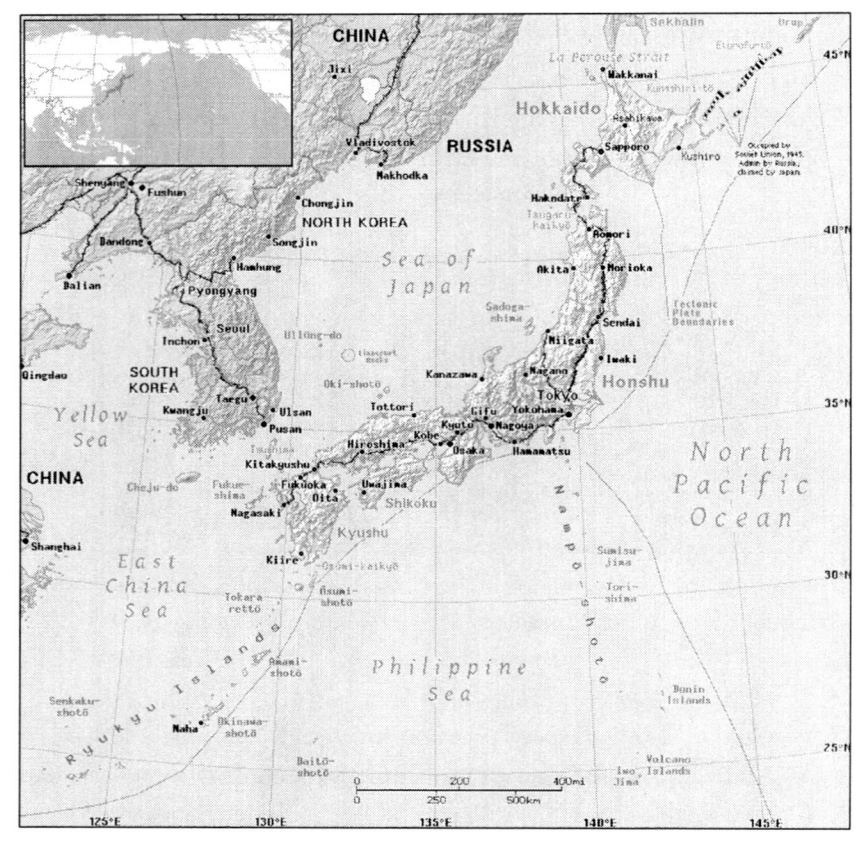

Map of Japan. http://ian.macky.net/pat/map/jp/jp.html.

poverty. Others were older or divorced or plain women who hoped to improve their marital prospects. A number were even upper-class women who turned to marital emigration in order to escape traditional Japanese social constraints. These women would frequently speak of having married America, not the man.[12] Last, a large number of picture brides were not Japanese at all but actually Okinawan or Korean women seeking to escape Japanese occupation.

In 1879, Japan had invaded and annexed Okinawa, which led to the widespread appropriation of land for sugarcane production, reduced the amount of farmland used for food, and left Okinawans starving and destitute as they were forced to depend on high-priced imported foods from Japan.[13] Japan's discriminatory taxation of the Okinawans further exacerbated these problems. For example, in 1882, Okinawa paid 655,279 yen in taxes to the central government, while it received only 455,136 yen in goods and services in return.[14]

Poverty forced many Okinawans, particularly young women, to seek work on the Japanese mainland under horrendous conditions and pervasive discrimination. Kikunaga Atsu, a fourteen-year-old girl who left Okinawa in 1910 to work at Tōyō Textile Mill in Wakayama Prefecture, described the harshness and desperation of life in the mills:

> Girls there came down with beri-beri one after another. Steam was pumped into the factory that had to be kept constantly warm and humid, making the air so bad it was a miracle if you didn't get sick. And standing at the machines working all day made the pain in our leg joints worse. But even when our legs swelled up, they told us it wasn't serious enough to be treated. I ended up in the hospital. . . . After that I wanted to go home, but they wouldn't let us leave until our contracts were up. I had to work at Tōyō for five years, longer than most of the other girls. One of them caught a lung disease and died while I was there.[15]

Similar experiences convinced thousands of Okinawans to leave Japan, and by the 1940s, one-sixth of the entire Okinawan population had immigrated abroad. Initially, many of these immigrants, both male and female, came to America,[16] but the 1907 Gentlemen's Agreement ended most of this immigration. Nevertheless, under the agreement Japanese wives were still permitted to enter America, so many Okinawan women became picture brides.[17]

The desire to escape Japanese domination and its ills effects was also an especially strong motivation for Korean picture brides.[18] In 1910, Japan annexed Korea, and thousands of Koreans suddenly lost their lands and way of life.[19] In addition, these men and women were sub-

Japanese picture brides at Angel Island in 1919. Wikimedia Commons.

ject to the deliberate and wide-scale destruction of their culture and identity.[20] However, the one "benefit" of annexation was that Korean women were now considered Japanese for purposes of the Gentlemen's Agreement, and thousands of Korean women subsequently became picture brides. As Phyllis Ahn Dunn, a fourteen-year-old Korean picture bride, recalled many years later, "I begged my mother to let me go to Hawai'i—I was not afraid."[21]

Asian women became picture brides for many of the same reasons that American women became mail-order brides, but the impact of U.S. immigration law added unique strains and pressures to Asian mail-order marriages. Unlike American mail-order brides, who would routinely reject objectionable fiancés, Asian picture brides rarely had that option. Before a Japanese, Okinawan, or Korean woman could even enter the United States, she was required to marry, meaning Asian picture brides had few options when confronted with an undesirable groom.[22] In most cases, their only choices were to marry or return home in disgrace.[23] Moreover, because most would-be grooms knew few women would consider returning home, these men frequently benefited from deception.

In 1918, Yoshiko Ueda traveled to America on the *Kashima Maru* and described his conversations with the many picture brides aboard the ship: "Having plenty of free time, we talked about our personal affairs and they spoke about their husbands, whom they had never seen. Some of them proudly said such things as: 'My husband is president of a company.' Or 'Mine is the manager of a large store.'" However, Ueda also noted that in most cases, these glowing descriptions turned out to be false: "[W]hen the boat finally landed, the 'president' and the 'manager' turned out to be unbearably disgusting, about 40 or 50 years old, and their humble job was working on the railroads."[24]

Unfortunately, Ueda's experiences were not unique. Many other observers also noted the large number of picture brides who had been lured by false promises of a young and wealthy husband. In 1917, a picture bride named Shika Takaya gave the following, unflattering description of many of the picture grooms: "Men who claimed to be owners of large stores, turned out to be running small fruit stands. Big farmers turned out to be share-croppers of five or six acres. And many of those men who had sent us splendid letters written in a fine hand, had had their letters written for them."[25] Korean picture brides also wrote of similar disappointment. One nineteen-year-old Korean woman provided the following heartbreaking description of meeting her husband:

> I came to Hawaii and was so surprised and very disappointed because my husband sent his 25 year old handsome looking picture. You know he was tall, six feet high. He came to the pier, but I see he's really old, 25 years more old than I am. My heart stuck. I was so disappointed, I don't look at him again. So I don't eat and only cry for eight days. I don't eat nothing, but at midnight when everybody sleeps I sneak out to drink water, so I don't die. ... If I don't marry, immigration law send me back to Korea free. Oh, I was thinking, thinking. I came once [to Hawaii],

better I marry and stay here. ... My parents would be very shame, so I can't go back. So after eight days, I [married him].[26]

A sixteen-year-old Korean picture bride named Nam Soo Young also remembered the bitter disappointment she felt upon meeting her husband: "When I see him, he was much older, an old man. I was surprised. He cheated his age ten years. He was twenty-five years older than I. 'How can I live with him?' I thought." Young considered refusing to marry and returning home, but in the end she decided against it. Thus, "with tears running down her cheeks," she married her husband.[27]

These experiences were common among Asian picture brides, but the women also developed a variety of methods to cope with their marital disappointments. Many focused on the benefits that their marriage and entry into America had afforded them, including, for some, religious and political freedoms. For example, many Korean picture brides began advocating for Korean independence. Large numbers of these women had been well educated back in Korea. Some had attended high school, a few even college.[28] This background helped them acquire leadership positions in the Korean American community and many became indispensable advocates for Korean freedom.[29]

Other picture brides dealt with their marital disappointment by taking advantage of America's economic opportunities. These women quickly realized that female scarcity in Asian immigrant communities meant they could earn a significant income performing traditional women's work such as cooking, cleaning, or serving.[30] In addition, picture brides further increased their economic prospects by forming mutual aid societies and pooling their earnings to facilitate loans so members could start businesses or buy real estate.[31] Due to these savvy business practices, many picture brides were able to significantly improve their economic circumstances. Most spent this money on their families, but some used it to leave unhappy marriages.

Divorce was not uncommon in Japan, but female-initiated divorce was rare. In America the situation was reversed. Wives started the majority of Japanese American divorce proceedings, and this demonstrated their growing economic power. Japanese American wives were able to seek divorces because, unlike traditional Japanese wives, they often had access to significant financial resources.[32] Specifically, most Japanese women were working at the time they initiated divorce,[33] so they could afford the legal help they needed to prevail.[34] For instance, 1915 records from the city of Sacramento indicate there were 491 married Japanese couples and 29 Japanese divorces, which was a rate significantly higher than the national average.[35] In addition, court records show that 24 of these divorces were female-initiated and that nearly all ended in a victory for the wife.[36] Similarly, in Seattle, which had a total Japanese population of 7,874 in 1920,[37] 105 Japanese divorce cases took place between 1907 and 1920.[38] Women initiated 70.5 percent of these cases and won nearly all of them.[39]

The grounds Japanese women cited for divorce also reveal the growing independence and self-sufficiency of these former picture brides. For example, the most common reason for divorce cited by petitioner wives was not abuse, but the husband's failure to work. These women, supporting themselves and their children, had clearly grown frustrated with caring for their unemployed husbands as well.[40] Related to this, the most common ground for divorce cited in male-initiated divorce petitions was the wife's desertion.[41] Many unhappy Japanese women did not bother with divorce but simply deserted their husbands.

Contemporary newspapers are full of stories of picture brides leaving their husbands and eloping with other men.[42] For example, in 1916, a Japanese paper described how Kimura Haru, wife of Kimura Masaki, had eloped with Shimizu Fudeki, a former employee of her husband's. After suffering a miscarriage, Haru went to Sacramento purportedly to regain her health, but while there, by prearrangement, she met Fudeki and the two ran off together.[43] In a similar case, a young picture bride named Ochiyo began work as a barmaid in order to support her much older, unemployed husband. She then fell in love with a fellow employee named Kawakita and the two eloped. Ochiyo's husband found them and captured Ochiyo, but she escaped and then sued her husband for divorce, arguing that he had "neglected and refused to support [her]."[44] The court agreed with Ochiyo and granted the divorce.

Women like Ochiyo and Kimura Haru demonstrate the resourcefulness and fortitude of Japanese picture brides.[45] However, many white Americans believed such actions were examples of Japanese immorality. As the number of Japanese picture brides increased, groups such as the Asiatic Exclusion League began claiming these women were actually prostitutes and that picture marriage was simply a way to import women "for sinister purposes."[46] The commissioner of San Francisco expressed similar views when he declared "[f]ifty percent of such women, lead immoral lives in this country."[47] In fact, even those supposedly supporting Japanese women, such as Margaret Lake, director of a missionary home for Japanese women in San Francisco, often claimed there was little difference between picture brides and prostitutes. According to Lake, these women were simply "taking [the] place" of former Chinese prostitutes.[48]

For many Americans, the perceived immorality of Japanese picture brides was particularly galling given the fact that the Gentlemen's Agreement had been intended to reduce the Japanese population in the United States and prevent the arrival of additional Japanese immigrants. Picture marriages thwarted this goal, and led to the birth of thousands of children who, pursuant to the Fourteenth Amendment, were automatically entitled to citizenship.[49] Suddenly, the United States was facing the prospect of a large population of Japanese American citizens. Many white Americans found this possibility terrifying, and racist politicians such as California senator James Phelan helped fuel these fears. In 1919, Phelan testified before the House Committee on Immigration and made exaggerated and inflammatory statements about a massive influx of picture brides. For example, he claimed that more than 5,000 picture brides had arrived in San Francisco, when the actual number was only 668.[50] Phelan also made erroneous statements

A picture bride being processed at Angel Island. Courtesy of California State Parks, 2015. Image 231–18–40.

about the Japanese birthrate, asserting that the picture brides were uncommonly fertile and would typically have a child "every year."[51]

Others critics added to these concerns by accusing picture-bride marriages of being shams. They claimed that the couple's proxy marriage in Japan indicated a lack of consent. They also worried these marriages demonstrated a disregard for love.[52] Few picture marriages were love matches, but such marriages were generally uncommon. In Japan, most couples married for practical and familial reasons, however, by the early twentieth century, the majority of Americans believed love was essential to a successful marriage and increasingly considered the loveless picture marriages cruel and barbaric.[53] The Japanese consul general informed the Japanese government the perceived lack of love in picture marriages was contributing to the growing anti-Japanese sentiment in America and he recommended that the "practice should be abolished because it is . . . in contravention of the accepted American conception of marriage."[54] Unfortunately, this recommendation came too late.[55]

Responding to the numerous and vociferous objections to picture marriages, Congress passed the Immigration Act of 1924, ending all Japanese immigration to the United States by barring the immigration of any persons not eligible for naturalization.[56] Consequently, after 1924, there were no more Japanese picture brides. Nevertheless, the experience and success of these women had not gone unnoticed. As other potential immigrant groups began to feel the effects of America's increasing immigration restrictions, substantial numbers of foreign women turned to mail-order marriage.

Nineteenth-century concerns regarding Asian immigration were accompanied by a growing anxiety regarding the much larger influx of European immigrants. Between 1880 and 1930, almost twenty-seven million people immigrated to the United States, many "undesirable" immigrants from Southern and Eastern Europe. This exploding immigrant population convinced the U.S. government to enact comprehensive immigration regulations, not just specific exclusion laws.[57] The result was the Immigration Act of 1882, which potentially affected all immigrants but made immigration particularly difficult for single women. As a result, marital immigration became an attractive option for single women seeking to immigrate to America.

The 1882 act had two critical components. First, it imposed a head tax of fifty cents on all immigrants and used this revenue to fund the salaries of immigration inspectors, pay for the erection and maintenance of detention facilities, and cover various other costs associated with increased immigration regulation.[58] Second, it delineated criteria that made a would-be immigrant ineligible for entry. The legislation dictated that "if on such examination there shall be found among such passengers any convict, lunatic, idiot, or any person unable to take care of himself or herself without becoming a public charge, they shall report the same in writing to the collector of such port, and such person shall not be permitted to land."[59]

Over time, revisions and additional categories of excludable immigrants were added to the 1882 act. In 1891, the public charge exclusion was expanded by changing "unable to take care of himself without becoming a public charge" to "likely to become a public charge" (LPC).[60] In 1903, the law was amended to add people with epilepsy as well as "persons who have been insane within five years previous [or] who have had two or more attacks of insanity at any time previously."[61] In addition, "prostitutes and persons who procure or attempt to bring in prostitutes or women for the purpose of prostitution" were also barred under this revision. In 1907, the terms "imbeciles" and "feeble minded persons" were added to the list of those barred. This revision also expanded the morality ban to include both prostitutes and women coming "for any other immoral purpose."[62] Finally, in 1910, the morality provision was amended again so that women who were chaste at the time of entry but became prostitutes or "immoral" at some point thereafter were eligible for deportation.[63]

As a result of the 1882 act and its subsequent revisions, the American immigration system was transformed from welcoming to mainly closed. Moreover, these changes were particularly challenging for single women who now faced the double hurdle of both LPC concerns and suspicions of immorality. Many female immigrants were ultimately unable to overcome these challenges. For example, when Etta Horowitz, a young Romanian widow with two children, arrived in the United States in 1910, she was excluded as LPC. Although she was a skilled seamstress who testified that she had always supported her family through her work, she was denied entry because immigration officials believed that, as a single mother, she would be "unable to devote sufficient time and energy to work outside the home."[64] Similarly, another seamstress named Rebecca Hercovici arrived with her mother in 1902 and was denied entry because immigration officials found the "only support appellants would have ... would be the earnings of the daughter as a tailoress."[65]

These examples demonstrate that even skilled women had difficulties convincing immigration officials of their financial viability, and women without demonstrable skills were at an even greater risk of an LPC determination. In fact, for these women the only reliable means of avoiding an LPC designation was to obtain the guarantee of a male relative. The case of Renee Berkoff is demonstrative. In 1922, Berkoff emigrated from Hungary to join her sisters who were working in America. She was single and unskilled, but her sisters earned a good income and assured immigration officials they could support Berkoff and that she posed no danger of becoming an LPC. Luckily, Berkoff was able to find an uncle willing to serve as her legal guarantor and she was eventually admitted to the United States. However, many other women were unable to find a male guarantor. For example, Vera Zimmerman, another single female immigrant, also attempted to rely on her sister's financial guarantees, but these were deemed insufficient, making her inadmissible. At the time of Zimmerman's arrival, her sister was earning twenty-two dollars a month as a domestic servant and had saved almost sixty dollars. This was a substantial amount of money, but immigration officials still informed Vera that she needed a male guarantor. Unfortunately, Vera did not have one and was forced to return to Austria.[66]

Immigration officials treated claims of female financial independence with skepticism, and women who arrived without a male guarantor ran a significant risk of inadmissibility. This risk was further increased if the woman was immigrating from a non–Western European country. At the turn of the century, there were strong efforts to link rates of poverty with ethnicity. As a result, certain immigrants, particularly Asians, Greeks, Jews, Mexicans, and southern Italians, were much more likely to be deported as LPCs than immigrants from other countries. In 1904, Asian and Southern and Eastern European immigrants constituted over half of all immigrants deported as paupers or likely paupers. Consequently, not only single women but also women of certain racial and ethnic backgrounds were especially vulnerable to LPC suspicions. Therefore, marriage to a man already living in America

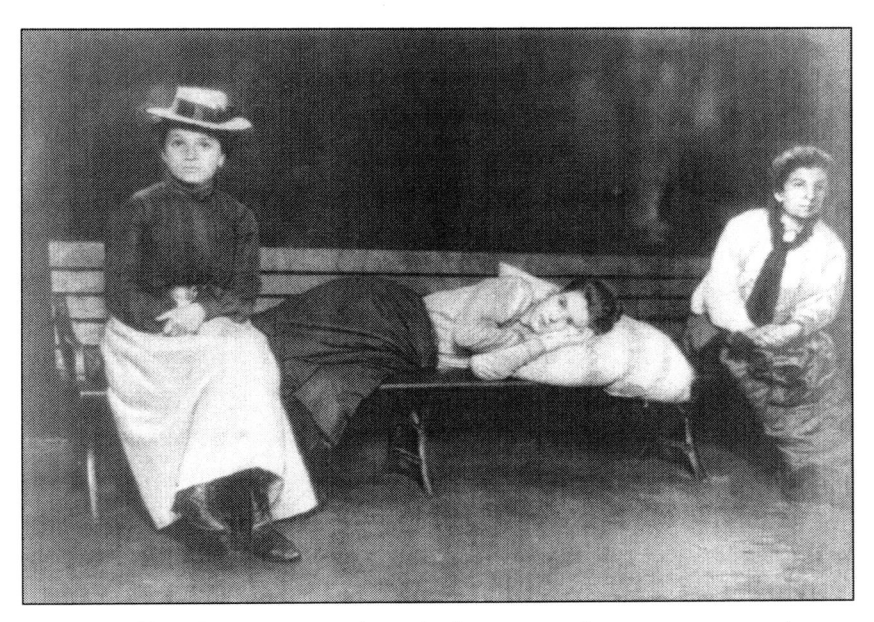

A group of female immigrants denied admission and waiting to return home. Library of Congress.

was one of the best ways single female immigrants, particularly those with these ethnic backgrounds, could avoid an LPC determination.[67]

Marriage also helped would-be female immigrants by protecting them from accusations of prostitution or other types of immorality that were frequently leveled at single female immigrants, preventing their entry into the United States. In 1881, in one of the first immigration "immorality" cases, Leong Shee arrived in San Francisco to reunite with her husband. At the time of Shee's immigration, American immigration officials suspected most Chinese women of immigrating for prostitution. However, Shee overcame this suspicion by convincing the officials that she was a legitimate wife. She argued that her bound feet indicated her "respectability."[68]

Similarly, Martha Ash, a young woman from New Zealand immigrating to meet her fiancé, was nearly denied entry in 1918 after immigration officials received allegations of improper behavior aboard the ship. Ash was accused by some passengers, including her fiancé's brother, of having become too friendly with a number of the boat's other passengers and behaving in a manner "not proper for young single women."[69] In the end, only the fact that Ash's fiancé was willing to marry her despite these rumors ultimately convinced immigration authorities of her moral character.[70] Shee and Ash used their status as wives to overcome suspicions of immorality, but single immigrant women lacked this protection. Marriage served as an important safeguard against inadmissibility.

The benefits of matrimonial immigration became even more pronounced after 1921, when the Quota Act radically limited the number of new immigrants permitted to enter the United States through quotas tied to country of origin and that country's percentage in the U.S. population in 1910 (later changed to 1890). The goal of the act was to limit the number of immigrants arriving from Eastern and Southern Europe, but these quotas did not apply to wives. Marital immigration thus made it possible for many otherwise ineligible women to immigrate to the United States. For these women, the benefit of admittance outweighed the negatives of marrying a stranger.

In the book *Rosa*, which recounts an Italian woman's journey to America, the author, Rosa, describes crossing the Atlantic in 1884 with two mail-order brides. At one point, one of the brides, Francesca, states, "Look at *me* . . . I'm going to marry a man I've never seen in my life. And he's not *Lombardo*—he's *Toscano*. But I'm not afraid." According to Rosa, "[Francesca] was so happy she was going to America and going to get married that she didn't care who the man was."[71] Mail-order marriage aided women like Francesca by increasing their likelihood of entry; it also helped by making the desire to immigrate more socially acceptable.

Francesca was Italian, and at the time of her immigration, Italian mores dictated that respectable women could travel with a husband or chaperone but never by themselves. This disapproval of single female

A European mail-order bride arrives on the SS *Baltic* in 1907. Library of Congress.

immigration is tellingly demonstrated in a popular Italian folk song from the period highlighting the dire consequences that could befall women who attempted immigration on their own. The song begins with a young woman begging her mother for money to immigrate to America:

> "Mother, mother, give me a hundred lire
> For to America I want to go."
> "I won't give you the hundred lire
> And to America no, no, no!"[72]

The girl then threatens to kill herself and eventually receives the money. She then leaves for America, but before she arrives is drowned at sea. The song served as a warning to single women that they should not try to immigrate to America. However, mail-order marriage provided

A group of mail-order brides on the SS *Baltic*. Library of Congress.

these women with an immigration solution and increased their marriage opportunities.

As Rosa notes in her memoir, Francesca was happy because she was going to America *and* because she was getting married. Like many of their predecessors, early twentieth-century mail-order brides often chose marital immigration because they believed it was their best marriage option. Marriage rates in Europe were extremely low during this period, and as a result, couples frequently had to live together outside of marriage. Immigration was a way to avoid this fate. For example, one recent German immigrant, whose own parents had waited years to afford marriage, noted this benefit of immigration and wrote a letter encouraging his sister to immigrate rather than attempt to marry in Germany. "[Rosina should] take care not to get involved with someone because she will get a husband here and women are more highly regarded in America than in Germany."[73]

For other European women, even finding a partner to live with in anticipation of future marriage was exceedingly difficult. In the Netherlands, for instance, the marriage market was so bad that approximately 20 percent of the female population never married.[74] Women who wanted to avoid this fate often became Dutch "letter brides" and immigrated to America to be wed.[75] Rachel Calof, a young Jewish woman from Russia, chose mail-order marriage for similar reasons.

In the 1890s, Calof, who was then known as Rachel Kahn, was working as a servant in her aunt's household when she fell in love with the local butcher's son. Unfortunately, this match was problematic. Calof was a poor orphan, but her extended family was of high status and disapproved of the match. As she noted in her autobiography, "Although I was nothing in the world myself, I was the granddaughter of Eda Velvel Cohen and because of this fact a friendship with this boy was out of the question."[76]

Calof's family considered status and connections more important than love, a not uncommon sentiment. At the turn of the century in Eastern Europe, love was not considered a reason to marry. In *A Walker in the City*, the Jewish author Alfred Kazin recalled the disdain his mother expressed when his American-raised cousin and her friends protested that they could never marry a man they didn't love. Kazin's mother exclaimed, "Liebe! [Love] Liebe! What is this love you make a stew about? You do not like the way he is holding his cigarette? Marry him first and it will all come out right in the end."[77] Although Calof left Russia shortly before Kazin's mother, she shared these sentiments. She did not believe love was the only reason to marry, so after Calof's grandfather rejected her request to marry the butcher's son, she began searching for other marital options. When she was presented with the opportunity to enter into marital correspondence with Abraham Calof, a man she had never met and certainly did not love, she seized it. "I hoped that I would be accepted," she wrote in her memoir. "I realized that I had to take the chance of going to a stranger in a strange land. No

Rachel Calof. From *Rachel Calof's Story*, edited by J. Sanford Rikoon. Copyright © 1995 Indiana University Press, Bloomington, Indiana. Reprinted with permission of Indiana University Press.

other avenue was open to me. I was already eighteen years old and time was against me."[78]

Mail-order marriage saved Calof from a life of domestic service and spinsterhood, but in some cases becoming a mail-order bride was literally lifesaving. In August 1922, the *King Alexander* arrived at Ellis Island with seven hundred picture brides from Turkey, Romania, Armenia, and Greece.[79] Almost simultaneously, a second ship, the SS *Constantinople*, arrived with another two hundred Greek and Armenian picture brides. Many of the boats' passengers were fleeing the horrors of the

Rachel Calof's family. From *Rachel Calof's Story*, edited by J. Sanford Rikoon. Copyright © 1995 Indiana University Press, Bloomington, Indiana. Reprinted with permission of Indiana University Press.

Greco-Turkish War. In fact, within days of the boats' arrival in New York, the largest and final offensive of the Turkish independence movement began.[80] Turkish forces recaptured the city of Smyrna, leading to the burning of the Greek and Armenian part of the city and the deaths of tens of thousands of Greeks and Armenians.

The arriving women escaped these horrors, but many were already survivors of the Armenian Genocide that had resulted in the murder of more than four hundred thousand Armenians.[81] Marital immigration allowed these persecuted women to enter America, yet astoundingly reports of their arrival fail to mention this horrific background. Instead, the newspaper accounts focused on whether the women found "love at first sight" or on their funny "foreign" customs. For example, one article mocked a bride for presenting her intended groom with an antique saddle, noting that "like most of his kind in the West at the present time, [the groom] transacts all of his business in an automobile and never indulges in horse riding."[82] One chilling exception to the superficial coverage of the women's arrival was an investigative report published by *Outlook* magazine. In this article, the reporter interviewed a young Armenian bride, named Tagavna, who was marrying an acquaintance of her uncle. When the reporter asked her if she was afraid to marry a man she had never seen, she responded, "It is better to marry a stranger than to be massacred."[83]

Mail-order marriage gave foreign women easy entry into the United States at a time when this was becoming increasingly difficult. Consequently, mail-order marriage greatly benefited many foreign women, but also led to significant criticism of marital immigration. Some of these were simply racist objections such as those spearheaded by the Asiatic Exclusion League. However, not all criticisms of mail-order marriage and foreign-born wives were bigoted. As more and more foreign-born women benefited from marital immigration, American women began to worry that these benefits were being achieved at their expense.

One of the earliest laws benefitting foreign wives was the act of February 10, 1855, which stated that "[a]ny woman who is now or may here-

Picture brides from SS *King Alexander* being introduced to their future husbands, July 3, 1922. https://historiful.wordpress.com/tag/museums-2/.

after be married to a citizen of the United States, and who might herself be lawfully naturalized, shall be deemed a citizen." This legislation clearly benefited foreign women who became automatically entitled to citizenship upon marriage to a citizen husband. As a result, some foreign women became citizens even before they set foot on American soil. For example, when Thakla Nicola arrived from Syria in 1908, she was denied admission by immigration authorities because she had contracted a contagious eye disease known as trachoma. However, Nicola was married to a citizen and argued that this made her a citizen, not a deportable alien. The court agreed; Nicola was a citizen at the time of her arrival and thus not subject to most immigration laws. According to the court, once she met the race requirements for naturalization, the law did not require her to satisfy any additional medical standards.[84]

For years the 1855 act had little direct impact on American women. However, in 1907, a corollary to the 1855 act was passed, stating, "any American woman who marries a foreigner shall take the nationality of her husband."[85] This Expatriation Act was a significant blow to American-born women. Not only did it deprive them of their citizenship, it did so right at the moment when they were close to achieving the right to vote, and thus when citizenship was becoming most valuable. In 1911, shortly after California granted women the franchise, the Expatriation Act was challenged as unconstitutional. The case was brought by Ethel MacKenzie, an American-born woman living in San Francisco. MacKenzie had helped campaign for women's suffrage, but because she was married to a foreigner (a popular Scottish tenor), she had lost her American citizenship and her right to vote. MacKenzie challenged this depatriation as unconstitutional. She argued that her American citizenship was a right conferred by the Constitution and beyond the power of Congress to take away without her consent. The Supreme Court disagreed and concluded that the "marriage of an American woman with a foreigner is tantamount to voluntary expatriation."[86] The Court's decision thus confirmed that after the 1907 act, American-born women like MacKenzie, who had lived their entire lives in the United States, now had fewer rights than the most recently arrived immigrant wives.[87]

Not surprisingly, the Expatriation Act angered American women and convinced them that obtaining the right to vote was the only way to overturn the act and prevent the passage of other similarly harmful legislation.[88] In addition, because foreign wives benefited from this law while native-born women did not, American women increasingly perceived foreign women as an obstacle to female equality. American Helen Papanastion, a social worker who lost her citizenship when she married a Greek man, exemplified this view: "A few days ago in my social work I visited a Greek woman, a 'picture bride,' married to a Greek, who is naturalized. She knows not one word of English and probably never will, for most of my Greek women ... have no intercourse with Americans. ... Well when I left this particular woman her husband followed me out in the street and wanted to know how soon his wife can vote. Presently, she will be voting and I who have read our literature, imbibed our standards, thrilled with our ideals, am an alien!"[89] Loretta Guignet, a marital expatriate living in France, expressed similar outrage. She recalled reading a *New York Herald* article announcing the quota-exempt arrival of fifteen Czech fiancées of naturalized men and described that moment as "the day I woke up from my Rip-van-Winkle sleep. . . . When I compared my children's and my own humiliation each time we enter my native land as aliens to the joy of those fifteen foreign born women about to enter the country as Americans, because the naturalized citizens who gave them the right to enter thus were men, and I was only a woman, I realized it was high-time that we American-born 'aliens' bestirred ourselves."[90]

The impression that foreign women threatened American women's rights was further strengthened by the fact that foreign women were often chosen as wives specifically because they were seen as unaffected by and uninterested in the American women's rights movement. For example, Italian men described mail-order brides as more "traditional" and "docile" than American women. As one social worker at the turn of the century noted, "it is a popular saying, particularly among young Italian immigrants, that girls who have been in America too long do not make good wives, that when a man wants to marry he had better send for a girl from the old country."[91]

Such sentiments led middle-class American feminists such as journalist Natalie De Bogory to declare mail-order marriages "death sentences to individuality and progress."[92] De Bogory also characterized foreign women's decisions to become mail-order brides as "simple-minded" and lamented, "The thought of those hundreds of women pouring into America, submissively accepting unknown husbands without friendship, romance, love, or any of those backgrounds which we have grown to regard as essential to marriage."[93] Considering her subject (Armenian refugees), De Bogory's views were particularly harsh. Nevertheless, her belief that loveless marriages perpetuated female subservience and harmed the fight for female independence was widespread.

Foreign wives whose marriages failed to conform to the ideal American love match were treated with animosity and contempt, and

Five French war brides arrive in Boston. Library of Congress.

this acrimony increased during both world wars as thousands of war brides entered the United States. Public reaction to these women was extremely negative. During World War I, they were frequently viewed as gold diggers and harlots, and many of the harshest criticisms came from those charged with helping the women immigrate. For example, when discussing the immigration of the war brides, Red Cross nurse Elizabeth Hutchin stated, "When I say that my personal feeling is that we are all co-operating in making entrance into America extremely easy for a far from desirable class of citizens, I am expressing myself with the utmost restraint."[94] Maude Cleveland, head of the American Expeditionary Force's office of war bride work in Antwerp, expressed a similar aversion to war brides. She accused the women of opportunism: "Living in Europe is hard, America is rich" and "the plum of free transportation is tempting even to those who are not unscrupulous."[95]

These views were then echoed by journalists, policy makers, and the public, many of whom quickly turned against the women.

During World War II, these same anxieties regarding opportunism reappeared. In addition, the animosity directed at war brides was further heightened by the substantial casualties suffered by American soldiers and the corresponding fear of an imminent "man shortage."[96] During the war, American women were warned that "no matter what happens, two to five million marriageable women in America are doomed to remain spinsters because of the male-female disproportion."[97] The anxiety caused by such predictions is apparent in the letter one concerned woman wrote to the New York Times in which she stated that "every British bride coming to our shores means just one less male for the native American."[98] Similarly, a Rhode Island woman was so distressed about the imminent man shortage that she wrote a letter to her senator, imploring him to stem this marital competition from "the dregs of Europe and Asia."[99]

As the latter comment demonstrates, racial animosity added to the resentment directed toward war brides. Prior to World War II, advocates of female immigration often argued that foreign brides were needed to help prevent interracial relationships. In fact, during the 1930s, this argument was used successfully to strike down restrictions on the immigration of Chinese wives of American citizens.[100] However, World War II war brides were often part of interracial relationships. As a result of the war and the subsequent occupation of Japan, American soldiers began forming relationships with Japanese women. Many of these men wanted to bring their new wives back to their homeland, but immigration law continued to forbid Japanese immigrants.[101] After years of petitioning, these immigration bans were eventually lifted, but the reaction to the Japanese war brides was far from positive.

In January 1952, the Saturday Evening Post ran an article titled "They're Bringing Home Japanese Wives," emphasizing the questionable origins of the Japanese brides and describing them as "all sorts of people."[102] Other critics were less reserved. For example, the writers

An American soldier and his Japanese bride. Library of Congress.

of the following letters to the *Cincinnati Enquirer* all expressed vehement objections to Japanese/American relationships. In the first, the author stated, "If we were put here in different colors, it must have been for a purpose. Why don't we stay that way. The boys . . . are getting like the man that had a cabin in the North Woods. No other human was there except an old Indian squaw. . . . One morning he got up and the old squaw looked like Hedy Lamarr . . . so he knew it was time to go back to civilization. Maybe it is time for our boys to come home."[103] A second writer wrote, "On the whole the American women have much higher ideals, morals, intelligence than Japanese women. Anyone connected with news knows the low morality among most Japanese women. Ask other servicemen that have been there! All these women that snared our GIs are only interested in entering the United States under any means, even to having children before marriage. . . . I'd like to bet two-thirds will be divorced before three years."[104] A third offered, "We do not hold our party girls and prostitutes in respect and envy as the Japanese do their 'geisha' girls. Apparently our standard of morals is higher than theirs. . . . It is absolutely criminal to allow interracial marriages to fill this country. We are all greatly opposed to extending the time limit for marriages and entry into this country, as enough damage has been done."[105]

By the time the Japanese war brides began entering the United States, Americans had been inundated with more than half a century of anti-foreign-bride sentiment, and the interracial aspect of these marriages just added to this already strong aversion. Foreign brides were considered immoral and opportunistic and were accused of stealing American men, corrupting America's racial purity, and delaying female equality. Moreover, as America entered the "golden age" of marriage in the 1950s, the need for mail-order brides virtually disappeared. Suddenly, everyone got married, and they were marrying younger than they had in more than half a century. By 1959, nearly half of all women were married by nineteen, 70 percent by twenty-four.[106] As a result, mail-order marriage was no longer necessary and the negative views of marital immigration became firmly entrenched. Mail-order marriages had provided women with social, political, and economic opportunities for centuries, but in the marital glow of the 1950s, this history was forgotten. All that remained was the unfavorable perception of mail-order marriage that persists today.

8

Mail-Order Feminism

Mail-order marriage virtually disappeared in the 1950s. It was unneeded, and almost everybody married. However, under a veneer of marital bliss, a backlash was brewing. As feminist historians have persuasively demonstrated, the mid-twentieth-century idealization of marriage created incredible stressors and deep unhappiness for many women. When the popular women's magazine *McCall's* ran an article in 1956 titled "The Mother Who Ran Away," it was the most widely read article in the magazine's history. "It was our moment of truth," said a former editor. "We suddenly realized that all those women at home with their three and a half children were miserably unhappy."[1] Similarly, when *Redbook* ran an article asking readers to explain "Why Young Mothers Feel Trapped," they got twenty-four thousand replies.[2]

By the 1960s, it had become clear that the marriage model of the male breadwinner and female homemaker was not working and that marriage was not providing the promised path to personal happiness.[3] Women began to rethink their expectations for marriage. They started postponing marriage in order to complete college or to establish careers; they used the pill to control their childbearing and commit more of their lives to work; and they fought for and won greater legal and civil rights.[4] During this same period, women also began to reform marriage and the long-standing roles of husband and wife. The ideal marriage slowly changed from the traditional male-headed household into the modern association of two, equal individuals.

Initially, the idea of marriage as an equal partnership was radical. In 1972, feminist Alix Kates Shulman's marriage and the contract she created with her husband, guaranteeing that each had "an equal right to his/her own time, work, values, and choices," was considered so astounding it became the subject of a cover story in *Life* magazine.[5] Then, barely six years later, the idea of marital equality had become so widely accepted that mainstream periodicals, like *Glamour* magazine, began running articles on how to write your own marriage contract.[6] Within a generation, the American marital landscape had changed drastically.[7] The average age for marriage rose, birthrates fell, and the divorce rate more than doubled. Women gained greater legal rights, increased access to education, birth control, and decent jobs,[8] and began rejecting the 1950s model of marriage as exploitative and oppressive.

Due to these changes, most Americans now take for granted the idea that marriage should be based on both love and equality. They also assume marriages deviating from this structure or formed for any other reasons, particularly monetary considerations, are problematic. Consequently, many Americans are highly uncomfortable with mail-order marriage, the very name of which implies the commodification of women. Moreover, many aspects of the modern, web-based mail-order marriage industry further fuel these commodification concerns.

There are currently more than four hundred international marriage broker agencies. Most of these operate websites that display photos of women interested in mail-order marriage and then charge men substantial fees to contact them. For example, on AnastasiaDate, one of the most popular mail-order websites, men purchase one-minute credits that allow them to chat with the women on the site. For $15.99, a man can buy twenty credits; and for $399.99 he may purchase one thousand. Smilies and emojis cost extra, and video chat costs even more.[9] Other matchmaking companies also sell a variety of extra services such as assistance selecting potential matches, help with letter writing and translation, legal assistance filling out visa forms, and even wedding planning services. In addition, increasing numbers of marriage broker agencies offer tour packages to help men visit the women with whom they have been corresponding.[10] These costly services add up quickly, and men seeking mail-order brides can easily wind up paying marriage broker agencies thousands of dollars. For many Americans, it looks like the men are buying a bride, and they find this highly alarming.

In the summer of 2009, *Glamour* magazine ran an article about mail-order marriage written by Lera Loeb, a Ukrainian mail-order bride married to American music producer Steve Loeb.[11] Lera was twenty-one and Steve forty-four when they met. According to Lera, the two had an instant connection. "I didn't expect to find love when I signed up with the agency, but I did," said Lera. "I feel very, very lucky." However, not everyone was so enamored of their relationship. Lera noted that she was shocked by the criticism and hostility directed at her marriage. She explained that in Russia, there is no stigma attached to mail-order marriages. "In my part of the world, in Russia, that's considered cool if you marry a foreigner. That's every girl's dream."[12] In America the reaction was quite different: "Most people never think of a 27-year-old career woman like me when they hear the words *mail-order bride*. They imagine someone who doesn't speak English, who's been shipped in, like property, to be subservient to her husband. 'Are you allowed to go out on your own?' an acquaintance once asked me. Another person wanted to know whether I had a curfew—seriously. If someone associates me with those kinds of stereotypes, Steve and I both get upset, because it's degrading. But I try not to take it too personally."[13] These types of reactions have made Lera defensive about her marriage, and she has tried to deflect the criticisms by embracing the label "mail-order bride." In fact, if you Google "Lera Loeb," mail-order bride is the top hit. "I say it as a joke," says Lera. "It's sort of super ironic. That's the attitude I've developed to it."[14]

The negative reactions described by Lera are not unusual. Americans are extremely hostile toward the idea of mail-order relationships, and the comments posted in response to Lera's article confirm the widespread discomfort many Americans feel about them. Although Lera stated that she was extremely happy in her relationship and felt very lucky to have married Steve, many readers were unable to view her as anything other than an abused and exploited woman. For example, one reader wrote, "This guy [her husband] just bought himself a \$20,000 pet. She's probably extremely docile, submissive and attentive. She probably has no say on any facet of their lives. Just stand there and be pretty." Similarly, another reader wrote, "Aren't the men who use this 'service' really just looking for a woman that they can isolate and control and who better than a young foreign woman with no friends or family here? The women who sign up for this bother me too but the men positively disgust me."[15]

The hostility and unease revealed in these comments is pervasive and not confined to Internet postings. For example, in her book *Wedded Strangers*, Dr. Lynn Visson recounts the typical responses she has received when asking women's groups for their views on American men seeking mail-order marriages. The women responded with comments such as it's "the dream of being the all-provider" and "it's not normal love interest that's driving them, it's fantasy."[16] Newspaper and magazine articles also routinely disparage these marriages, calling the women "desperate" and the men "losers" or, as the *St. Petersburg Times* put it, "stiffs, weirdos, and those who drink too much."[17] Fictional portrayals of men and women in these relationships are similarly unflattering. In the open call ad for the "husband" in the indie feature *Mail Order Bride*, the desired candidate was described as "35–45, white male, imperfections a plus, overweight, bald, etc."[18] However, the most damning critique of these relationships is not that the men are "losers" but that they are actually using mail-order marriage to find women to abuse or traffic.

One of the most widely cited sources for the proposition that mail-order marriage encourages abuse is the book *Mail Order Brides: Women for Sale*, written by Mila Glodava and Richard Onizuka. In this book, Glodava recounts working with mail-order brides who were victims of domestic violence. Based on these experiences, Glodava and Onizuka concluded that "those who have used the mail-order bride route to find a mate have control in mind more than a loving and enduring relationship."[19] The book identifies thirty mail-order brides who called the domestic abuse shelter during a nearly ten-year period. However, although the book clearly shows that mail-order brides can be subject to abuse, it provides little support for the statement that men turn to mail-order marriage because they are looking for women to control and that they will enforce this desire "with fists."[20] As anthropology professor Nicole Constable has noted in her lengthy criticism of *Mail Order Brides*, "Glodava and Onizuka are no doubt correct that there are men who meet their wives through correspondence (as well as other means) who are guilty of spousal abuse. But they overlook the possibility that these men and women are a highly diverse group, and that there are also men who are critical of such sexist and chauvinistic behavior and intentions."[21] *Women for Sale* shows that mail-order brides can be abused but presents little support for its main premise, which is that such marriages have higher rates of abuse than others.[22]

Other mail-order marriage critics also fail to provide evidence for their general claims that mail-order marriages lead to abuse.[23] For example, the Tahirih Justice Center, which advocates on behalf of immigrant women and is extremely opposed to mail-order marriage, describes men seeking these brides as "predators." It strongly warns women to avoid these marriages and reverse the "growing number of matches ... made between foreign women and abusive U.S. men."[24] However, like Glodava and Onizuka, the center provides little support for these increased abuse claims. In fact, despite its statements that large numbers of mail-order brides are abused, it acknowledges on its website, under the inflammatory heading "How Widespread Is the Problem of Abuse?," that there are "no national statistics reflecting what the prevalence of abuse is in brokered marriages."[25] More accurately, there are no statistics indicating that this form of introduction, including marriage brokers, pen pal clubs, and so on, increases the risk of abuse at all.[26] As doctoral student Lisa Simons discovered during her research on mail-order brides, most of the citations for the claim that mail-order marriage increases abuse actually stem from two newspaper articles from the 1980s, containing no statistical research,[27] or are based on studies regarding domestic violence in general.[28] In addition, she also notes that most studies that have investigated mail-order marriages have actually found a "generally high level of marital satisfaction and a generally low level of physical violence."[29]

The perception of mail-order marriages as abusive began in the 1980s, but increased significantly after the highly publicized murders of two mail-order brides in Washington State.[30] These murders, one in 1995 and the second in 2002, appeared to highlight the particular vulnerability of mail-order brides and served as the catalyst for subsequent legal reforms. However, despite the widespread belief, it is not at all clear that mail-order marriage increases a foreign woman's risk of abuse. In fact, because mail-order brides immigrate legally, they are probably less likely to face abuse than many other foreign wives.

Studies show that immigrant women experience higher rates of domestic violence than do nonimmigrant women, and that the risk of abuse is even greater for married immigrant women.[31] At the same time, this fact has little bearing on whether mail-order marriage in particular makes a foreign woman likely to experience abuse. In fact, the different rates of abuse of foreign women are much more likely to be tied to their immigration status.

Documented and undocumented wives maintain a vastly different position relative to each other.[32] Mail-order brides, by definition, enter the country legally.[33] Most immigrate to the United States on fiancée or K-1 visas,[34] which permit them to enter the United States and then stay for ninety days. This period provides potential brides with a chance to spend time with their fiancé and learn about his life and community before agreeing to marry. Then, once the woman is married, she becomes a two-year conditional resident with all the rights and privileges of residency.[35] Conditional residents can work, drive, and attend school. Consequently, as soon as a mail-order bride marries, she can earn her own money, have her own friends, learn English, get a job, and travel, all without worrying about deportation. After two years, she is then eligible to change her conditional residency status to permanent residency. Then, once she becomes a permanent resident her immigration status is no longer contingent on her marriage and she cannot be deported if her marriage ends.[36] In addition, mail-order brides are also given specific protections against domestic abuse, including information regarding U.S. domestic abuse laws and a criminal background check on her intended husband.

In contrast, undocumented foreign wives face a very different situation and consequently a much greater likelihood of abuse. Undocumented women who enter the country illegally remain subject to deportation regardless of their subsequent marriage to an American citizen.[37] Under the Illegal Immigration Reform and Immigrant Responsibility Act of 1996, all undocumented immigrants are eligible for deportation, and those who have been in the United States for more than one year may be subject to a ten-year ban on reentry.[38] As a result, undocumented wives live with the constant fear of deportation and the potential separation from their children.[39] Furthermore, because any attempt to seek employment, education, or a social network could reveal their immigration status and threaten their ability to stay in the country, undocumented wives are also likely to be isolated and wary of seeking out government benefits or assistance. Last, because such women's undocumented condition has no time limit, deportation remains an ever-present threat. This leaves many undocumented wives isolated and dependent on their husbands, factors known to make women particularly vulnerable to abuse.

The 2001 Amendments to the Violence Against Women Act (VAWA) were enacted to address concerns regarding the abuse of undocumented wives.[40] These amendments permit battered immigrant wives to self-petition for adjustment of immigration status and to avoid an otherwise applicable ten-year inadmissibility bar. These same amendments also give mail-order brides the right to self-petition and seek an immediate change in immigration status. The two groups are given similar protection from abuse, but undocumented wives appear to have a much greater need for this protection. This finding was unexpected. When passing the VAWA amendments, Congress assumed mail-order brides were the immigrant wives particularly vulnerable to domestic abuse. In fact, after enacting the amendments, Congress asked the Immigration and Naturalization Service (INS) to examine the self-petitions made by abused immigrant women in order to determine "the extent of domestic abuse in mail order marriages."[41]

At a minimum, between four thousand and six thousand mail-order brides enter the country each year,[42] but the INS found that of the 1,170 VAWA self-petitions they examined for this study, only 7 were the result of marriages arranged through the mail-order bride industry.[43] These results contradicted widely held assumptions about mail-order marriages, but they are actually not surprising. Although the VAWA self-petition provision protects mail-order brides and undocumented wives in similar ways, the two groups hold vastly disparate immigration statuses, and studies on immigration status and abuse demonstrate that immigration status can have a substantial effect on the likelihood abuse.

For example, in her work regarding the willingness of battered immigrant women to seek police assistance, American University professor Leslye Orloff demonstrated that immigration status had a significant impact on foreign women's likelihood of reporting abuse. Specifically, Orloff found that the reporting rate for women with stable permanent immigration status was 43.1 percent, that it dropped to 20.8 percent for women who were in the United States legally but on temporary nonimmigrant visas, and that it dropped to 18.8 percent if the woman was undocumented.[44] Orloff's study did not include K-1 visa holders like mail-order brides, but based on her research, these brides (who hold a conditional but legal immigration status) should be more likely to report abuse than undocumented women.[45] Thus, Orloff's work indicates that it is inaccurate to assume comparable abuse rates among women with different immigration statuses. In addition, her study suggests that the rates of mail-order abuse as a percentage of the total rates of abuse against immigrant wives are lower than what the INS study found since undocumented women are less likely than mail order brides to report abuse.

The possible reasons for the different reporting rates observed by Orloff further counsel against conflating the experiences of undocumented wives with those of mail-order brides. Many scholars have suggested that undocumented women are reluctant to report abuse because they live in perpetual fear of deportation. They argue that undocumented women have a significant distrust of the legal system and find it difficult to accept that the same government that can expel them is also interested in protecting them from domestic abuse.[46] In contrast, mail-order brides enter legally and thus are unlikely to view the U.S. government with a similar level of suspicion. In fact, mail-order brides may even be inclined to trust the government, at least with regard to protection from domestic abuse, given that by the time they arrive in the United States the government has already demonstrated its commitment to their safety by providing them with information regarding their rights in the event of domestic abuse and a detailed criminal history of their intended spouse.

The 2008 International Marriage Broker Regulation Act (IMBRA) protects foreign brides by requiring that all fiancée visa holders be informed of their right to be free of domestic and sexual abuse and of their right to self-petition in case of abuse.[47] Specifically, the act obliges U.S. Immigration and Customs Enforcement to inform foreign brides that domestic abuse and child abuse are both illegal in the United States and requires them to provide these women with a booklet outlining the legal rights and resources available to immigrant victims of domestic violence and to provide them with information about domestic abuse and sexual assault hotlines.[48]

IMBRA also aims to reduce potential mail-order bride abuse by requiring matchmaking organizations to provide information on the U.S. citizen client to both the foreign woman and the Department of Homeland Security. Pursuant to the act, these organizations must conduct a search of the sex offender public registries,[49] and provide documentation regarding the client's criminal history, including any arrests for alcohol or substance abuse. In addition, the U.S. client must provide a personal history indicating how many times he was previously married, the dates these marriages ended, whether the client had previously sponsored any foreign fiancées, the ages of any minor children, and all states and countries he has resided in since he was eighteen years old.[50] Last, the act places a limit on the frequency and number of fiancée visas that can be applied for.[51]

Both IMBRA and VAWA are good laws that seek to prevent the abuse of foreign spouses. However, the fact that these laws specifically single out mail-order brides as the foreign wives most in need of protection does not prove these marriages have higher rates of abuse. Instead, these laws simply reveal how widespread the perception of abuse in such marriages has become. Moreover, this is not the only misconception about mail-order marriages. The belief that mail-order brides are trafficked women is similarly pervasive but also based on little evidence.

Many of the harshest critics of these marriages argue that there is no such thing as a consenting mail-order bride; mail-order marriage is simply another name for human trafficking. Natalia Khodyreva, a well-known feminist researcher and activist in Russia, espoused this view when she unapologetically described all mail-order brides as victims and insisted, "all marriage agencies are trafficking women." Nevertheless, when asked for documentation of this "fact," Khodyreva admitted she had no proof, she simply insisted no proof was needed because it is well known.[52]

The Cambodian government used similar reasoning to defend its various mail-order bride bans. Over the past ten years, thousands of Cambodian women have left the country to become the mail-order brides of Korean men. In response, Cambodia instituted a number of marriage bans, including a prohibition on marriages between Cambodian women and foreign men over fifty; a ban on marriage between Cambodian women and Korean men; and, in 2008, a ban on all marriages with foreigners.[53] After issuing these bans, the government sent a formal statement to the Korean embassy explaining that the ban on marriage with Korean men was justified because it would "prevent the trafficking of Cambodian women."

Like Khodyreva, the Cambodian government was unable to distinguish between mail-order brides and "traffick[ing] victims." Dr. Shin Hei-soo, a prominent women's rights activist and representative of the National Movement for the Eradication of Sex Trafficking, noted this problem when she recounted a conversation with a Cambodian official in which she was shocked to discover the Cambodian official "viewed [all] marriages to Korean men as trafficking." Hei-soo then had to explain to him that "a marriage through a broker doesn't mean trafficking."[54]

Other opponents of mail-order marriage often conflate these brides with human trafficking victims by employing expansive definitions of either one or both of these terms. For example, the Philippine Women Centre of British Columbia is able to include mail-order brides within their definition of trafficking by "oppos[ing] any 'narrow definition' of trafficking that attempts to isolate 'abuse and coercion.'"[55] According to this view, a woman who is neither abused nor coerced but willingly chooses to marry a foreign husband may still be trafficked. George Washington law professor Suzanne Jackson's critique of mail-order marriages has a similar definitional problem. In her work on trafficking victims, Jackson includes foreign prostitutes whom American men are to paid marry and bring to the United States within her definition of "mail-order brides." These women are certainly trafficking victims, but they do not meet any traditional definition of mail-order bride.

Studies on Russian trafficking victims also show no connection between trafficking and mail-order marriages. Instead, these studies indicate that the trafficking of Russian women is done through job agencies and tourist firms, not marriage brokers. As Kateryna Levchenko, the director of the antitrafficking organization La Strada (based in Kiev), notes, "we do not have any evidence that marriage agencies are a major part of trafficking networks."[56] An examination conducted by the Ukrainian government also found no evidence that mail-order marriage companies are used to traffic women.[57] It is clear that the perception of mail-order brides as trafficked is based on opinion rather than proof.

There is little evidence that American mail-order brides are trafficked or subject to higher rates of domestic abuse. Nevertheless, even if the majority of Americans could be convinced of this fact, most would still consider these relationships objectionable. This is unfortunate. As this book has repeatedly shown, mail-order marriage has always carried risks and uncertainty, but has also empowered women and increased marital equality. Modern mail-order marriages offer similar benefits, which is perhaps not surprising given that the factors driving mail-order marriage have also remained very similar over the past four hundred years.

Historically, mail-order marriages were the result of significant gender disparities that created the desire for increased female immigration and the willingness to provide the legal, political, and financial incentives necessary to convince foreign women to immigrate. The factors leading to modern American mail-order marriages are comparable. The male and female populations in the United States are roughly equal, but the increasing marginalization of many blue-collar and lower-middle-class American men is decimating their marriage prospects and creating a significant gender disparity in the marriage market. As a result, growing numbers of these men have begun seeking mail-order marriages. At the same time, favorable immigration laws, improved financial prospects, and a desire for gender equality continue to motivate foreign women to become mail-order brides.

Initially, the idea that American men are seeking mail-order brides because there is a shortage of marriageable American women may seem unlikely. There is no dearth of women in America, and women actually slightly outnumber men.[58] Nevertheless, gender parity does not mean a wife for every man. For a growing segment of American men, the pool of marriageable women—those willing to marry them—is shrinking drastically. For these men, marriage is becoming more and more elusive. At the same time, marriage remains important. For lower-middle-class and working-class families, and for men in particular, marriage is often the difference between success and failure.

As Berkeley law professor Melissa Murray has noted, in America marriage "*is* the social safety net—or at the very least, the means by which we patch what is left of the disintegrating social safety net."[59] For many lower-income families, marriage provides access to health care, child care, and a second income. It also means that the loss of a job is difficult, not devastating. Moreover, because men are the ones increasingly facing job instability and unemployment, marriage is particularly important for their financial well-being.[60] These economic benefits of marriage are significant, but the social benefits may be even more important.[61] Marriage is a choice. If you are married, someone considers you worthy of his or her commitment. Failure to marry signals the opposite, and American women are increasingly looking at American men and finding them unworthy. For these men, mail-order marriage provides a possible solution.

In recent years, growing numbers of journalists, commentators, politicians, and pundits have begun referring to the declining rates of marriage as a "crisis." In 1960, 72 percent of Americans were married, now it is less than 50 percent.[62] At the same time, cohabitation rates are skyrocketing. Modern couples are fifteen times more likely to live together outside of marriage than they were back in 1960, and almost half of these cohabitating couples include children. Nevertheless, the decline in marriage is not the same as a decline in the desire to marry. A study by the Pew Research Center found that although "40 percent of unmarried adults believe marriage is obsolete," half of these participants still stated they wished to marry.[63] These men and women understand that, at least in America,[64] marriage represents the highest form of commitment.[65] In fact, it is this belief in the superiority of marriage that was at the core of the biggest marriage issue of our time: whether same-sex couples had the right to marry.

In *Perry v. Schwarzenegger*,[66] the case concerning the constitutionality of California's Proposition 8, which defined marriage as a heterosexual relationship, the only issue before the court concerned the expressive function of marriage.[67] By this time, California's same-sex couples were already entitled to the same rights and privileges as heterosexual couples. The sole difference was that they could not legally call their relationships "marriage."[68] Nevertheless, the California district court found this semantic distinction significant, recognizing that "marriage is widely regarded as the definitive expression of love and commitment in the United States."[69] The *Perry* court understood that in America, whether you are married or unmarried makes all the difference.[70]

The same-sex marriage debate brought attention to the issue of marriage exclusion, but because the discussion of same-sex marriage focuses on a legal impediment to marriage, it tends to obscure the fact that there are many other marriage barriers. For example, in his book *Is Marriage for White People?*, Professor Ralph Richard Banks looks at the exclusion of African American women from the institution of marriage. His book focuses on the financial and educational success of African American women and shows how the achievements of these women have outpaced those of African American men. According to Banks, this disparity has created a situation in which many women choose to forgo marriage altogether rather than marry a man with inferior financial and educational prospects.

Banks's book concerns the African American community, but he notes that the trends he discusses are increasingly mirrored in the general population.[71] The educational and financial prospects of women across all racial and ethnic groups have been rising for decades, while the possibilities for men have stagnated or declined. For the first time in American history, women earn more than men. On average, studies show that women between the ages of twenty-one and thirty now earn 117 percent of wages of men of the same age group.[72] Women are also more educated. For example, a 2005 study from New York revealed that

53 percent of working women in New York had college degrees, while only 38 percent of working men did.[73] These changes have not gone unnoticed. Journalist Hanna Rosin recently wrote a best-selling book titled *The End of Men and the Rise of Women*, in which she shows the extent to which men are faltering.[74] Rosin refers to the current generation of American men as "Cardboard Men," by which she means men unable to adapt to changing times who insist on keeping their lifestyle and ambitions the same despite the fact that traditional male jobs and roles have changed.[75]

Books like Rosin's credit women's increasing success to their ability to adapt while also noting that men have been less successful at adjusting to the new "knowledge economy." In the past, manufacturing jobs offered stable, well-paid employment to unskilled male workers, but these jobs have largely been eliminated or outsourced, so men without college degrees no longer have a clear path to upward mobility.[76] These less educated men are also failing to obtain the skills and training they need to take advantage of available employment opportunities, and most are now facing a significant decline in wages and lifestyle. Moreover, as men's job prospects have faltered, their marriage prospects have suffered as well.[77]

Books like *Is Marriage for White People?* and *The End of Men* demonstrate that American women continue to want marriage but are increasingly unwilling to marry lower-status men.[78] Rosin notes that most of the upwardly mobile women she interviewed would like to marry, but only if they could find men of comparable achievements and motivations or those who, at the very least, would not be a drain on the family's resources.[79] In one telling example, Rosin describes a grocery store encounter with a single mother named Bethenny, who explained her unwillingness to consider her child's father as a marriage prospect by gesturing to a package of granola bars in her shopping cart and stating, "Calvin would just mean one less granola bar for the two of us."[80]

Economic and cultural changes have allowed women like Bethenny to decide they are better off single, but these shifting dynamics have been devastating for men.[81] Married men do better, and the health benefits alone are shocking. Studies show married men are less likely to develop heart disease, cancer, high blood pressure, diabetes, and serious depression. One interesting study even showed that married male heart attack victims arrive at the hospital half an hour before single men.[82] In fact, the health benefits of marriage are so great, they led Bernard Cohen and I-Sing Lee, researchers studying this phenomenon, to conclude that "being unmarried is one of the greatest [health] risks that people voluntarily subject themselves to."[83] Nevertheless, for many men, their single status is not voluntary, and their inability to marry and provide for a family is upending not only their health, but their very sense of themselves.[84]

Geoffrey Canada, the founder, president, and CEO of the Harlem Children's Zone, aptly captures this loss in his observation that "[i]t used to be where it was clear [that being a man] was about having a job and providing for your family. I think men struggled—we maybe weren't the most enlightened folk, but at least we knew who we should be."[85] As Canada recognizes, modern men are losing not only their ability to earn a living, but also the very definition of what it means to be a man. When men cannot achieve the positive characteristics of "being a man," they often turn to roles that are self-defeating and self-destructive.[86] As Guy Garcia writes in his book *The Decline of Men*, "The symptoms of the male malaise are already showing as men of all ages become increasingly angry, suspicious, reactionary and isolated. Men are opting out, coming apart, and falling behind. They are losing their sense of place in society and their direction as individuals."[87]

In *Is Marriage for White People?*, Banks advises African American women to increase their dating pool by looking outside of their racial group. American men considering mail-order marriage seem to be making a similar calculation. As these men are increasingly rejected by American women, they are turning to foreign women in the belief that these women will consider them more desirable marriage partners, a belief that appears to be correct.[88]

Studies demonstrate that many of the men seeking mail-order brides are precisely those who have been left behind by the rise of women. A 1998 study of the men using mail-order services found that only 50 percent had two or more years of college.[89] That means that half of the men seeking mail-order brides are those most hurt by the changing job market and most likely to be excluded from marriage. Letters from these men to potential mail-order brides confirm their experience with rejection by American women.[90] For example, in a letter written to a Russian woman named Olga, the suitor stated that he wanted a woman who was not a "feminist" and lamented the fact that American women are "only interested in their own careers." This man wrote that he turned to mail-order marriage because he was looking for a "wife who'll take care of our home and children." The man worked as an installer of garage doors.[91]

Critics of mail-order marriage seize upon the antifeminist aspects of such letters as proof that men seeking mail-order marriages are looking for women to dominate and oppress. However, the antifeminist rhetoric in these letters is misleading. As feminist author Susan Faludi has noted, "feminism" is often simply a "scapegoat for wider feelings of social and economic displacement and powerlessness, including a diminished sense of male power in relation to assumptions of women's real or imagined social gains."[92] Although men's letters to potential mail-order brides frequently express a rejection of feminism and feminists, their actions tell a different story. In many instances, the same men who write that they are looking for women who are not "feminists" are specifically choosing to court smart, well-educated, and accomplished women. For example, when asked about the type of women entering mail-order marriages, the vice consul for immigrant visas at the U.S. embassy in Moscow stated, "For the most part these women are far better educated than the men. I see women doctors, scientists, etc. being petitioned for by truck drivers, gas station attendants, farmers with very little money. Some of them can barely afford to do this because they need to earn an income that is 25 percent above poverty level."[93]

The irony is that American men considering mail-order marriage often seem to be searching for a foreign version of the type of woman who is rejecting them at home.

Jen, the manager of a pen pal agency in Beijing, made similar observations about the men seeking Chinese brides. She noted that in her experience, American men, unlike their Chinese counterparts, were happy to marry women significantly more successful than themselves. According to Jen, many "educated, professional women in their mid-thirties and forties or older who are divorced" become mail-order brides because "local men want younger women and often are not comfortable with a woman who is successful or who earns more money than they do."[94] Filipina women express analogous sentiments regarding the appeal of mail-order marriage. As one Filipino women's advocate explained, "Powerful, educated Filipinas intimidate [Filipino men]. Accomplished women might as well be attracted to foreigners because a Filipino man wouldn't want them anyway."[95]

The fact that American men frequently seek highly educated and professionally successful brides suggests that despite the antifeminist rhetoric in their letters, American men considering mail-order marriages are not actually opposed to female success. Instead, their objection seems to be with the fact, as they perceive it, that this success has led American women to reject marriage and family and these men in particular.[96]

Interviews with men considering mail-order marriage confirm their frustration with the domestic dating scene. In one poignant example, a man on one of the Russian bride tours made the following observation:

> The foreign women say in their personal ads they want to love and be loved. In contrast, American women have numerous demands like exact height and weight of a guy, a salary over $100,000, fit body, must like specific sports, films, etc. I find all this makes me ineligible with such women. I don't have enough money and I am not fit enough. I consider myself average looking, but it is not good enough for most

American women I would be interested in meeting. I like the fact that Ukrainian women are impressed that I have a job at all, they don't seem to care what I do, but simply that I have been at it for as long as I have [he has been a UPS driver for twenty years] shows them I am reliable.[97]

In her book *Marriage Confidential*, author Pamela Haag similarly demonstrates that successful American women are unlikely to marry lower achieving men. In 2008, Haag compiled a sample of 120 wedding announcements from the *New York Times* and the *Baltimore Sun* and found only one example of a non-college-educated man marrying a college-educated woman. In that case, the man, Mr. Wright (his true name), met his future wife while providing a CPR refresher course to the crew of a sailboat designed by his wife's company. However, in every other example, the couples had the same level of education and most also attended schools of comparable prestige.[98]

The accusation that men seeking mail-order marriages are looking for women to dominate as opposed to simply date is also called into question by the fact that the women are often quite assertive in these relationships. For example, in reference to the stereotype of the submissive mail-order bride, an American doctor named Timothy described his Filipina wife, Mary, as the "classic case of false advertising! In our house, she's the boss!"[99] Similarly, many of the women acknowledge taking charge of the family finances or actively steering their husband's career prospects. In an interview about her relationship, a Russian mail-order bride named Masha, described her husband Paul, a forty-year-old math teacher from Indiana, as patient and attentive, but terrible with money. She recalled how, early in the marriage, she had asked Paul about their numerous bills and received a dreadful shock when he informed her of his significant debt. "How can you owe that much?" she remembered asking in disbelief. When Masha recovered from the initial shock, she vowed to fix Paul's financial problem and immediately took charge of the money. Within a few years, Masha and Paul were out of debt and saving to buy a house.[100]

In her book *Confessions of a Mail Order Bride*, the author, a Thai mail-order bride named Wanwadee Larsen, also recounts the despair she felt when she discovered the family's desperate financial situation and the fact that her "professor" husband would soon be out of a job "for having made no progress [on his] Ph.D." She writes, "What kind of twisted dream is this that I have come so far to live? To have a husband with no job—in America?"[101] Larsen did not leave her husband, but she also did not accept his aimless lifestyle. Instead, she engaged in a persistent campaign against her husband's lack of ambition and high marijuana use, until he changed his life around.[102] Her perseverance paid off, as by the end of the book her husband had received a permanent academic position and Larsen was on her way to attaining an art degree and her own academic career.

These descriptions of men relying on their mail-order wives stand in stark contrast to the usual portrayal of such men and also show how American men benefit from these marriages. Nevertheless, the biggest beneficiaries of mail-order marriage are usually the women. It is widely assumed that only the poorest, most vulnerable, and most desperate women would agree to such marriages, but contrary to this pervasive view and in keeping with the long history of American mail-order marriage, modern mail-order brides typically benefit from their decision to become marital immigrants.[103]

Men seeking mail-order brides frequently claim they are looking for "traditional" wives who will be happy to take care of the home and family, statements that make most American feminists shudder.[104] American women have largely rejected the separate spheres ideology of the male breadwinner and the female homemaker, but there is no evidence that foreign women find abandoning this traditional family structure emancipatory.[105] In fact, mail-order marriage participants routinely indicate frustration with forced gender equality. The correspondence between Polina, a young Russian woman from Smolensk, and her American suitor demonstrates such concerns. In the following letter, Polina disparages gender equality because, at least in Russia, it has been a raw deal for women:

> I've got a gentle character. I never was able to be active in a relationship. But over the last 70 years Russian men have stopped feeling they are the head of the family and a pillar of support for women. From childhood on we were told that men and women are equal in everything. Many of our men are infantile and women have to decide everything for them. A new type of woman has been formed in the Soviet Union. Deep down, a woman has become more of a man than a woman. Our poet Evtushenko was right in saying that the "best men are women." In my character there are no such male traits, although, like all women in our country, I have to hustle—rush to work, study, stand on line, do housework. Gradually, all of this leads to a loss of one's feminine core, to a roughness of which I am very frightened.[106]

As Polina's letter illuminates, equality in Russia has meant women are now doing everything, which has been far from liberating.[107]

In her book *Romance on a Global Stage*, Professor Nicole Constable also remarks on this fact, noting that what is often lacking in the "critique of marriage and gender relations [is] an appreciation of the variety of ways in which women in different sociocultural contexts might define liberation. To work for a wage might be liberating to a middle-class American woman, but not to a woman who has worked in fields or factories for subsistence since childhood."[108] Moira, a forty-five-year-old Chinese mail-order bride exemplifies this idea. Moira was well educated with a good job, but she felt burdened by the stigma of having been divorced. She hoped that marriage to an American would give her a fresh start. Career success was less important than excelling as a wife. She stated she would happily give up her career and commit herself entirely to her husband, if that was what he preferred. Moira wanted the opportunity to live with "more open-minded people" who would allow her to "escape her past and begin anew," and whether she achieved this goal as a working wife or as a "traditional" wife was nearly irrelevant.[109] Sentiments like Moira's are common among mail-order brides, yet it is interesting to note that most of them do work. At the same time, they are quick to point out that their desire to work is not "feminist." For example, when Olga, a Russian music teacher, was asked if she saw herself working after marriage, she replied, "Yes. I'm going to be a teacher. ... I wouldn't want to be entirely dependent on my husband and I don't want to just sit around at home." Olga then further clarified, "I don't want a career. I'm not a feminist. My family will be my first priority, but I do want to have a job and make some money."[110] One Russian bride site even specifically states that men should expect their wives to work and advises that "within a few months after arriving in America, their wives will likely become bored and want to get a job."[111] Interestingly, few men seem to object.

As the above examples demonstrate, the relationship between mail-order marriage and feminism is complicated. Men and women in these relationships frequently conform to outdated and often disparaged gendered roles, yet at the same time the women commonly describe their marriages as liberating and empowering. Moreover, although anti-feminist rhetoric is widespread in letters to and from mail-order brides, with the men typically saying they are looking for women who are not feminists and the women claiming they have no feminist intentions, both parties actually use these marriages for the very feminist goal of increasing choice and combating disempowerment.

Interviews with potential mail-order brides reveal that these women view foreign marriages as a means of reasserting control over their lives. Similarly, interviews with the potential husbands demonstrate that they also turn to mail-order marriage as a way of combating their own disempowerment, typically in relation to American women.[112] Thus, as researcher Lisa Simons, who conducted numerous interviews with mail-order marriage participants, has noted, both groups use mail-order marriages to resist the "sense of disempowerment and rejection from the state of gender relations in their own country and community." Simons also suggests that "their coming together across unequally stratified national boundaries [is] one possible way of bridging those differences" and reasserting control.[113]

Men seeking mail-order brides typically see themselves as victims of the changing role of men and women, but rather than viewing these men as opposing female empowerment, it may be more accurate to describe them as objecting to male decline. Many of these men support female equality, but also believe it has been bad for men. Edward, an American man married to a Russian mail-order bride, typifies these complicated feelings. When asked about his views on gender equality, he made the following statement: "During the seventies I supported the equality and equal opportunity for women that they worked for. And I still do. It's the way I was raised. Somewhere in the seventies the women's movement was hijacked. 'Women of the world unite against bourgeois-proletarian male domination!' The net result was that women were taught to view all male-female relationships as power struggles where somebody wins and somebody loses. Every American woman I met at some point turned our relationship into a struggle for power."[114] Edward's statement reveals that he is not opposed to increased power and opportunities for women, but he does object to the idea that female equality must mean male decline. Edward is far from alone in conflating these two ideas. For example, the title of Rosin's book, *The End of Men and the Rise of Women*, links these two ideas explicitly. However, Rosin also notes that objecting to or fearing male decline should not be considered antifeminist. Instead, she describes such concerns as an understandable reaction to the "specter of a coming gender apocalypse."[115]

At one point in *The End of Men*, Rosin interviews a man named David, whose girlfriend makes significantly more money than he does, and she asks him why he has such uneasiness with the changing roles of marriage. After thinking about the question, he responds, "It's because our team is losing. All the things we need to be good at to thrive in the world we imagine existing in ten or twenty or even fifty years from now are things that my female friends and competitors are better at than me. Than us."[116]

It is not unreasonable for men like David to feel discomfort regarding their growing sense of disempowerment, but mail-order marriage can actually help combat these feelings. According to a 2000 UN report on masculinity, "[M]ost men remain disempowered in relation to elites (composed of both men and women) that wield political and economic power. . . . It is this experience of disempowerment that potentially connects some men and women across the patriarchal divide, and offers the possibility of linking a gender politics that challenges patriarchy with wider politics of social transformation."[117] Consequently, for many of these struggling men, the appeal of a mail-order marriage is not that it introduces them to women they can dominate, but that it connects them with sympathetic partners who have experienced similar struggles.

The idea that mail-order marriage increases marriage equality may seem counterintuitive, but it is an idea repeatedly expressed by those who work with mail-order brides. Despite the widespread perception that mail-order marriages are "antifeminist," many mail-order brides seek foreign husbands precisely because they see them as less patriarchal and more egalitarian than their male countrymen. As Harvey Balzer, director of Georgetown University's Russian Area Program, noted, Russian women are tired of "domestic dictators": "Even [the Russian] men I know who write about women's rights wouldn't get up from the dinner table to help clear the dishes." Therefore, Balzer notes that the American man who claims to be seeking an "unliberated woman" looks to the Russian woman like a "liberated man."[118] Vera, the owner of a mail-order bride service in Russia, echoed these sentiments: "Russian men can't provide for the family and they don't pay attention to their families. ... That really doesn't agree with us women. ... Plus, they don't value what we do for them. And men in our country are prone to alcoholism."[119]

Interviews with Russian mail-order brides show that many turn to this type of marriage in order to achieve more egalitarian relationships and that they often view gender divisions as beneficial. For example, Zina stated that what specifically attracted her to her husband Robert was his request for a traditional wife "who would build a home life for him," and for whom he could fulfill the traditional male role of protector and provider. As Zina noted, "In Russia, all the men know what women's obligations are—to sew, to cook, they know all that by heart. But they have no idea whatsoever what their obligations might be. Here it's just the opposite. The men know what is wanted of them and what their obligations are."[120] Peter, a man married to a Russian mail-order bride, confirmed this fact. He stated that his wife's appreciation of his willingness to assume the male protector/provider role was one of the biggest advantages of a foreign bride. He noted, "She's so much more feminine and appreciative than American women."[121]

Tamara, a beautiful blonde-haired, blue-eyed, thirty-two-year-old secretary from Irkutsk, expressed similar appreciation for her bald, forty-seven-year-old, TV repairman husband. Although outsiders might be skeptical of this pairing, it is clear that Tamara believes she is the lucky one in the relationship. She explained that at first her friends were dubious of her decision to become a mail-order bride, but now her friends back in Russia are "tearing their hair out from jealousy."[122]

Many non-Russian mail-order brides also express similar views about the greater equality available through their marriages and an appreciation of defined gender roles. For example, a Chinese mail-order bride named Meili explained that she was looking for a foreign husband because "[t]hey say what is on their mind" and they are "more likely to want an 'equal' relationship with women." When pressed to explain what she meant by "equal," she clarified that she was looking for a "balanced" division of labor, the kind that could be satisfied by the traditional male breadwinner, female homemaker structure.[123]

The enhanced gender equality provided by mail-order marriage also manifests as greater marital opportunities for single mothers. A large proportion of mail-order brides are divorced women with children, but in many foreign countries single mothers are stigmatized. For example, Russia has the largest proportion of single-mother households (as compared with other Eastern European countries), yet having children from a previous marriage significantly lowers a Russian woman's chance of remarriage. In *Dreaming of a Mail-Order Husband*, gender researcher Ericka Johnson interviewed dozens of potential Russian mail-order brides. She noted being "a little surprised how categorical the women were in their characterizations of Russian men as uninterested in older women with children (and by older I mean mid-twenties)."[124] In contrast, she found that the American men seeking mail-order brides were also often divorced and looking for a "loving mother to [their] children" and quite happy to marry a woman who had already proven her interest in motherhood.[125]

Studies of modern mail-order brides also indicate that these women seek such marriages because they believe foreign men are more respectful toward women.[126] Mail-order brides consistently express the belief that Western men are held to a higher standard of ethics in their relationships with women.[127] Tanya, a twenty-four-year-old Russian woman with a three-year-old child, expressed this view when she explained that what attracted her to Peter, a twenty-nine-year-old engineer from Wisconsin, was that he was kind and would listen to her. She noted, "He calls me every day from work to see if I need anything. Very few Russians would do that."[128] Similarly, in describing why she listed with a mail-order bride company, Olga, a twenty-nine-year-old music teacher from Russia, stated,

Everyone knows that life in America is much better than here in Russia. Even poor people there have cars, houses and color TVs. And there's always plenty of food to eat. But the most wonderful thing about America is the men. They're much more handsome than Russian men. They don't have gold fillings in their mouth or rotted teeth like all my old boyfriends. And they don't boss you around and treat you like you're their slave. I dream every night of going to the United States, marrying a handsome man and having children. I can't wait to go. As soon as I find the right man, I'm going to apply for an exit visa.[129]

Both statements demonstrate that part of their reason for seeking an American husband is the belief that American men treat their wives with greater respect than do Russian men, and this belief is not limited to Russian women; other foreign women also express these sentiments. For example, Filipina mail-order brides frequently note that American men know how to "take care of" their wives and describe them as less likely to have an affair and more likely to allow their wives social freedom than Filipino men. Similarly, Chinese mail-order brides describe Western men as "more open-minded and less controlling than Chinese husbands."[130]

While some of the above descriptions may be overly rosy, they show that foreign women view mail-order marriage as a way to achieve respect and equality in their marriages and not as a desperate and dreaded last resort. In fact many brides bristle at the suggestion they are seeking such marriages out of desperation. A Filipina named Mary Beth provided the following explanation of her motivations for seeking a mail-order marriage and her frustration with the victim stereotypes: "I was aware of pen pal clubs, but had not thought to use one myself until I met an American man in Manila who had come to meet his girlfriend. We became friends and he encouraged me to try this way of meeting someone. I was suspicious at first. I had heard reports and comments of people who assumed you had to be desperate to do this. I didn't consider myself desperate. I had a good job. I didn't need to get married or seek better opportunities elsewhere."[131] Constable's book also refutes this stereotype of the "desperate" mail-order bride. Constable describes a fabulous dinner she had in 1999 with two potential Chinese mail-order brides, noting that "after a feast of jiaozi (dumplings), the conversation moved smoothly from Beethoven and Bach to Elizabeth Taylor's latest marriage, Prince William, the trade accord, the pros and cons of hormone therapy for menopause, and the election of Taiwan's new president."[132] This anecdote was just one of many Constable used to show that many modern mail-order brides are a far cry from the commonly depicted sad and hopeless women.

One final objection to mail-order marriage is the belief that it commodifies something that should not be commodified and therefore exploits women. As marriage historian Nancy Cott has written, "American rhetoric and popular culture . . . put love and money on opposite sides of the street. Mercenary or cold-blooded motives for marrying [are] labeled crass, unethical, and destined for disastrous fate."[133] Since at least the 1920s, Americans have viewed the love aspect of marriage as not only essential but almost divine. For example, in her book on the history of marriage, Cott cites a study from 1925 showing that Americans believed that "only through some 'mysterious attraction' that 'just happens' [are] young people supposed to find each other." She notes that the study further added that Americans viewed "romance in marriage [as] something which, like the religion, must be believed in to hold society together."[134]

In contrast to this idealized "love match," mail-order marriages do not "just happen." Most mail-order brides consider these relationships a bargained exchange and are quite open about that fact that financial considerations played a role in their decision.[135] This aspect of these marriages is unsettling to many Americans who believe in the superiority of romantic marriage.[136] Nevertheless, love has not always been considered an important or even desirable part of marriage. Well into the nineteenth century, the romanticization of marriage was often treated with concern. Novels, which provided fictionalized accounts of romantic love, were seen as harming young women by encouraging unrealistic expectations of marriage. In the 1857 marriage manual *The Young Lady's Counsellor*, the Reverend Daniel Wise expressed dismay at the "multitude [of young women] who form their notion of love and marriage from sickly novels, from theatrical performances, and from flippant conversations."[137] The nineteenth-century English domestic advice writer Sarah Ellis expressed similar sentiments regarding romantic love. According to Ellis, women need to reduce their expectations regarding marriage, and a wife "should place herself, instead of running the risk of being placed, in a secondary position."[138]

Despite these various objections to love matches, romantic ideals eventually took hold. Nevertheless, it was not until the late twentieth century that a majority of American women finally indicated that love outweighed all other considerations in choosing a partner.[139] Today, most Americans believe in the superiority of romantic marriage, but with a divorce rate hovering around 50 percent, there is reason to question this preference. In 2002, Robert Epstein, former editor of *Psychology Today*, published a controversial editorial arguing that it is the idealization of the love marriage that prevents happy marriages. According to Epstein, the American "love marriage" based on physical attraction and romance is "really, really horrible."[140]

Mail-order brides often marry for financial reasons, but this does not preclude the possibility of love after marriage. For example, studies show that the commodification of caregiving relationships does not hurt either the quality or the sincerity of the care, and it tends to greatly benefit female caregivers.[141] For example, Dartmouth professor Deborah Stone has noted that study after study of nursing home aides, home health aides, child care workers, nannies, and au pairs demonstrates that despite the fact they were paid to care for strangers, women in these professions commonly formed a bond with their clients and quickly came to consider them family. As one child care provider lovingly explained, "these children, they are so close to you. You're like a second mom to them. And you being there when they come home after school—you listen to the different little things they want to talk with you about. It becomes a personal thing, where, you know, they can't get to mom right away. But they can get to you."[142]

Conversations with mail-order brides also show that financial considerations do not prevent the formation of true, loving bonds. As Masha, the Russian woman who married Paul, explained, her first consideration was to secure a decent life for her child, and she was willing to give "love" to whoever could provide this for her and her son. Masha stated, "The way I fe[lt] about Paul is this: you're giving me a decent life for myself and my child, and so I'm giving you love. After all, what I was thinking about back in Kharkov wasn't where can I find love but will I have money today to buy bread for my child?"[143] At the same time, it is clear this bargain also facilitated genuine affection. Asked whether she loved Paul, Masha replied, "How can I not love a man who's being so kind to me and my child?"[144]

As the marriage between Masha and Paul shows, the exchange of care and affection in return for money, security, and a decent lifestyle is often explicit in mail-order marriages, but this arrangement does not preclude the development of love. In fact, a number of feminist scholars have even argued that it is the failure to commodify marriage that actually creates the greatest harm to women.[145] According to these scholars, our modern concept of marriage encourages women to provide their services for free and devalues women and the work they do in marriage.[146] As Professor Robin West has written, by encouraging a wife to work for free, we are encouraging a woman to think of herself "as the conduit for the pleasures of *others*, rather than ... acting toward the maximization of her own."[147] According to West, "a woman who routinely performs harmful altruistic acts" (acts where she consistently puts the needs of others before her own) "loses the sense of *integrity* necessary to at least liberal conceptions of individualism."[148] West believes there is no reason why the family *should* be any more altruistic than the marketplace, particularly when this altruism harms women.[149]

Mail-order marriages avoid these harms. Unlike conventional marriages, they are often explicit exchanges. Therefore, according to West's analysis, they may actually be more beneficial to women than the idealized, romantic marriage. A mail-order bride who makes her sacrifices and performs caregiving for her husband and family as part of a contractual understanding is empowered by her actions in a way the "loving" altruistic wife is not.[150] As Svetlana, a potential Russian bride from Moscow, noted, "Love has become a luxury. . . . I'll be old and gray before we [Russian women] can afford love."[151] Encouraging women like Svetlana to wait for "love" may be the least helpful thing we can do.

Conclusion

Statistics on the success rates of mail-order marriages are hard to verify. Encounters International, one of the largest match-making agencies, claims 104 marriages and 4 divorces in seven years. Similarly, a lawyer who specializes in fiancée visas, noted that in eight years he had seen 600 mail-order marriages and 21 divorces.[1] In addition, at least one study claims the success rate for mail-order marriages is 80 percent after five years,[2] which makes it comparable to conventional domestic marriages,[3] or perhaps slightly better since the mail-order marriage statistic includes remarriages (which have significantly higher divorce rates).[4] Regardless, even if these marriages have a lower divorce rate than traditional marriages, no one is arguing that they should become the norm.

Throughout history, mail-order marriages have always carried risks and uncertainties. Modern mail-order marriages continue to present these concerns. However, they have also consistently provided substantial benefits. Since the founding of Jamestown, women have used mail-order marriage as a source of empowerment. In the colonial era, it was a way to share in the economic and nation-building opportunities of colonization. Mail-order brides were considered important to the success of the North American colonies, and this gave colonial women legal and political opportunities rarely available to their contemporaries. A similar pattern was repeated during the frontier period: female scarcity was considered a problem of national significance, so substantial legal and political incentives were offered to incentivize their immigration. The experiences of early American mail-order brides show these women were neither desperate nor exploited, but were making a rational decision to increase their marital opportunities and hopefully improve their lives.

Early American mail-order marriages also demonstrated the difference between successful and disastrous marital immigration programs. In order to be successful, mail-order marriage requires consent and significant benefits and protections for the marital immigrant. The programs of Jamestown, New France, and the American West conformed to these criteria. They gave single women substantial economic, social, and legal advantages as well as meaningful protections such as safe passage, the right to divorce, and the right to control their separate property. In the Louisiana colony, marital immigrants were not given these protections. They were lied to and many were kidnapped, producing a disastrous result.

In the post–Civil War period, mail-order marriage continued to increase. Changes in communication and transportation technology made it possible for men and women to arrange their own unions, but the basic purpose of mail-order marriage remained the same. Men and women continued seeking these marriages because they believed they offered them opportunities otherwise unavailable. Matrimonial advertisements brought isolated women into contact with an infinitely greater number of potential partners. These ads also enabled single women to contact like-minded men and to state explicitly what they desired in a marriage. Consequently, mail-order marriage gave nineteenth-century women increased control over their marital futures.

As the nineteenth century progressed, growing numbers of foreign women began seeking this type of marriage. Most of these women were racially or financially inadmissible, but by becoming mail-order brides, they found a way around America's harsh immigration restrictions. Most foreign brides benefited from their mail-order marriages and the ability to immigrate, but the circumstances of their arrival contributed to the growing concerns regarding mail-order marriage. These brides were no longer seen as supporting American goals and policies but instead seemed to be defying them. Foreign brides were seen as undermining federal immigration law and policy, increasing the population of those perceived to be racially and ethnically undesirable, and undermining the women's rights movement. These negative views were further reinforced during both world wars when large numbers of foreign women entered the country as war brides, and they continue to inform modern perceptions of mail-order marriage.

The negative views of mail-order marriage are well entrenched, but they are often unjustified and obscure the fact that these relationships continue to benefit both men and women. Mail-order marriages increase the marital options of those who find their domestic marriage opportunities limited and disempowering. The grooms in modern mail-order marriages are often men who have been excluded from the American marriage market. The brides are typically women unhappy in their home countries and particularly with the available men there, but with few emigration opportunities. Mail-order marriage connects these two groups and enables both to reassert control over their lives by expanding their marital opportunities. Moreover, given that mail-order marriage provides one of the most effective paths to U.S. immigration, it is likely to remain an attractive choice for many foreign women and, increasingly, for foreign men as well.

After the U.S. Supreme Court decided *United States v. Windsor* in 2013 and struck down part of the Defense of Marriage Act as unconstitutional, the secretary of the Department of Homeland Security, Janet Napolitano, issued the following statement: "After last week's decision by the Supreme Court holding that Section 3 of the Defense of Marriage Act (DOMA) is unconstitutional, President Obama directed federal departments to ensure the decision and its implication for federal benefits for same-sex legally married couples are implemented swiftly and smoothly. To that end, effective immediately, I have directed U.S. Citizenship and Immigration Services (USCIS) to review immigration visa petitions filed on behalf of a same-sex spouse in the same manner as those filed on behalf of an opposite-sex spouse."[5] As a result of this decision, immigration petitions for same-sex spouses increased exponentially. Michael Sisitzky, an attorney with Immigration Equality, an organization devoted to helping binational same-sex couples, described the *Windsor* decision as having "completely changed the landscape." According to Sisitzky, fifteen hundred couples contacted Immigration Equality in the week after the decision, more than had contacted the organization the entire previous year.[6] For LGBT people in the United States, the *Windsor* decision was a clear statement that things are improving, but the thousands of same-sex immigration petitions also demonstrated that the growing acceptance of LGBT individuals in America stands in stark contrast to their treatment in many other countries.

As of May 2015, there were seventy-nine countries where homosexuality was considered a crime,[7] and many more where gay men and women are subject to significant homophobia. For example, in Russia, homosexuality is not technically illegal, but it is highly denigrated and frequently met with violence. Moreover, the situation in Russia is getting increasingly worse. In June 2013, Russia enacted an anti-LGBT propaganda law, which was purportedly passed to prevent the distribution of "non-traditional sexual relationships" ideas among minors, but was seen by many as a thinly veiled attempt to criminalize homosexuality. Since the law was enacted, violence against LGBT individuals has increased markedly, and not surprisingly, the number of Russian LGBT people seeking asylum in the United States has risen fourfold.[8]

Unfortunately, asylum is rarely granted, so it is not surprising that a growing number of gay men from Russia and Ukraine have begun considering marital immigration. In fact, a number of same-sex marriage websites have sprung up to meet this demand. They are similar to those that cater to heterosexual Western men. Like traditional mail-order bride sites, same-sex marriage sites emphasize their clients' desire for long-term marital relationships based on love and compatibility. For instance, on the Gay Marriage Agency "Golden Boys" website, which lists the profiles of Ukrainian men interested in same-sex marriages, the agency proudly states that "during [the] time of our work dozens of lonely people have met and found their happiness together. We are sure our agency was born under [a] lucky star because all couples who met through [the] matchmaking service of our gay marriage agency are very happy together."[9] However, unlike traditional mail-order brides' sites, these sites tend to be much more explicit about the political factors that have influenced their clients' desire to immigrate.

The bottom of the Golden Boys webpage includes a link to a newspaper article describing two recently proposed pieces of antigay legislation.[10] In addition, the contact information page includes a chilling disclaimer: "Most guys listed in our catalog provide their contact phone numbers to our disposal, but not all of them. As we cooperate with genuine gay guys from the province, some of them hesitate to do it due to [the] high degree of homophobia in our country."[11] Similarly, on the Gay Fiancés website, which also caters to Western men seeking Ukrainian or Russian spouses, the "news" section describes the dismal state of gay rights in Russia and Ukraine and notes that "[a]ccording to research institute Levada, only one percent of all Russians respect gay rights." It further adds, "Hostility towards gays is strong in Ukraine as well."[12]

For gay men living in countries that afford them few rights and protections, marital immigration offers an attractive alternative.[13] As a result, the future of mail-order marriage will likely be somewhat less female and may mean we can finally discard the term "mail-order bride." However, in most other ways, future mail-order marriages are likely to remain very similar. As this book has shown, throughout U.S. history the motivations of mail-order brides have remained fairly constant. Women choose martial immigration when it offers them the opportunity to improve their marital, economic, and political circumstances. Potential same-sex foreign spouses are interested in marital immigration for comparable reasons and seem unlikely to change the contours of these relationships drastically. The larger question, though, is whether these marriages should change.

Most Americans perceive mail-order marriage as problematic. They are uncomfortable with the fact that mail-order brides are often motivated by reasons other than love and worry that this makes these relationships too different from modern American love matches. However, the defining feature of modern marriage is not love but choice.[14] Choice is what facilitated the rise of the love match, and this fact is crucial for understanding how mail-order marriage fits within the context of modern marriage. For more than four hundred years, mail-order marriage helped men and women increase their marital choice and form advantageous and empowering relationships. Modern mail-order marriages are created for the same reason. Today's mail-order brides and grooms are not a throwback to an earlier, unenlightened time. Instead, like most of us, they are simply men and women who believe marriage will improve their lives, and we should support their choice.

NOTES

INTRODUCTION

1 The heroic Sarah from a beloved children's novel, Patricia MacLachlan, *Sarah, Plain and Tall* (New York: HarperCollins, 1985), is one such example.

2 Rose Wilder Lane, "Object, Matrimony," *Saturday Evening Post* 207, no. 9 (September 1, 1934).

3 Wilder was the author of the "Little House on the Prairie" series, which chronicled her family's life as pioneers on the western frontier.

4 Lane, "Object Matrimony," 5. The story doesn't give a precise date. However, railroads did not arrive in South Dakota until 1873.

5 Ibid.

6 Ibid., 7.

7 Ibid., 58.

8 John Bowe, "The Mail-Order Bride," *GQ: Gentlemen's Quarterly* 76, no. 4 (April 2006): 194.

9 Ibid., 196.

10 Ibid., 252.

CHAPTER 1. LONELY COLONIST SEEKS WIFE

1 See Julia Cherry Spruill, *Women's Life and Work in the Southern Colonies* (New York: Norton, 1972), 3. See also *Boddie v. Connecticut*, 401 U.S. 371, 376 (1971) and *Griswold v. Connecticut*, 381 U.S. 479, 496 (1965) (Goldberg, J., concurring).

2 See, e.g., Peter N. Moogk, "Reluctant Exiles: Emigrants from France in Canada before 1760," *William and Mary Quarterly* 46, no. 3 (July 1989): 463, 465, 475. See also Gwenaël Cartier, "City of Québec 1608–2008: 400 Years of Censuses," *Canadian Social Trends*, June 3, 2008, 62, http://www.narea.org/2008meeting/City%20of%20Quebec%201608–2008.pdf (Quebec City was founded one year after Jamestown, in 1608).

3 Michael L. Cooper, *Jamestown, 1607* (New York: Holiday House, 2007), 1.

4 Spruill, *Women's Life*, 5.

5 Lynn Betlock, "New England's Great Migration," in *A Survey of New England: 1620–1640*, http://www.greatmigration.org/new_englands_great_migration.html. Between 1629 and 1640, over twenty thousand men, women, and children emigrated from England in order to form a religious community. The proportion of New England immigrants who arrived in family groups was the highest

in American immigration history. Moreover, unlike colonists who settled in other parts of the United States, the Puritan colonists came seeking spiritual rather than economic rewards. See ibid.

6 The colony did make some attempts to attract religious dissenters. For example, Governor Dale was a Puritan army officer and was specifically hired to attract other religious immigrants. Phillip Abbott, *Political Thought in America: Conversations and Debates*, 4th ed. (Long Grove, IL: Waveland, 2010), 20.

7 The women were Mrs. Forrest, who was married to Virginia colonist Thomas Forrest, and her maid, Anne Burras. See Margaret Pickett and Dwayne Pickett, *The European Struggle to Settle North America: Colonizing Attempts by England, France and Spain, 1521–1608* (Jefferson, NC: McFarland, 2011), 137.

8 Spruill, *Women's Life*, 3–5. See also Betlock, "New England's Great Migration." The English recruitment problems were not unique. France also had difficulties attracting large numbers of immigrant women, but they were uninterested in encouraging family migration. In 1669, a French official explained that family immigration was "'a bad practice' since 'one hundred persons, composing twenty-five families, will cost as much to the king as one hundred bachelors,' who, presumably, would all be productive workers." Moogk, "Reluctant Exiles," 483.

9 See Spruill, *Women's Life*, 4.

10 In 1607, when Jamestown was founded, the population of the settlement was entirely male. See Spruill, *Women's Life*, 3.

11 See Betlock, "New England's Great Migration"; see also Spruill, *Women's Life*, 8.

12 Spruill, *Women's Life*, 8.

13 See ibid.

14 The memberships of the Virginia Company and the Houses of Lords and Commons overlapped considerably. "Many of the House of Lords and about one hundred and forty members of th[e] House of Commons were also members of the Virginia Company of London." Alexander Brown, "The Parliaments of James I and the Plantation of America," *Green Bag* 6 (1994): 39.

15 Spruill, *Women's Life*, 8.

16 This was one of a number of suggestions made by Martin to improve the colony's long-term prospects. Ibid.

17 Edward Duffield Neill, *History of the Virginia Company: With Letters to and from the First Colony Never before Printed* (Albany, NY: Joel Munsell, 1869), 70.

18 Ibid., 71.

19 Thomas A. Foster, ed., *New Men: Manliness in Early America* (New York: New York University Press, 2011), 9.

20 Spruill, *Women's Life*, 8.

21 Ibid., 3.

22 Ibid., 8.

23 The money was raised by the Earl of Southampton and other gentlemen who recognized "that the plantation [could] never flourish" until families settled there. See ibid., 8–9.

24 See ibid., 9 (stating that the company had sent ninety maids in 1620 and another fifty maids in 1621 and 1622).

25 Jana Voelke Studelska, *Women of Colonial America* (North Mankato, MN: Compass Point Books, 2007), 6.

26 Alfred A. Cave, *Lethal Encounters: Englishmen and Indians in Colonial Virginia* (Santa Barbara, CA: Praeger, 2011), 75.

27 Ibid., 75.

28 In 1610, the entire population of Jamestown consisted of 60 colonists. Between 1610 and 1618, 3,000 new settlers arrived and another 4,000 between 1619 and 1623. However, between disease, starvation, and Indian massacres, the attrition rate was nearly 60 percent. Thus, despite these large influxes of new colonists, the population of Jamestown in 1624 was only 1,300. Joseph R. Conlin, *The American Past: A Survey of American History* (Boston: Wadsworth, 2011), 37–38.

29 Frank E. Grizzard, Jr. and D. Boyd Smith, *Jamestown Colony: A Political, Social, and Cultural History* (Santa Barbara, CA: ABC-CLIO, 2007), 88–89.

30 Smith mistakenly believed that a puberty ritual practiced by the Virginia Indian tribes involved sacrificing their own children to the devil. Alfred A. Cave, *The Pequot War* (Amherst: University of Massachusetts Press, 1996), 14.

31 Ronald Niezen, *Spirit Wars: Native North American Religions in the Age of Nation Building* (Berkeley: University of California Press, 2000), 31.

32 Richard Godbeer, *Sexual Revolution in Early America* (Baltimore: Johns Hopkins University Press, 2002), 160.

33 Cave, *Lethal Encounters*, 97.

34 J. Martin Evans, *Milton's Imperial Epic*: Paradise Lost *and the Discourse of Colonialism* (Ithaca, NY: Cornell University Press, 1996), 58.

35 Godbeer, *Sexual Revolution*, 159.

36 Lyon Gardiner Tylor, *Narratives of Early Virginia, 1606–1625* (New York: Charles Scribner's Sons, 1907), 153–54.

37 Rebecca Anne Goetz, *The Baptism of Early Virginia: How Christianity Created Race* (Baltimore: Johns Hopkins University Press, 2012), 64. Strachey was both attracted to and repelled by Indian women, whom he described as "full of their own country-disease (the Pox)." Ibid., 64.

38 Cave, *Lethal Encounters*, 98 (noting that unlike the colonies in New Spain, no mestizo class ever emerged in America: "Despite the marriage of Rolfe and Pocahontas, Indian maidens were not esteemed as prospective wives by respectable Englishmen in the colony").

39 Ibid., 97.

40 Rolfe and Pocahontas's marriage was one of only a handful of "officially" recorded intermarriages. Dagmar Wernitznig, *Europe's Indians, Indians in*

Europe: European Perceptions and Appropriations of Native American Cultures from Pocahontas to the Present (Lanham, MD: University Press of America, 2007), 12. However, there were many unofficial intermarriages. See Roger Thompson, *Women in Stuart England and America: A Comparative Study* (London: Routledge & Kegan Paul, 1974), 43 (noting that the marriage between Rolfe and Pocahontas was not "an isolated incident" and citing sources describing such marriages as "common"). See also Grizzard and Smith, *Jamestown Colony*, 1.

41 Thompson, *Women in Stuart England and America*, 44. The effects of the colony's intermarriage concerns were long-lasting. In 1691, Virginia became the first colony to prohibit white-Indian marriages. The 1691 statute stated, "Whatsoever English or other white man or woman being free shall intermarry with a negroe, mulatto, or Indian man or woman bond or free shall within three months after such marriage be banished and removed from this dominion forever." This law expanded an earlier 1662 law that already "made fornication between the races illegal." Heidi Hutner, *Colonial Women: Race and Culture in Stuart Drama* (New York: Oxford University Press, 2001), 13. This ban remained in place for more than 250 years and ended only after the U.S. Supreme Court's landmark decision in *Loving v. Virginia*, 388 U.S. 1 (1967), declared all such bans unconstitutional.

42 See Phillip Alexander Bruce, *Social Life of Virginia in the Seventeenth Century: An Inquiry into the Origin of the Higher Planting Class, Together with an Account of the Habits, Customs, and Diversions of the People* (Richmond, VA: Whittet & Shepperson, 1907), 228.

43 David R. Ransome, "Wives for Virginia, 1621," *William and Mary Quarterly* 48, no. 1 (January 1991): 12.

44 Spruill, *Women's Life*, 8.

45 Ransome, "Wives for Virginia, 1621," 10.

46 John C. Miller, *The First Frontier: Life in Colonial America* (Lanham, MD: University Press of America, 1966), 26 (giving the company their choice of which felons, simply barring "those guilty of rape, murder, burglary or witchcraft"). Descriptions referring to the felons as able-bodied and "fit to be ymployied in forraine discoveries of other services beyond the Seas" imply that these first felons were all men. Ann Jones, *Women Who Kill* (New York: City University of New York, Feminist Press, 2009), 44. The first clear record of female felons arriving was not until 1635. Ibid., 46.

47 Ibid., 27.

48 Anthony S. Parent, Jr., *Foul Means: The Formation of a Slave Society in Virginia 1660–1740* (Chapel Hill: University of North Carolina Press, 2003), 26.

49 Don Jordan and Michael Walsh, *White Cargo: The Forgotten History of Britain's White Slaves in America* (New York: New York University Press, 2007), 128.

50 Brandon Marie Miller, *Good Women of a Well-Blessed Land: Women's Lives in Colonial America* (Minneapolis, MN: Lerner, 2003), 21.

51 Jordan and Walsh, *White Cargo*, 135.

52 Bruce, *Social Life of Virginia*, 228.

53 Jordan and Walsh, *White Cargo*, 121.

54 Edward Eggleston, *The Beginners of a Nation: A History of the Source and Rise of the Earliest English Settlements in America with Special Reference to the Life and Character of the People*, 3rd ed. (New York: Appleton, 1896), 72, https://ia801408.us.archive.org/1/items/beginnersofanatioooo6ombp/beginnersofa-natioooo6ombp.pdf.

55 Miller, *First Frontier*, 26.

56 Ransome, "Wives for Virginia, 1621," 16.

57 See Bruce, *Social Life of Virginia*, 234; see also Spruill, *Women's Life*, 9.

58 Spruill, *Women's Life*, 9 (explaining that women would be married not to servants but to freemen "with the means of maintaining them").

59 Ibid.

60 In addition, if a young woman came to the colonies and did not like any of her marital choices, she could easily find work "as a domestic servant or agricultural laborer" and quickly earn more than the cost of her transportation to the colonies. See Bruce, *Social Life of Virginia*, 229.

61 Ransome, "Wives for Virginia, 1621," 6.

62 Amanda Vickery, *The Gentleman's Daughter: Women's Lives in Georgian England* (New Haven, CT: Yale University Press, 2003), 82.

63 Henry Kamen, *Early Modern European Society* (London: Routledge, 2000), 159.

64 David Cressy, *Birth, Marriage & Death: Ritual, Religion and the Life-Cycle in Tudor and Stuart England* (Oxford: Oxford University Press, 1997), 249–50.

65 See Bruce, *Social Life of Virginia*, 233 (explaining that many of the young women brought from England were from lower orders of English society but were chosen for their good character). See also Miller, *Good Women of a Well-Blessed Land*, 22 (noting that eleven of the women were orphaned, another eleven had lost their fathers, and three were widows).

66 According to one study, as many as 60 percent of young English men and women worked as servants. Stephanie Coontz, *Marriage, a History: From Obedience to Intimacy or How Love Conquered Marriage* (New York: Viking Penguin, 2005), 126.

67 Immigration to the colonies provided other types of freedom as well. A study of seventeenth-century Somerset County in Maryland shows "that about one-third of immigrant women ... were pregnant at the time of the ceremony—nearly twice the rate in English parishes. There is no indication of community objection to this freedom so long as marriage took place." Lois Green Carr and Lorena S. Walsh, "The Planter's Wife: The Experience of

White Women in Seventeenth-Century Maryland," *William and Mary Quarterly* 34, no. 4 (October 1977): 551.

68 Coontz, *Marriage, a History*, 126.

69 Georges Duby et al., eds., *A History of Women in the West, Vol. III: Renaissance and the Enlightenment Paradoxes* (Cambridge, MA: Harvard University Press, 1993), 27.

70 The youngest bride was fifteen-year-old Jane Dier. Ransome, "Wives for Virginia, 1621," 11.

71 However, some have argued that these health risks were probably no greater than those a seventeenth-century woman would have faced "moving from her village to London." See Carr and Walsh, "Planter's Wife," 547.

72 Ibid., 552. See also Elizabeth Abbott, *A History of Marriage* (New York: Seven Stories Press, 2011), 107 (noting that the average male life expectancy in the colonies was between "twenty to thirty years").

73 Spruill, *Women's Life*, 341; see generally William Blackstone, *Commentaries on the Laws of England, Vol. 1: The Rights of Persons* (Philadelphia: Lippincott, 1893), 1:430.

74 Spruill, *Women's Life*, 356.

75 H. R. McIlwaine, ed., *Journals of the House of Burgesses of Virginia, 1619–1658/59: Report of the Proceedings of the General Assembly of 1619* (Richmond: Colonial Press, 1905), 6–7; *Records of the Virginia Company* (London: 1619), 1:566.

76 Spruill, *Women's Life*, 9. This was the same year the colonists requested the first shipment of women. Ibid., 8.

77 Benjamin Trumbill, *A General History of the United States of America* (Boston: Farrand, Mallory, 1810), 67.

78 "Maides for Wives," *Virginia Magazine of History and Biography* 50, no. 4 (October 1942): 315–17. The 1622 Indian massacre was a turning point in white/Indian relations in the Virginia colony. Nearly four hundred colonists, or one-third of the population, were killed, ending the illusion that the English and Indians could live peacefully together. According to survivor William Capps, "the last massacre killed all out counnie. . . . Beside them they killed, they burst the heart of all the rest." David A. Price, *Love and Hate in Jamestown: John Smith, Pocahontas and the Start of a New Nation* (New York: Vintage, 2003), 208.

79 See Jones, *Women Who Kill*, 58.

80 Richard B. Morris, *Studies in the History of American Law: With Special Reference to the Seventeenth and Eighteenth Centuries* (New York: Columbia University Press, 1930), 128–29.

81 See Marylynn Salmon, "The Legal Status of Women in Early America: A Reappraisal," *Law and History Review* 1, no. 1 (Spring 1983): 129–51. See also Mary Beth Norton, "The Evolution of White Women's Experiences in Early North America," *American Historical Review* 89, no. 3 (June 1984): 593–619.

82 See Joan Hoff, *Law, Gender, and Injustice: A Legal History of U.S. Women* (New York: New York University Press, 1991), 83–84. See also Laurel Thatcher Ulrich, *Good Wives: Image and Reality in the Lives of Women in Northern New England* (New York: Vintage, 1991). See also Louis P. Masur, ed., *The Challenge of American History* (Baltimore: Johns Hopkins University Press, 1999), 101–2.

83 Hoff, *Law, Gender, and Injustice*, 87.

84 Linda E. Speth, "More Than Her 'Thirds': Wives and Widows in Colonial Virginia," *Women & History* 1, no. 4 (1983): 10.

85 Hoff, *Law, Gender, and Injustice*, 85. This was also the case in Maryland. See also Carr and Walsh, "Planter's Wife," 556.

86 If the children were all minors, the widow controlled the property until the oldest son came of age, and only if she did not remarry. Carr and Walsh, "Planter's Wife," 557–58 (describing a study of three English villages and noting that in only one did women tend to receive a life interest in the estate and suggesting this village was unusual).

87 This meant they were given the responsibility for paying his debts and preserving the estate. Speth, "More Than Her 'Thirds,'" 23–24.

88 Ibid., 33.

89 Ibid., 22.

90 Moreover, contracts between widows and their new husbands to protect the woman's property were common. Carr and Walsh, "Planter's Wife," 561.

91 Elizabeth Frost-Knappman and Kathryn Cullen-DuPont, eds., *Women's Suffrage in America: An Eyewitness History*, 2nd ed. (New York: Facts on File, 2005), 2.

92 Speth, "More Than Her 'Thirds,'" 27 (examining three eighteenth-century Virginia counties and noting that fewer than 9 percent of widows remarried).

93 Ibid.

94 The ratio was still three to one "as late as the 1680s." Marilyn Yalom, *A History of the Wife* (New York: HarperCollins, 2001), 141. See also Carr and Walsh, "Planter's Wife," 543.

95 Abbott, *Political Thought in America*, 106.

96 Carr and Walsh, "Planter's Wife," 550. However, in some cases, it was the wealthy widows who were doing the marital "purchasing." On March 15, 1771, the *Virginia Gazette* published an announcement regarding the marriage of "Mr. William Carter, third son of Mr. John Carter, aged twenty-three, to Mrs. Sarah Ellyson, Relict of Mr. Gerard Ellyson, deceased, aged eighty five, a sprightly old Tit, with three Thousand Pounds Fortune." Spruill, *Women's Life*, 161.

97 Thompson, *Women in Stuart England and America*, 36.

98 Ibid., 37.

99 See Alexander Brown, *The First Republic in America: An Account of the Origin of This Nation, Written from Records Then (1624) Concealed by the Council, Rather*

Than from the Histories Then Licensed by the Crown (Boston: Houghton Mifflin, 1898), 564.

100 Ibid.

101 Virginia General Assembly, House of Delegates, *Journal of the House of Delegates of the Commonwealth of Virginia* [House Doc. 1] 24 (1919), http://books.google.com/books/download/Journal_of_the_House_of_Delegates_of_the.pdf?id=TSMSAAAAYAAJ&output=pdf&sig=ACfU3U38QwtirpMBm BvpilJoG_1KeFnYtQ.

102 Brown, *First Republic in America*, 564.

103 Ibid.

104 Ibid. The charter of 1606 established the colony and set out that it was to be governed by a council of thirteen men, although only seven were specifically named. These men were to choose their own successors and elect their president. The Virginia Council had many powers, including the right to act as a court, but they were ultimately under the control of the Council of Thirteen, which was a group appointed by the king to look after the Crown's interest in Virginia. See Alexander Brown, *The Genesis of the United States: A Narrative of the Movement in England, 1605–1616, Which Resulted in the Plantation of North America by Englishmen, Disclosing the Contest between England and Spain for the Possession of the Soil Now Occupied by the United States of America* (Boston: Houghton Mifflin, 1897), 64–75.

105 Brown, *First Republic in America*, 564.

106 Ibid. In the seventeenth century, the word "nice" was commonly used to describe something as a "fine or subtle" distinction. See Fadzilah Amin, "Words and Phrases Subject to Fashionable Change," *Star Online*, August 2, 2013, http://thestar.com.my/english/story.asp?file=/2012/4/24/lifefocus/1114 9264&sec=lifefocus.

107 Brown, *First Republic in America*, 564.

108 *Pathway: A Family History, Cecely Reynolds Baley Jordan—Records of the Virginia Company*, http://biographiks.com/pleasant/cecely.htm.

109 See Saskia Lettmaier, *Broken Engagements: The Action for Breach of Promise of Marriage and the Feminine Ideal, 1800–1940* (Oxford: Oxford University Press, 2010), 22.

110 Leah Leneman, *Promises, Promises: Marriage Litigation in Scotland 1698–1830* (Edinburgh: NMS Enterprises, 2003), 9. For example, in her study of declaratory actions filed in Scotland between 1700 and 1829, historian Leah Leneman found that of the 417 cases she examined, 371 were raised by women and only 46 were instigated by men. Earlier periods also seem to have had similar ratios. A study of marriage suits before the marriage courts in Basel found that women initiated 82 percent of the suits brought between 1550 and 1592, 78 percent of the suits brought between 1585 and 1589, 85 percent of the suits brought between 1645 and 1649, and 71 percent of the suits brought between 1685 and

1689. Joel Francis Harrington, *The Unwanted Child: The Fate of Foundlings, Orphans, and Juvenile Criminals in Early Modern Germany* (Chicago: University of Chicago Press, 2009), 327n72.

111 See Leneman, *Promises, Promises*, 24–25 (describing the 1797 case of *Lowe v. Allardyce*, in which a Scottish man had sexual relations with a young woman and promised her father that he would marry her in the future and the court held this promise for future marriage to be a binding promise of marriage).

112 See Lettmaier, *Broken Engagements*, 27. In five breach-of-promise cases that were studied, three of the plaintiffs were men and all three men were awarded substantial damages. Ibid.

113 *Harrison v. Cage & Wife*, 1 Ld. Raym. 387 (1698).

114 See also Lettmaier, *Broken Engagements*, 24.

115 The council clearly believed there had been an engagement. See Edward D. Neill, *The History of Education in Virginia during the Seventeenth Century* (Washington, DC: Government Printing Office, 1867), 10 (also found at http://babel.hathitrust.org/cgi/pt?id=miun.aen6394.0001.001;view=1up; seq=102). The reference to "certain women" within the colony having contracted themselves to two men at once was understood as a clear reference to the Jordan/Pooley engagement. See Brown, *First Republic in America*, 564–65. See also National Society of the Colonial Dames of America, "Celebration of the Three Hundredth Anniversary of the First Legislative Assembly in America" (1919), 18.

116 See Neill, *History of Education*, 10.

117 Ibid.

118 See ibid.

119 Spruill, *Women's Life*, 151.

120 Spragg was simply required to stand before the congregation in church, acknowledging her offense, and ask "God's and the Congregation's forgiveness." See ibid.

121 Ibid.

122 See ibid., 152.

123 Ibid.

124 The Chesapeake colonies were the colonies with the greatest scarcity of women and were where most colonial mail-order brides settled.

125 Marilyn French, *From Eve to Dawn, A History of Women in the World, vol. II, The Masculine Mystique: From Feudalism to the French Revolution* (New York: City University of New York, Feminist Press, 2008), 267. See also Walter Hart Blumenthal, *Brides from Bridewell: Female Felons Sent to Colonial America* (Rutland, VT: Charles E. Tuttle, 1962), 54 (stating that "in the first decades of the Virginia settlement, ninety inveigled 'maydes' had been shipped over to the Virginia colony by the heartless London Company. . . . During the next two years, fifty more, lured from city slums and rural areas by unscrupulous

agents. . . . These 140 were the tobacco maids sold at Jamestown for about their weight in leafage. They were not felons, but were, to all intents, shanghaied as 'breeders' for the colony").

126 French's portrayal is far from unique. It is quite common for critics of these marriages to describe these women as "sold." For example, in her book *Regulating the Lives of Women*, Mimi Abramovitz describes the Jamestown brides as part of a scheme devised by an English sea captain to "sell 'wives' for 120 pounds of leaf tobacco—or about $80." Mimi Abramovitz, *Regulating the Lives of Women: Social Welfare Policy from Colonial Times to the Present*, rev. ed. (Cambridge, MA: South End Press, 1996), 46. In the next sentence, Abramovitz discusses the documented kidnapping of other women who were forcibly brought to the colonies, and thus clearly invites a comparison between the two groups. Ibid., 46.

127 See, e.g., Christine Chun, "The Mail-Order Bride Industry: The Perpetuation of Transnational Economic Inequalities and Stereotypes," *University of Pennsylvania Journal of International Economic Law* 17 (1996): 1155; Donna Lee, "Mail Fantasy: Global Sexual Exploitation in the Mail Order Bride Industry and Proposed Legal Solutions," *Asian Law Journal* 5 (1998): 139; Eddy Meng, "Mail-Order Brides: Gilded Prostitution and the Legal Response," *University of Michigan Journal of Law Reform* 28 (1994): 197; Vanessa Vergara, "Abusive Mail Order Bride Marriage and the Thirteenth Amendment," *Northwestern University Law Review* 94 (2000): 1547.

CHAPTER 2. THE FILLES DU ROI

1 See Allan Greer, *The People of New France* (Toronto: University of Toronto Press, 1997), 17.

2 See Hubert Charbonneau, Mario Boleda, and Real Bates, *The First French Canadians: Pioneers in the St. Lawrence Valley*, trans. Paola Colozzo (Newark: University of Delaware Press, 1993), 23, 27; Moogk, "Reluctant Exiles," 463.

3 See Moogk, "Reluctant Exiles," 465.

4 Bernd Horn, *Battle Cries in the Wilderness: The Struggle for North America in the Seven Years' War* (Toronto: Dundurn Press, 2011), 30–31.

5 See Moogk, "Reluctant Exiles," 475.

6 Charbonneau, Boleda, and Bates, *First French Canadians*, 36.

7 Paul R. Magocsi, ed., *Encyclopedia of Canada's Peoples* (Toronto: University of Toronto Press, 1999), 540.

8 Charbonneau, Boleda, and Bates, *First French Canadians*, 79.

9 Before 1650, 73.3 percent of immigrants to New France returned to France. The rate for the entire seventeenth century was about 67 percent. Ibid., 213n31.

10 See Sarah E. Meltzer, *Colonizer or Colonized: The Hidden Stories of Early Modern French Culture* (Philadelphia: University of Pennsylvania Press, 2012), 116 (describing the growing fear that intermarriages caused French men "to

become barbarians and make themselves similar to [the Indians]"). This lifestyle was particularly common among the "coureurs du bois," which meant "runner of the woods" and referred to French men who traded with the Indians, adopted their lifestyle, married Indian women, and lived as part of an Indian village. "The Coureur de Bois," in *Chronicles of America*, http://www. chroniclesofamerica.com/french/coureur_de_bois.htm.

11 Sophie White, *Wild Frenchmen and Frenchified Indians, Material Culture and Race in Colonial Louisiana* (Philadelphia: University of Pennsylvania Press, 2012), 112.

12 See Greer, *People of New France*, 17; see also Guillaume Aubert, "'The Blood of France': Race and Purity of Blood in the French Atlantic World," *William and Mary Quarterly* 61, no. 3 (July 2004): 451.

13 Aubert, "'Blood of France,'" 453.

14 See also ibid. (explaining that none of the money that was set aside for Indian dowries was ever used. By 1683, the Indian character of the fund was abandoned and the money was spent to support the marriage of French girls). In fact, it was specifically abandoned at the same time that the filles du roi began arriving. See Greer, *People of New France*, 450.

15 Aubert, "'Blood of France,'" 453.

16 Ibid., 455. Compared to those of the French, the intermarriages in the English colony were miniscule. John Smith had noted that the Virginia Indians were amazed that the Englishmen "had no women, nor cared for any of theirs." Godbeer, *Sexual Revolution*, 160. French desertions numbered in the hundreds. See Eric J. Dolin, *Fur, Fortune, and Empire: The Epic History of the Fur Trade in America* (New York: Norton, 2011), 97; Harold Innis, *The Fur Trade in Canada: An Introduction to Canadian Economic History* (Toronto: University of Toronto Press, 1930), 63.

17 Betheny Ruth Berger, "After Pocahontas, Indian Women and the Law: 1830 to 1934," *American Indian Law Review* 21 (1997): 25.

18 See Kathleen DuVal, "Indian Intermarriage and Métissage in Colonial Louisiana," *William and Mary Quarterly* 65, no. 2 (April 2008): 283 (noting that associations with the French could benefit Indian women because they could use Catholic principles "to avoid marriages they did not want, escape abusive husbands, or to mold marital relationships"). There is considerable debate regarding whether native women liked sororal polygamy. It was often practiced in communities where there was a dearth of men and, thus, provided women with a way to marry. In 1637, a missionary among the Mistantee Cree reported that his admonishments that "a man should have only one wife ... [were] not well received, by the women; for since they are more numerous than the men, if a man can only marry one of them, the others will have to suffer." However, such objections do not mean that native women actually preferred polygamy, simply that they saw it as their least worst option. Carol Devens, *Countering*

Colonization: Native American Women and Great Lakes Missions, 1630–1900
(Berkeley: University of California Press, 1992), 27. But see John D'Emilio and
Estelle B. Freedman, *Intimate Matters: A History of Sexuality in America*, 2nd ed.
(Chicago: University of Chicago Press, 1997), 87 (arguing that many Indian
women would have found polygamy beneficial since it "offered women the
benefit of sharing domestic work with other wives" and "also lessened the
reproductive labors of each wife"). William E. Farr and William W. Bevis, eds.,
Fifty Years after The Big Sky: *New Perspectives on the Fiction and Films of A. B.
Guthrie, Jr.* (Helena: Montana Historical Society Press, in association with the
O'Connor Center for the Rocky Mountain West, University of Montana,
Missoula, 2001), 131 (noting that "[s]ororal polygyny tended to strengthen a
woman's position rather than weaken it. Sisters protected one another from
domestic aggression, and sisters were often able to present a united front to
further their interests").

19 French men also had a reputation as much better lovers than native men. David
Royot, *Divided Loyalties in a Doomed Empire: The French in the West: From New
France to the Lewis and Clark Expedition* (Cranberry, NJ: Associated University
Presses, 2007), 120.

20 David Hackett Fischer, *Champlain's Dream* (New York: Simon & Schuster,
2008), 507 (estimating the population at 9,700).

21 Trevor W. Harrison and John W. Friesen, eds., *Canadian Society in the Twenty-
First Century: An Historical Sociological Approach*, 2nd ed. (Toronto: Canadian
Scholars' Press, 2010), 192.

22 Aubert, "'Blood of France,'" 451 (citing Marc Lescarbot, *History of New France*,
trans. W. L. Grant [Toronto: Champlain Society, 1907]).

23 Lescarbot, *History of New France*, 160.

24 See Thomas N. Ingersoll, *To Intermix with Our White Brothers: Indian Mixed
Bloods in the United States from Earliest Times to the Indian Removals*
(Albuquerque: University of New Mexico Press, 2005), 280n104. See Aubert,
"'Blood of France,'" 450.

25 See Aubert, "'Blood of France,'" 450.

26 Sylvia Van Kirk, "From 'Marrying-In' to 'Marrying-Out': Changing Patterns of
Aboriginal/Non-Aboriginal Marriage in Colonial Canada," *Frontiers: A Journal
of Women's Studies* 23, no. 3 (2002): 3.

27 Jennifer S. H. Brown, *Strangers in Blood: Fur Trade Company Families in Indian
Country* (Vancouver: University of British Columbia Press, 1980), 4.

28 In the United States, Indian women routinely lost their legal status as wives
when marriageable white women moved into former Indian territory.
Intermarriages that had previously been tolerated and even encouraged were
suddenly stripped of legal protections in order to encourage white husbands to
leave their Indian wives without fear of legal reprisals. For example, in the case
of Delilah and David Wall, the court claimed to be citing Choctaw law when it

held that "the husband may at pleasure dissolve the relation. His abandonment is evidence that he has done so." Kevin R. Johnson, ed., *Mixed Race America and the Law: A Reader* (New York: New York University Press, 2003), 77. Similarly, nineteenth-century Canadian cases also include numerous instances of white husbands abandoning their Indian wives. Van Kirk, "From 'Marrying-In' to 'Marrying-Out,'" 5.

29 The filles du roi represented a changed view about the type of women who should help populate New France. Native women were no longer viewed as acceptable wives. Greer, *People of New France*, 17 (purporting that the "'king's daughters' program represented a racial reorientation as much as a demographic developmentalist agenda").

30 Karen Elizabeth Bush, *First Lady of Detroit: The Story of Marie-Thérèse Guyon, Mme Cadillac* (Michigan: Wayne State University Press, 2001), 186.

31 Catherine Cangany, *Frontier Seaport: Detroit's Transformation into an Atlantic Entrepôt* (Chicago: University of Chicago Press, 2014), 233n16.

32 Sylvia Van Kirk, *Many Tender Ties: Women in Fur Trade Society, 1670–1870* (Norman: University of Oklahoma Press, 1980), 23 (Hearne's description was written in the 1770s).

33 Greer, *People of New France*, 24.

34 See Charbonneau, Boleda, and Bates, *First French Canadians*, 27 ("[T]he Crown took on the responsibility of recruiting and transporting female immigrants").

35 See ibid., 28 (noting that the king's daughters "crossed over to Canada at the King's expense").

36 Ibid. (the intendant was the government official who controlled the colony's entire civil administration).

37 Abbott, *History of Marriage*, 10. See Charbonneau, Boleda, and Bates, *First French Canadians*, 28.

38 Aubert, "'Blood of France,'" 454. A livre was the French unit of currency. "A family could probably have lived decently on 25 livres a month," but an unskilled worker might earn as little as 10 livres a month. Andrew Trout, *City on the Seine: Paris in the Time of Richelieu and Louis XIV, 1614–1715* (New York: St. Martin's, 1996), xi. Trout further estimates that in 1669 one livre was worth about $40 (of 1990 dollars).

39 Aubert, "'Blood of France,'" 454.

40 Ibid.

41 In 1669, 410,000 livres was approximately the same as £31,000 (British pounds). See http://www.pierre-marteau.com/currency/converter/eng-fra.html. That amount translates to approximately £4.3 million at today's rates and into about $6 million. The economic cost of the project was approximately £689,000, which is more than $1 billion. See Lawrence H. Officer and Samuel H. Williamson, "Five Ways to Compute the Relative Value of a UK Pound

Amount, 1270 to Present," *MeasuringWorth*, 2015, http://www.measuringworth. com/calculators/ukcompare/relativevalue.php?use%5B%5D=CPI&use%5B%5 D=NOMINALEARN&year_early=1669&pound71=31000&shilling71=&penc e71=&amount=31000&year_source=1669&year_result=2014. The filles du roi would fulfill Williamson's definition of a project, which includes "a government expenditure, such as the financing of Medicare or a war." Ibid., "Glossary of Terms."

42   Greer, *People of New France*, 17.

43   See Charbonneau, Boleda, and Bates, *First French Canadians*, 28.

44   Abbott, *History of Marriage*, 10. The particular characteristics of the individual women were considered relatively unimportant, and no consideration was given to whether they would make a good match for any individual male colonist. At the same time, this lack of individualized focus was not limited to mail-order brides. A 1667 bill of lading sent to Quebec by Colbert included only one adjective. It described "400 good men, 50 filles, 12 mares and 2 stallions." Jan Noel, *Along a River: The First French-Canadian Women* (Toronto: University of Toronto Press, 2013), 76.

45   Abbott, *History of Marriage*, 10.

46   See ibid., 11–12.

47   See Charbonneau, Boleda, and Bates, *First French Canadians*, 138.

48   Abbott, *History of Marriage*. 11.

49   Ibid., 10.

50   See Charbonneau, Boleda, and Bates, *First French Canadians*, 205.

51   Ibid., 205.

52   See, e.g., "Les Filles du Roi (The King's Daughters)," http://richardnelson. org/Parent-Frost%20Website/Filles%20du%20Roi%20master.htm.

53   Marie-Florine Bruneau, *Women Mystics Confront the Modern World: Marie de l'Incarnation (1599–1672) and Madam Guyon (1648–1717)* (Albany: State University of New York Press, 1998), 93. He was not alone in this belief. In her correspondence to her son, the nun Marie de l'Incarnation (she joined the Ursulines after being widowed) writes, "We no longer want to ask for anyone but village girls suitable for work like men. Experience makes one see that those who have not been raised in this way are not right for here, where they find themselves in a state of inescapable need." Ibid.

54   Aimie Kathleen Runyan, "Daughters of the King and Founders of a Nation: Les Filles du Roi in New France" (master's thesis, University of North Texas, 2010), 15, http://digital.library.unt.edu/ark:/67531/metadc28470/m2/1/high_res_d/ thesis.pdf (quoting Yves Landry, *Les Filles du roi au XVIIe siècle: Orphelines en France, pionnières au Canada. Suivi d'un répertoire biographique des filles du roi* [The daughters of the king in the seventeenth century: Orphaned in France, pioneers in Canada followed by a biographical directory of the daughters of the King] [Ottawa: Leméac, 1992], 62–63).

55 Runyan, "Daughters of the King," 14–15. According to Landry's study, "of the 770 women, 486 were from cities, 215 were from the countryside, and 69 were of indeterminate origin." Ibid.

56 The "declarations of their marriage certificates and contracts suggest that close to 65% of them lost their fathers before they reached adulthood." See Magdalena Paluszkiewicz-Misiaczek, "From Strength to Weakness— Changing Position of Women in Societies of New France and British North America," in *Place and Memory in Canada: Global Perspectives Third Congress of Polish Association for Canadian Studies and Third International Conference of Central European Canadianists* (Krakow: Polish Academy of Arts and Sciences, 2004), 381, http://www.ptbk.org.pl/userfiles/file/paluszkiewicz_misiaczeko4.pdf.

57 Ibid.

58 Ibid., 380.

59 Francis Parkman, *The Old Régime in Canada* (Boston: Little, Brown, 1875), 219.

60 Ibid., 220.

61 Abbott, *History of Marriage*, 10.

62 Parkman, *Old Régime*, 222.

63 See generally Peter J. Gagné, *Before the King's Daughters: The Filles à Marier, 1634–1662* (Pawtucket, RI: Quintin, 2002), 13. In fact, even without all the incentives offered by the government, an earlier group of women known as the Filles à Marier (marriageable girls) had made the same journey to the colony to seek husbands and a better life. Ibid.

64 Gillian Hamilton, "Property Rights and Transaction Costs in Marriage: Evidence from Prenuptial Contracts," *Journal of Economic History* 59 (1999): 69. Not all parts of France followed the Coutume de Paris.

65 The only exceptions to this rule were "immeubles propres," types of nontransportable property such as land and houses. The husband could not sell these types of property, but the wife also lacked the right to alienate this property. See Jennifer L. Palmer, "Atlantic Crossings: Race, Gender and the Construction of Families in Eighteenth-Century La Rochelle" (PhD diss., University of Michigan, 2008), 155 (citing Simon-François Langloix, *Principes Généraux de la Coutume de Paris*, 3rd ed. [Paris: Prault Père, 1746]). See also Paluszkiewicz-Misiaczek, "From Strength to Weakness," 380 (noting that French law guaranteed that husbands did not have the power to alienate the family property that a woman brought when she entered marriage).

66 The women were significantly more educated than the men they would marry. See Cornelius J. Jaenen, *The Role of the Church in New France*, 2nd ed. (Ottawa: Canadian Historical Association, 1985), 19, http://www.collectionscanada.gc.ca/obj/008004/f2/H-40_en.pdf.

67 See Natalie McNair, *New France* (Aurora, Ontario: St. Andrew's College Intranet Kilby document), H17, http://kilby.sac.on.ca/faculty/nMcNair/7%20

HIS%20Documents/His7_Unit1.pdf. Marital contracts for such purposes were permissible; Hamilton, "Property Rights," 68–69; Janine Lanza, *From Wives to Widows in Early Modern Paris: Gender, Economy, and Law* (Farnham, Surrey: Ashgate, 2007), 45; Suzanne Boivin Sommerville, *Késsinnimek—Roots— Racines*, http://www.kateritekakwitha.org/roots/suzanne4–7.htm#_edn9.

68 Sommerville, *Késsinnimek*.

69 See McNair, *New France*, H17.

70 See Hamilton, "Property Rights," 81.

71 Ibid., 80.

72 Parkman, *Old Régime*, 224.

73 Bettina Bradbury, ed., *Canadian Family History: Selected Readings* (Toronto: Copp Clark Pitman, 1992), 18.

74 Parkman, *Old Régime*, 226.

75 Abbott, *History of Marriage*, 90. The first question most of the women asked their potential suitors "was whether the suitor had a house and a farm." Parkman, *Old Régime*, 224.

76 Jack Verney, *The Good Regiment: The Carignan-Salières Regiment in Canada 1665–1668* (Montreal: McGill-Queen's University Press, 1992), 105.

77 Charbonneau, Boleda, and Bates, *First French Canadians*, 90.

78 Parkman, *Old Régime*, 226.

79 Ibid., 226.

80 The law technically required marriage within fifteen days after the arrival of a bride ship. However, since the women were not forced to marry, the specific time limit does not appear to have been enforced. Instead, men were required to attempt to marry as quickly as possible. Ironically, Talon never married. Parkman, *Old Régime*, 226; see also Will Ferguson, *Canadian History for Dummies*, 2nd ed. (Hoboken, NJ: John Wiley, 2005), 81.

81 Thomas Chapais, *The Great Intendant: A Chronicle of Jean Talon in Canada 1665–1672*, vol. 6, *Chronicles of Canada*, ed. George M. Wrong and H. H. Langton (Toronto: Glasgow, Brook, 1914), 56.

82 Ibid. Moreover, had Lenoir's father lived in the colony, he would have been punished as well. See Parkman, *Old Régime*, 225 (explaining that fathers who failed to marry off their sons at age twenty and their daughters at age sixteen were fined, and were required to report to the authorities every six months to explain the delay).

83 Chapais, *Great Intendant*, 57.

84 Ibid., 56–57.

85 Parkman, *Old Régime*, 225.

86 This sum was referred to as "the King's gift." See ibid., 225 ("[t]wenty livres were given to each youth who married before the age of twenty, and to each girl who married before the age of sixteen").

87 Ibid., 227–28. See also J. M. S. Careless, "A Century of New France: 1663–1763,"
    in *Canada: A Celebration of Our Heritage* (Bowmanville, ON: Canadian
    Heritage Gallery, 1994), http://www.canadianheritage.ca/books/canada3.htm.

88 See Marilyn Barber, *Immigrant Domestic Servants in Canada* (Ottawa: Canadian
    Historical Association, 1991), 12, http://www.collectionscanada.gc.ca/
    obj/008004/f2/E-16_en.pdf; Charbonneau, Boleda, and Bates, *First French
    Canadians*, 111.

89 Charbonneau, Boleda, and Bates, *First French Canadians*, 201.

90 Adam Shortt and Arthur G. Doughty, eds., *Canada and Its Provinces: A History
    of the Canadian People and Their Institutions by One Hundred Associates*
    (Toronto: Glasgow, Brook, 1914), 42, https://archive.org/stream/canadaitspro
    vinc15shoruoft#page/42/mode/2up/search/knelt.

91 Records show that widows "conceived almost four times as frequently" as
    single women, indicating the significant freedom they enjoyed in the French
    colony. Charbonneau, Boleda, and Bates, *First French Canadians*, 129–30.

92 See *Jugements et Déliberations du Conseil Souverain de la Nouvelle-France; publiés
    sous les auspices de la Legislature de Québec* (Quebec: A. Coté et cie, 1885),
    https://archive.org/stream/jugementsetdlio1newf#page/n5/mode/2up.

93 Typically, the *chivaree* involved a raucous group of people engaging in a noisy
    uproar in front of the couple's new home and demanding money or whiskey.
    However, such groups could quickly become frightening mobs and cause
    significant property destruction, injury, or even death. William Bell, a
    Presbyterian minister in Upper Canada described an 1845 *chivaree* of a neighbor
    in which the mob broke down the groom's door and became so rowdy that he
    had to call the magistrates for protection. In some instances, *chivarees* lasted up
    to two weeks. There were also instances where the bridegrooms shot or even
    killed some of their assailants. W. Peter Ward, *Courtship, Love, and Marriage in
    Nineteenth-Century English Canada* (Montreal: McGill-Queen's University
    Press, 1990), 114–15. See also Abbott, *History of Marriage*, 58 (describing the
    chivaree that occurred after a runaway slave married an Irish woman in which "a
    mob that included the sons of prominent families broke into his house, dragged
    him from his bed, and rode him on a rail. Naked in the freezing night, the
    just-wed bridegroom died at their tormenting hands").

94 Colonial widows were not subjected to *chivaree* despite the fact that the general
    custom was imported into Canada. See William S. Walsh, *Curiosities of Popular
    Customs and of Rites, Ceremonies, Observances, and Miscellaneous Antiquities*
    (Philadelphia: J. B. Lippincott, 1898), 209, https://archive.org/stream/
    curiositiespopuoowalsgoog#page/n4/mode/2up. This lenient treatment is
    particularly interesting given that *chivaree* was widespread in France and
    persisted despite its prohibition by the Council of Tours and the disapproval of
    the French parliament. See ibid., 211.

95 Leslie Choquette, "'Ces Amazones du Grand Dieu': Women and Mission in Seventeenth-Century Canada," *French Historical Studies* 17, no. 3 (Spring 1992): 630.

96 Ibid., 632.

97 Ibid., 654.

98 In addition, their presence could also provide tangible benefits to nonreligious women. For example, female missionaries, like the Ursulines, made education available to all women, not just the daughters of the elite. In fact, in 1657, Marguerite Bourgeoys opened a school for girls in Montreal. However, not everyone approved of general female education. According to one critic, the education of country girls "made them frivolous and lazy like so many of their contemporaries from the social elite living in the principal towns." Jaenen, *Role of the Church*, 19–20.

99 The end of the bride shipments was not an end to the gender imbalance in Canada. However, by 1681, the younger population was beginning to reach equilibrium. In the over-thirty population, there were still two men for every woman, but the colony was quickly reaching gender parity due to the high birth rates. Greer, *People of New France*, 16. See also Charbonneau, Boleda, and Bates, *First French Canadians*, 37 (noting that only an additional 201 women "arrived after the last contingent of King's Daughters of 1673").

100 Gilbert Parker and Claude G. Bryan, *Old Quebec: The Fortress of New France* (New York: Macmillan, 1903), 98, http://www.gutenberg.org/ files/30367/30367-h/30367-h.htm#CHAPTER_VI.

101 Parkman, *Old Régime*, 222.

102 See Jan G. Coombs, *Our Tangled French Canadian Roots: A History of the People Who Were Part of Our Gregoire, Adam, Martel and Beaudry Lines* (Middleton, WI: Jan Gregoire Coombs, 2009), 48 ("Very few of the King's Daughters created problems in their communities. Only five appeared in court on charges of adultery, prostitution, or debauchery, and one was executed, along with her son-in-law, for a serious crime, the nature of which is unknown because their court records were lost"), http://books.google.com.au/books?id=S-s2maBGn hoC&printsec=frontcover&source=gbs_ge_summary_r&cad=0#v=onepage &q&f=false. In addition, since the aim of the program was to send *fertile* women to the colony to marry and reproduce, the idea of sending filles de joie, among whom venereal disease was common, would have was been completely contrary to the king's design.

103 See Peter J. Kastor and François Weil, eds., *Empires of the Imagination: Transatlantic Histories of the Louisiana Purchase* (Charlottesville: University of Virginia Press, 2009), 41–42; Louis Houck, *A History of Missouri: From the Earliest Explorations and Settlements Until the Admission of the State into the Union* (Chicago: R. R. Donnelley & Sons, 1908), 25; Addison Erwin Sheldon, *History and Stories of Nebraska* (Chicago: University Publishing, 1913), http://

www.olden-times.com/oldtimenebraska/n-csnyder/nbstory/story3.html. Interestingly, even these obvious fabrications took nearly a century to be fully exposed. In fact, for nearly a hundred years after his memoir was published, maps of America continued to contain "The Long River." *The United States Service Magazine* (New York: Charles B. Richardson, 1864), 1:359, https:// archive.org/stream/unitedstatesseroounkngoog#page/n11/mode/2up.

104 Women convicted of prostitution in France were exiled to the French islands of the Caribbean—Martinique and Saint-Christophe (present-day Saint Kitts). No prostitutes were knowingly sent to Canada. See also Peter J. Gagné, *King's Daughters and Founding Mothers: The Filles du Roi 1663–1673*, 2 vols. (Pawtucket, RI: Quintin, 2001), 1:22.

105 Runyan, "Daughters of the King," 30.

106 See, e.g., Gustave Lanctot, *Filles de Joie ou Filles du Roi: Étude sur l'Émigration Féminine en Nouvelle-France* (Montreal: Editions du Jour, 1966), 158; Mordecai Richler, *Oh Canada!, Oh Quebec! Requiem for a Divided Country* (Toronto: Penguin, 1992), 102; Sarah Gahagan, "Les Filles du Roi," in *moé pi toé*, ed. Rhea Côté Robbins (2003), http://www.fawi.net/ezine/vol3no4/FASWST2003/Gahagan.html.

CHAPTER 3. CORRECTIONS GIRLS AND CASKET GIRLS

1 The program began similarly but soon became very different. Joan M. Martin, "*Placage* and the Louisiana *Gens de Couleur Libre*," in *Creole: The History and Legacy of Louisiana's Free People of Color*, ed. Sybil Kein (Baton Rouge: Louisiana State University Press, 2000), 60–61.

2 The king granted the permission as long as the Indian women converted. Martha Elizabeth Hodes, ed., *Sex, Love, Race: Crossing Boundaries in North American History* (New York: New York University Press, 1999), 41.

3 Ibid., 41 ("To illustrate their point, Hall and others often insist that the seventeenth-century French colonial policies that tolerated and sometimes encouraged sexual interactions between French male settlers and Indian or African women in New France … were transplanted and persisted unabated in eighteenth-century French Louisiana").

4 Hodes, *Sex, Love, Race*, 42.

5 See Aubert, "'Blood of France,'" 467.

6 Elizabeth Reis, ed., *American Sexual Histories*, 2nd ed. (Hoboken, NJ: John Wiley, 2012), 63.

7 Randy J. Sparks, *Religion in Mississippi* (Jackson: University Press of Mississippi, 2001), 11.

8 See Aubert, "'Blood of France,'" 467.

9 Marcel Giraud, *A History of French Louisiana, Vol. 1: The Reign of Louis XIV, 1698–1715*, trans. Joseph C. Lambert (Baton Rouge: Louisiana University Press, 1974), 167.

10 Hodes, *Sex, Love, Race*, 38.

11 Ibid., 41.

12 In 1714, there were only 215 Louisiana colonists, compared with over 250,000 English colonists. Mathé Allain, *Not Worth a Straw* (Lafayette: Center for Louisiana Studies, 1988), 64.

13 In fact, even supporters worried such mixing could "produce in the colony only children of a hard and idle character." Hodes, *Sex, Love, Race*, 45.

14 Aubert, "'Blood of France,'" 469. In these views, one can see the beginning of the arguments regarding racial inferiority that would justify the horrors of slavery in the South.

15 Ibid., 469 ("Commissary Jean-Baptiste Dubois Duclos forcefully refuted 'the plan and the proposal of Mr. De La Vente' to allow marriages between French men and 'sufficiently instructed Sauvagesses.' Permitting such unions, Duclos argued, 'would be of no utility for the increase of families'").

16 Allain, *"Not Worth a Straw,"* 83.

17 See John Hugh Reynolds, ed., *Publications of the Arkansas Historical Association* (Fayetteville: Arkansas Historical Association, 1908), 335.

18 Jennifer M. Spear, *Race, Sex, and Social Order in Early New Orleans* (Baltimore: Johns Hopkins University Press, 2008), 47.

19 In the twentieth century, a full-size, authentic replica of the *Le Pelican* was built at La Malbaie in Quebec. Construction on the ship began in 1987, but there were numerous problems with the project, and it was not completed until 1992. The *Le Pelican* was then purchased and brought to Donaldsonville, Ascension Parish, Louisiana, in 2002 as a tourist attraction. The ship sank in 2002 and was raised, it sank again in 2004, and in 2008 the sunken ship was hit by a barge. "Barge Hits Sunken Warship Replica," *USA Today*, January 20, 2008.

20 Gail Alexander Buzhardt and Margaret Hawthorne, *Rencontres sur le Mississipi, 1682–1763* (Jackson: University Press of Mississippi, 1993), 63.

21 Spear, *Race, Sex, and Social Order*, 47.

22 See Allain, *"Not Worth a Straw,"* 86. The bishop of Quebec described the colony as "well provisioned." Ibid.

23 Spear, *Race, Sex, and Social Order*, 47.

24 Giraud, *History of French Louisiana*, 1:155.

25 See Dauphin Island History Archives, *Archive of Historical Data, Books, Maps and Other Materials*, http://www.dauphinislandhistory.org/kennedy/pelican_expand318x228.htm.

26 Giraud, *History of French Louisiana*, 1:155.

27 Allain, *"Not Worth a Straw,"* 86. "Starving times" refers to a famine that gripped the colony during this time, coupled with the colony's severe lack of provisions from France. Ibid.

28 See Robert Lowry and William H. McCardle, *A History of Mississippi: From the Discovery of the Great River by Hernando DeSoto Including the Earliest Settlement*

Made by the French under Iberville to the Death of Jefferson Davis (Jackson, MS: R. H. Henry, 1891), 29, https://books.google.com/books/about/A_History_of_Mississippi.html?id=1meUmjGDshUC. See also *Mississippi History Timeline,* http://mdah.state.ms.us/timeline/zone/1699–1762-french-dominion.

29 Lowry and McCardle, *History of Mississippi,* 29.

30 See David G. Sansing et al., *Natchez, an Illustrated History* (Natchez, MS: Plantation Publishing, 1992), 27.

31 Ibid.

32 John R. Spears and A. H. Clark, *A History of the Mississippi Valley: From Its Discovery to the End of Foreign Domination* (New York: A. S. Clark, 1903), 61.

33 Susan Tucker, ed., *New Orleans Cuisine: Fourteen Signature Dishes and Their Histories* (Jackson: University Press of Mississippi, 2009). See also Lowry and McCardle, *History of Mississippi,* 29.

34 Boisrenaud "refused to marry under the pretext she was of the nobility." Giraud, *History of French Louisiana,* 1:155.

35 See Spear, *Race, Sex, and Social Order,* 47.

36 Compare this with the treatment of the filles du roi and the care taken to ensure their grievances were addressed and did not affect further immigration. Specifically, in a 1667 letter, Talon expresses great concern upon learning that some of the women, particularly the higher class ones, were complaining about the neglect and hardships they had suffered on the voyage over. He particularly worries that if he cannot "soothe their discontent," the women will convey their grievances to people back in France, and that such complaints will hinder the immigration of additional brides. Parkman, *Old Régime,* 1258.

37 See, e.g., Michelene E. Pesantubbee, *Choctaw Women in a Chaotic World: The Clash of Cultures in the Colonial Southeast* (Albuquerque: University of New Mexico Press, 2005), 94.

38 Giraud, *History of French Louisiana,* 1:167 (noting that between 1706 and 1708 the number of children in the colony decreased from "thirty-four to twenty-five").

39 See Jennifer M. Spear, "They Need Wives," in Hodes, *Sex, Love, Race,* 35.

40 Ibid., 48.

41 Allain, *"Not Worth a Straw,"* 85.

42 Spear, "They Need Wives," 48.

43 Even before the women left France, there were indications they would be treated differently than the filles du roi. When the boat docked in Rochfort, the women began to hear rumors about the true conditions in the colony and some deserted. In order to prevent this, the women were no longer permitted to leave the ship as they pleased. Giraud, *History of French Louisiana,* 1:152.

44 Spear, "They Need Wives," 49.

45 Ibid. ("Many of these women did not come voluntarily to Louisiana. In 1719 ninety-five women arrived aboard the *Mutine,* 'sent by the king,' while thirty-eight 'exiled women' arrived aboard the *Deux Frères* and *Duc de Noailles*").

46 Ibid., 48.

47 Spear, *Race, Sex and Social Order,* 47.

48 Ibid., 48.

49 For example, the entire country of Australia was originally founded as a penal colony. See generally John Hirst, *Freedom on the Fatal Shore: Australia's First Colony* (Collingwood, Victoria: Black, Inc., 2008). Britain also sent convicts, including women, to the American colonies, although their immigration was not intended as a marital solution. See Blumenthal, *Brides from Bridewell,* 65–75; see generally Daniel Defoe, *Moll Flanders* (London: Chetwood, 1721).

50 This legislation was ignored by the Crown, which found immigration a convenient and cheap way of dealing with criminals. Susan F. Martin, *A Nation of Immigrants* (New York: Cambridge University Press, 2010), 21–22.

51 Marcel Giraud, *A History of French Louisiana, Vol. 2: Years of Transition 1715–1717,* trans. Brian Pearce (Baton Rouge: Louisiana State University Press, 1993), 34. D'Orléans ended the policy of forced immigration (for both men and women) only after the dragnet became so broad it began sweeping up business visitors to Paris. Ned Sublette, *The World That Made New Orleans: From Spanish Silver to Congo Square* (Chicago: Lawrence Hill Books, 2008), 53.

52 Henry B. Wheatley, *The Historical and the Posthumous Memoirs of Sir Nathaniel William Wraxall, 1772–1784* (New York: Scribner and Welford, 1884), 1:54. See also Michel Lincourt, *In Search of Elegance: Towards an Architecture of Satisfaction* (Montreal: McGill-Queen's University Press, 1999), 134 (describing these "orgies" including one occasion on which d'Orléans invited his private butler to join in, who "thanked his master but said that he would never debase himself by joining such a corrupt company. The regent laughed").

53 Spear, *Race, Sex and Social Order,* 44 (noting that the ban was lifted in 1717).

54 See Spear, "They Need Wives," 48–49.

55 Allain, *"Not Worth a Straw,"* 84.

56 Sublette, *World That Made New Orleans,* 52.

57 Ibid., 53.

58 Ibid., 52–53.

59 See Spear, "They Need Wives," 47; Pesantubbee, *Choctaw Women in a Chaotic World,* 94.

60 See Spear, "They Need Wives," 50. In colonies such as Virginia, which had a similar surplus of single men, prostitution was virtually nonexistent. Thompson, *Women in Stuart England and America,* 42 (describing one English visitor "who searched Williamsburg in vain for a whore" in 1720).

61 The policy of forced migration "officially" ended in March of 1720, but the practice continued well beyond that date.

62 Herbert Asbury, *The French Quarter: An Informal History of the New Orleans Underworld* (New York: Knopf, 1936), 11–12.

63 Ibid., 12.

64 Ibid.

65 Marcel Giraud, *A History of French Louisiana, Vol. 5: The Company of the Indies 1723–1731*, trans. Brian Pearce (Baton Rouge: Louisiana State University Press, 1991), 262.

66 Asbury, *French Quarter*, 12–13.

67 Allain, "Not Worth a Straw," 85. According to Captain Jean François Dumont de Montigny, a duel was nearly fought over the last girl. However, it should be noted that de Montigny also claimed to have "captured a frog two feet long and 18 inches thick, weighing 36 pounds." See Robert Bingham Downs, ed., *The Bear Went over the Mountain: Tall Tales of American Animals* (New York: Macmillan, 1964), 139.

68 Asbury, *French Quarter*, 13. See also Rosary O'Neil, *New Orleans Carnival Krewes: The History, Spirit and Secrets of Mardi Gras* (Charleston, SC: History Press, 2014), 23 (noting that if every one of these claims were correct, "each 'casket girl' bore 162 children").

69 See Blumenthal, *Brides from Bridewell*, 95–96 ("Diligent search for the name of the ship on which the lauded 'casket girls' were supposed to have come in 1728, and for the list of twenty-three 'virtuous maidens' celebrated by all American historians of Louisiana as the precious cargo of this vessel, revealed the voyage and the flawless contingent as *mythical*. ... The 'correction girls' and the 'casket girls' were *one and the same*. Review of manuscript authorities seems to prove that the girls from La Salpêtrière who came in the *Baleine* in 1721/2 and are variously declared to have numbered from eighty to ninety-six—were in fact the 'casket girls'").

70 For example, the records of the 1724 voyage of the *Loire* show the hiring of a carpenter with an indemnity paid for his wife. Similarly, the records of the *Aurore* show that one of the passengers was a stave splitter who was accompanied by his daughter and that her passage had been paid by the Company of the Indies. Giraud, *History of French Louisiana*, 5:261.

71 Allain, "Not Worth a Straw," 85.

72 The council was founded in 1712 and was modeled on other governmental organizations in other colonies. "The Council had original and, at first, exclusive jurisdiction to decide disputes arising anywhere in Louisiana." Morris S. Arnold, *Colonial Arkansas 1686–1804: A Social and Cultural History* (Fayetteville: University of Arkansas Press, 1991), 125.

73 Spear, "They Need Wives," 50.

74 Jean-Francois-Benjamin Dumont de Montigny, *The Memoir of Lieutenant Dumont, 1715–1747: A Sojourner in the French Atlantic*, ed. Gordon M. Sayre and Carla Zecher, trans. Gordon M. Sayre (Chapel Hill: University of North

Carolina Press, 2012), 32 (noting that "La Chaise had been sent to the colony to investigate charges of malfeasance, including smuggling and profiteering, which eventually resulted in Bienville's recall to France").

75 See Spear, "They Need Wives," 50.

76 The ship actually arrived in 1727. Kelly Burgess, "Here Come the Brides?," *Ancestry Magazine*, November–December 2009, 22, 26. See also Workers of the Writers' Program of the Works Progress Administration in the State of Louisiana, *Louisiana: A Guide to the State* (New York: Hastings House, 1941), 320.

77 There is no mention of any additional women. Burgess, "Here Come the Brides?," 26. See also Emily Clark, *Masterless Mistresses: The New Orleans Ursulines and the Development of a New World Society, 1727–1834* (Chapel Hill: University of North Carolina Press, 2007), 54 (describing the history of the Ursuline nuns in Louisiana yet making no mention of the casket girls they supposedly brought with them).

78 Martin, "*Placage* and the Louisiana *Gens de Couleur Libre*," 61.

79 See Chun, "Mail-Order Bride Industry"; Lee, "Mail Fantasy"; Meng, "Mail-Order Brides"; Vergara, "Abusive Mail-Order Bride Marriage."

80 See, e.g., Violent Crime Control and Enforcement Act of 1994, Pub. L. No. 103–322, 108 Stat. 1796 (giving abused immigrant women the right to self-petition and, thus, removing their immigration status from their husband's control); Illegal Immigrant Reform and Responsibility Act of 1996, Pub. L. No. 104–208, § 652(e)(1)(A), 110 Stat. 3009 (requiring matchmaking organizations to disseminate information regarding their immigration status and information about battered spouse waivers); Title IV; INA 204(a)(1)(A)(iii)(I) &(II); Victims of Trafficking and Violence Protection Act of 2000, Pub. L. No. 106–386, § 107, 114 Stat 1464 (stating that the government will aid in protecting victims of trafficking).

CHAPTER 4. WELL DISPOSED TOWARD THE LADIES

1 Brian Roberts, *American Alchemy: The California Gold Rush and Middle-Class Culture* (Chapel Hill: University of North Carolina Press, 2000), 233.

2 Farnham was not the only reformer to propose mail-order brides as a cure for lawlessness. A few decades later, the women of Tucson, Arizona, created the Busy Bee Club to recruit mail-order brides for the town's black miners. The women proposed the idea after repeated shoot-outs occurred over the hand of the few single women. The organizers hoped the club would prevent further violence. Chris Enss, *Object Matrimony: The Risky Business of Mail Order Matchmaking on the Western Frontier* (Guilford, CT: Globe Pequot Press, 2013), 31–34.

3 JoAnn Levy, *Unsettling the West: Eliza Farnham and Georgiana Bruce Kirby in Frontier California* (Berkeley, CA: Heyday Books, 2004), 17.

4   Alfred L. Hurtado, *Indian Survival on the California Frontier* (New Haven, CT: Yale University Press, 1988), 169.

5   Jack actually survived the wound and then killed the woman with a knife. Ibid., 176.

6   Ibid., 180 (noting that the term to "obtain a squaw" was often just a euphemism for rape). See also Irene I. Blea, *The Feminization of Racism: Promoting World Peace in America* (Westport, CT: Praeger, 2003), 30.

7   Hurtado, *Indian Survival on the California Frontier*, 182.

8   Ibid., 188.

9   Roberts, *American Alchemy*, 234.

10   Members of the movement included female celebrities such as Catharine Beecher, Harriet Beecher Stowe, and Lydia Maria Child. Dolores Hayden, *The Grand Domestic Revolution: A History of Feminist Designs for American Homes, Neighborhoods and Cities* (Cambridge, MA: MIT Press, 1982), 316.

11   Faith Rogow, *Gone to Another Meeting: The National Council of Jewish Women 1893–1993* (Tuscaloosa: University of Alabama Press, 1993), 4.

12   "Wives Wanted," *Burlington Free Press*, August 25, 1837, http://chroniclingamerica.loc.gov/lccn/sn84023127/1837–08–25/ed-1/seq-2/#date1=1837&sort=relevance&rows=20&words=impudence&searchType=basic&sequence=0&index=8&state=&date2=1837&proxtext=impudence&y=9&x=17&dateFilterType=yearRange&page=2.

13   Ibid.

14   "Female Emigrants," *Edgefield Advertiser*, March 14, 1849, http://chroniclingamerica.loc.gov/lccn/sn84026897/1849–03–14/ed-1/seq2/#date1=1849&index=0&rows=20&words=unfeminine&searchType=basic&sequence=0&state=&date2=1849&proxtext=unfeminine&y=12&x=13&dateFilterType=yearRange&page=1.

15   Levy, *Unsettling the West*, ix.

16   Roberts, *American Alchemy*, 233. Other endorsers of the mission included "Quaker philanthropist Isaac Hopper, former U.S. Attorney Benjamin F. Butler and Superior Court Judge John W. Edmonds." Levy, *Unsettling the West*, 4.

17   Levy, *Unsettling the West*, 1.

18   Ibid., 1.

19   Ibid., 2.

20   Chris Enss, *Hearts West: True Stories of Mail Order Brides on the Frontier* (Guilford, CT: TwoDot, 2005), 175. At the same time, however, the proposal was not without critics. See Teresa S. Neal, *Evolution toward Equality: Equality for Women in the American West* (Lincoln, NE: iUniverse, 2006), 76 (noting that some critics believed mail-order marriage was not only inappropriate, but actually just "an elaborate prostitution scheme"). See also Levy, *Unsettling the West*, 174 (stating that Farnham's plan was undermined by rumors and gossip). According to Professor Kerry Abrams, one of these rumors was that some of

the recruits were black mill workers. See Kerry Abrams, "The Hidden Dimension of Nineteenth-Century Immigration Law," *Vanderbilt Law Review* 62, no. 5 (October 2009): 1358.

21 Carter Goodrich and Sol Davison, "The Wage-Earner in the Westward Movement II," *Political Science Quarterly* 51, no. 1 (March 1936): 79–80.

22 See Matthew Lavallee, "Immigration in Lowell: New Waves of Nativism," *WR: Journal of the Arts and Sciences Program*, no. 3 (2010–11), http://www.bu.edu/writingprogram/journal/past-issues/issue-3/lavallee/.

23 Stanley Lebergott, "Wage Trends, 1800–1900," in *Trends in the American Economy in the Nineteenth Century*, ed. Conference on Research in Income and Wealth (Princeton, NJ: Princeton University Press, 1960), 452.

24 This was the safety valve approach to immigration, and was also commonly suggested as the solution to the unrest of male wage earners. See Goodrich and Davison, "Wage-Earner," 117.

25 Western states were frequently posting ads to attract the immigration of wage earners. However, the difficulty these potential immigrants faced was amassing enough money to finance the high cost of moving. Goodrich and Davison, "Wage-Earner," 133.

26 Ibid., 93–94.

27 "Not Good for Man to Be Alone," *Windham County Democrat*, April 13, 1853, http://chroniclingamerica.loc.gov/lccn/sn84022807/1853-04-13/ed-1/seq-4/#date1=01%2F01%2F1836&index=0&date2=12%2F31%2F1922&searchTy pe=advanced&language=&sequence=0&lccn=sn84022807&words=domestic +efficacies&proxdistance=5&rows=20&ortext=&proxtext=domestic+efficacie s&phrasetext=&andtext=&dateFilterType=range&page=1.

28 "Female Emigration," *Daily Dispatch*, July 20, 1855, http://chroniclingamerica. loc.gov/lccn/sn84024738/1855-07-20/ed-1/seq-2/#date1=1855&index=0&row s=20&words=EMIGRATION+FEMALE&searchType=basic&sequence=0&s tate=&date2=1855&proxtext=Female+Emigration&y=0&x=0&dateFilterType =yearRange&page=1.

29 This organization was created in response to the 1857 depression and once again suggested immigration as a solution to female unemployment. Farnham was one of the group's founders, and thus the WPES's emphasis on emigration is not surprising. Levy, *Unsettling the West*, 158. Other such societies included the Philadelphia Women's Industrial Aid Association.

30 "Appeal of the Women's 'Protective Emigration Society,'" *New-York Daily Tribune*, December 14, 1857, http://chroniclingamerica.loc.gov/lccn/sn83030213/1857-12-14/ed-1/seq-4/#date1=1857&index=0&rows=20&words= Emigration+Protective+Society+Woman&searchType=basic&sequence=0&st ate=&date2=1857&proxtext=Woman%27s+Protective+Emigration+Society&y =14&x=14&dateFilterType=yearRange&page=1. Between November 10, 1857,

and March 3, 1858, the WPES "sent out between 100 and 150 women a month." See Goodrich and Davison, "Wage-Earner," 93.

31 Goodrich and Davison, "Wage-Earner," 93.

32 Eastern states began hiring significant numbers of female schoolteachers only after the beginning of the Civil War and the loss of many male schoolteachers to the battlefield. See James M. Volo and Dorothy Denneen Volo, *The Antebellum Period* (Westport, CT: Greenwood, 2004), 80. However, by the 1840s, the need for teachers in the West had led to a growing willingness to hire female teachers. In fact, in some western states, they were even paid salaries comparable with those of their male peers. See Mary Hurlbut Cordier, "Prairie Schoolwomen, Mid-1850s to 1920s, in Iowa, Kansas, and Nebraska," *Great Plains Quarterly* 8 (Spring 1988): 106.

33 Women were specifically desired as teachers because of their perceived moral superiority.

34 Other organizations created to bring female schoolteachers West included "the Board of National Popular Education in Cleveland and the American Women's Educational Association." Carol Lasser and Stacey Robertson, *Antebellum Women: Private, Public, Partisan* (Lanham, MD: Rowman & Littlefield, 2010), 33.

35 "Come to the West," *Weekly Indiana State Sentinel*, March 8, 1855, http:// chroniclingamerica.loc.gov/lccn/sn82014286/1855-03-08/ed-1/seq-2/#date1= 1855&sort=relevance&rows=20&words=Slade&searchType=basic&sequence= 0&index=6&state=&date2=1855&proxtext=Slade&y=10&x=18&dateFilterTyp e=yearRange&page=6.

36 *The White City: The Historical, Biographical, and Philanthropical Record of Virginia and West Virginia and Their State Exhibits at the World's Columbian Exposition* (Chicago: Chicago World Book, 1893), 20, http://books.google. com/books?id=8HYBAAAAMAAJ&pg=RA3-PA20&dq=%22slade's+girls%22 &hl=en&sa=X&ei=iXmGUtXiO4uPkAf_gYGwAw&ved=0CDkQ6AEwAg#v =onepage&q=%22slade's%20girls%22&f=false.

37 Reprinted in "Yankee Girls," *Weekly Indiana State Sentinel*, May 24, 1855, http:// chroniclingamerica.loc.gov/lccn/sn82014286/1855-05-24/ed-1/seq-1/#date1=1 855&index=1&rows=20&words=Girls+Slade&searchType=basic&sequence=0 &state=&date2=1855&proxtext=Slade%27s+Girls&y=8&x=9&dateFilterType= yearRange&page=1.

38 Reverend James Hill, "Some Yankees Enlarged," *New England Magazine* 46–47 (1912): 88.

39 Ibid., 89.

40 Levy, *Unsettling the West*, 4.

41 Ibid., 5.

42 Roberts, *American Alchemy*, 238.

43 Abbott, *History of Marriage*, 139.

44 One nineteenth-century exposé (Jacob A. Riis, *How the Other Half Lives: Studies among the Tenements of New York* [New York: Charles Scribner's Sons, 1890], 9) of the urban poor described their living quarters as "the hot-beds of the epidemics that carry death to rich and poor alike; the nurseries of pauperism and crime that fill our jails and police courts; that throw off a scum of forty thousand human wrecks to the island asylums and workhouses year by year; that turned out ... [a] half million beggars ... that maintain a standing army of ten thousand tramps." Abbott, *History of Marriage*, 147.

45 S. J. Kleinberg, *The Shadow of the Mills: Working-Class Families in Pittsburgh, 1870–1907* (Pittsburgh: University of Pittsburgh Press, 1989), 88.

46 Farnham would eventually remedy this mistake when she helped found the Women's Protective Emigration Society. However, in 1849, her belief in the superiority of women did not overcome her dislike for the lower classes. Levy, *Unsettling the West*, 158.

47 In at least one letter, Farnham did state that her "chief difficulty is that of getting money." Letter to Lydia Sigourney, April 11, 1849, quoted in Levy, *Unsettling the West*, 35. Others have suggested that potential recruits were dissuaded from emigrating after they heard gossip that Farnham's California's Association of American women was a ploy for prostitutes. JoAnn Levy, *They Saw the Elephant: Women in the California Gold Rush* (Norman: University of Oklahoma Press, 1992), 174.

48 Levy, *Unsettling the West*, 37.

49 In England, these rules were quite restrictive, but their impact was weakened by the fact that the law was extremely decentralized. In contrast, in America, the law of coverture was far stricter. America received the coverture rules as a complete body of law, which the courts were then expected to implement in a uniform manner with little room for discretion or equitable considerations. Moreover, when American courts needed guidance on how to apply these rules, they looked to the female-adverse commentaries of William Blackstone. This rigid adherence to Blackstone's interpretation of the law of coverture was devastating for women's rights. Coverture, as William Blackstone explained, was the legal fact that upon marriage, "the very being or legal existence of the woman is suspended ... or at least is incorporated and consolidated into that of the husband." Hendrik Hartog, *Man and Wife in America: A History* (Cambridge, MA: Harvard University Press, 2009), 120–21.

50 See, e.g., Jodi O'Brien, ed., *Encyclopedia of Gender and Society* (Thousand Oaks, CA: SAGE, 2008), 743. In fact, during this period, entire communities were created that directly challenged the laws of love and marriage. Groups like the Oneida Community rejected traditional marriage in favor of group marriage. In addition to "free love," the group also practiced gender equality and communal child rearing. Similarly, the Modern Times Commune in Long Island also

rejected many of the restrictions of nineteenth-century marriage and replaced them with the practice of gender equality and sexual freedom. See, e.g., Ann D. Braude, *Radical Spirits, Spiritualism and Women's Rights in Nineteenth-Century America* (Bloomington: Indiana University Press, 1989), 133. These communities were extreme examples of the growing opposition to oppressive marriage laws, but by midcentury, large numbers of American women were seeking to achieve greater respect and independence in their marriages.

51 Under the civil law property regime, wives had joint ownership of the marital property. See Calvin R. Massey, *Emanuel Law Outlines: Property: Keyed to Dukeminier/Krier/Alexander/Schill,* 7th ed. (New York: Aspen, 2010), 85.

52 Donna C. Schuele, "'None Could Deny the Eloquence of This Lady': Women, Law, and Government in California, 1850–1890," in *Taming the Elephant: Politics, Government, and Law in Pioneer California,* ed. John F. Burns and Richard J. Orsi (Berkeley: University of California Press, 2003), 169.

53 Ibid., 172. Although California's law was nearly identical to that of other former Spanish and French colonies, which retained their civil law tradition, it is clear that most of the California delegates viewed this as reforming the common-law system rather than keeping the status quo. See generally Susan Westerberg Prager, "The Persistence of Separate Property Concepts in California's Community Property System, 1849–1975," *UCLA Law Review* 24 (1976): 1–82, 46.

54 Schuele, "'None Could Deny the Eloquence of This Lady,'" 172. Halleck began his argument with the quip, "I am not wedded to the common law, or the civil law, or yet to a woman." Burns and Orsi, *Taming the Elephant,* 7.

55 Levy, *They Saw the Elephant,* 189.

56 This high regard for women was not limited to California. In at least one Texas town, it translated into community protection from abuse. In northeastern Texas, around the time of the California gold rush, it became known that a local man was biting and pinching his wife "just for his own independent amusement." The couple had moved from Pennsylvania, where the law offered the woman little protection from abuse. Nevertheless, her new Texas community decided to protect her by subjecting her husband to one hundred lashes. After that punishment, the husband never hurt her again. Hartog, *Man and Wife in America,* 165.

Enticing female immigrants was difficult. Even married men could have problems convincing their wives to follow them west. In 1883, the married Warren Cochran placed a marital advertisement in the *Omaha Bee* after speanding nearly a decade trying to get his wife Letitia to permanently relocate to Nebraska with him. Three months after finally abandoning his attempts, he placed the following ad: "Wanted—To correspond with a Christian lady of culture and refinement between the ages of 25–50, without children, who could unite with a genial husband to make his nice home in Omaha one of prosperity and happiness. This is in good faith and deemed a proper method of introduction." A few months later he sued Letitia for divorce based on desertion. Hartog, *Man and Wife in America*, 21.

57 Roberts, *American Alchemy*, 228.

58 Ibid., 228–29.

59 Levy, *They Saw the Elephant*, 176.

60 Hartog, *Man and Wife in America*, 98.

61 Ibid., 137.

62 Ibid., 151.

63 Ibid., 153.

64 Hartog, *Man and Wife in America*, 247.

65 In the West, women were so valuable that parents would actually discourage suitors because "the departure of a daughter depleted the household's real, and potential, income." Cathy Luchetti, *I Do! Courtship, Love and Marriage on the American Frontier* (New York: Three Rivers Press, 1996), 97.

66 Levy, *They Saw the Elephant*, 189.

67 Ibid., 173.

68 A letter to the *Boston Journal* after the discovery of gold describes the craziness of gold fever and its impact on women's employment opportunities, noting that "[e]very woman who chooses can now find ready employment in making up clothing for the gold diggers, and at a great price." Levy, *Unsettling the West*, 5. Shortly after her arrival, Farnham also remarked on these opportunities: "Women are more in requisition than gold or anything else. Those who came out with me had immediately offers of employment at $75 and $100 per month. If there had been five hundred instead of five, they could all have engaged immediately on similar terms." Ibid., 44.

69 Levy, *They Saw the Elephant*, 175.

70 The actual numbers were likely even higher than these records indicate because some of the tabulators ignored prostitutes, as well as many other women who were living "unseen aboard ships." Levy, *They Saw the Elephant*, 177.

71 Albert Hurtado, *Intimate Frontiers: Sex, Gender and Culture in Old California* (Albuquerque: University of New Mexico Press, 1999), 76.

72 In fact, California was having so little trouble attracting women that the property incentive enacted in the 1849 constitution quickly disappeared. As early as 1850, the California state legislature passed property laws that expressly undermined certain aspects of the constitutional guarantee. Schuele, "None Could Deny the Eloquence of This Lady," 174. For example, contrary to the express provisions of the convention, California husbands were given the right to manage and control all property, including the wife's separate property. In addition, wives could not even will their own property. The only limitation on the husband's control was that he could not sell or encumber the property

without the wife's consent in writing and confirmed outside the presence of the husband. A few years later, in 1857, these rights were further undermined when the legislature ended the right to no-fault, equal division of common property upon divorce and eliminated the wife's right to "testamentary control over half of the common property." Ibid., 174. These changes were rapid and significant. By 1870, California women were living under the most repressive property regime in the country. Ibid., 176.

73 Enss, *Hearts West*, 48.

74 Reprinted in "Puget's Sound Wife Market," *Burlington Free Press*, October 28, 1859, http://chroniclingamerica.loc.gov/lccn/sn84023127/1859-10-28/ed-1/seq-1/#date1=1836&index=1&date2=1922&searchType=advanced&language=&sequence=0&lccn=sn84023127&words=compensation+higher&proxdistance=5&rows=20&ortext=&proxtext=higher+compensation&phrasetext=&andtext=&dateFilterType=yearRange&page=1.

75 Ibid.

76 "Varieties," *Cincinnati Daily Press*, October 12, 1860, http://chroniclingamerica.loc.gov/lccn/sn84028745/1860-10-12/ed-1/seq-1/#date1=1860&index=6&rows=20&words=girls+wives&searchType=basic&sequence=0&state=&date2=1860&proxtext=no+girls+there+for+wives&y=10&x=13&dateFilterType=yearRange&page=1.

77 During the Civil War, thousands of women entered the wage force primarily as seamstresses. This competition, coupled with inflation of nearly 80 percent, meant that "[r]eal wages in general declined by about 20 percent." See Paul A. Cimbala and Randall M. Miller, eds., *An Uncommon Time: The Civil War and the Northern Home Front* (Bronx, NY: Fordham University Press, 2002), 178. See also Herbert J. Lahne, *The Cotton Mill Worker* (New York: Farrar & Rinehart, 1944), 73 ("After the Civil War the cotton mill was even less attractive in comparison with other occupations"); Nancy F. Cott, *No Small Courage: A History of Women in the United States* (New York: Oxford University Press, 2004), 281.

78 Judith E. Harper, *Women during the Civil War: An Encyclopedia* (New York: Routledge, 2004), 210.

79 Enss, *Hearts West*, 48.

80 Ibid.

81 Ibid., 49.

82 Abrams, "Hidden Dimension," 1404.

83 Few family groups immigrated to places like Albany, which were logging and trapping towns. Abrams, "Hidden Dimension," 1362.

84 Cong. Globe, 27th Cong., 3d Sess. 24 (1843).

85 One of the unintended side effects of this was it also increased the number of child brides. Julie Roy Jeffrey, *Frontier Women: "Civilizing" the West? 1840–1880*, rev. ed. (New York: Hill & Wang, 1998), 76.

86 Abrams, "Hidden Dimension," 1404.

87 Ibid.

88 Ibid., 1356.

89 Ibid., 1401. The 1860 "census showed only 302 people lived in Seattle, and fewer than 12,000 (non-Indians) in the entire Territory." Ibid., 1363.

90 Peggy Pascoe, *What Comes Naturally: Miscegenation Law and the Making of Race in America* (New York: Oxford University Press, 2009), 98n58. It was only after the white, single female population had increased significantly that such bans finally became enforceable. Specifically, in 1858, the ban was amended to nullify all future interracial marriages, and by 1866 the law was further amended to deny even common-law recognition to interracial marriages. See Coll-Peter Thrush, *Native Seattle: Histories from the Crossing-Over Place* (Seattle: University of Washington Press, 2007), 56–57.

91 Abrams, "Hidden Dimension," 1404.

92 Ibid., 1405.

93 Sarah Carter, ed., *Montana Women Homesteaders: A Field of One's Own* (Helena, MT: Farcountry Press, 2009), 32.

94 Because it was unclear what year the "alleged" marriage took place, the court could not simply find the relationship barred by the state's antimiscegenation statute, which was valid in 1867 but repealed in 1868. See Jason A. Gillmer, "Crimes of Passion: The Regulation of Interracial Sex in Washington, 1855–1950," *Gonzaga Law Review* 47 (2012): 428. Consequently, the court held that their union violated the state's antimiscegenation statute if it was in place when they married, but also that the relationship would have been void if it had actually occurred a year later when the statute was no longer in force. *In re Estate of Wilbur v. Bingham*, 8 Wash. 35 (1894).

95 In a similar case, the court essentially declared all Indian wives prostitutes by condemning the entire notion of Indian customary marriages, stating, "It is clearly apparent white men had no difficulty in obtaining Indian women to live with them by paying money to their relatives" and that "such arrangements could hardly amount to marriages under any law." Pascoe, *What Comes Naturally*, 103.

96 *In re Estate of Wilbur*, 35.

97 Washington University State Historical Society, *Washington Historical Quarterly* 6–7 (1915): 225–26, http://books.google.com/books?id=vZMeAQAAMAAJ&pg=PA226&lpg=PA226&dq=#v=onepage&q&f=false.

98 Ibid. What these employment prospects actually were is somewhat unclear. When the governor of Massachusetts was asked what the women would do in Seattle, he stated they would become teachers. However, Seattle consisted of barely three hundred people, almost none of whom were children, leading one reporter to make the following observation: "How your Washington bachelors

can be fathers is a subject rather for a hearty guffaw than for any serious debate. So it seems rather more likely than otherwise that when 'the girls' reach their intended home, they will find they have been 'carrying coals to Newcastle.'" Abrams, "Hidden Dimension," 1375.

99 Abrams, "Hidden Dimension," 1364.

100 Ibid., 1366.

101 Ibid.

102 See Mary Avery, *Washington: A History of the Evergreen State* (Seattle: University of Washington Press, 1964), 249 (noting it opened with Mercer as president and teacher, and thirty-one students).

103 He hoped to recruit as many as seven hundred women. Abrams, "Hidden Dimension," 1388.

104 Ibid., 1367.

105 Many of the women also contributed to their passage. Mercer's advertisements listed various costs for the voyages ranging from "a very low rate of $200" to $50 for "orphans and poor girls." Ibid., 1371.

106 Roger Conant, *Mercer's Belles: The Journal of a Reporter*, ed. Lenna A. Deutsch (Pullman: Washington State University Press, 1992), 103.

107 Ibid.

108 Ibid., 104.

109 Ibid.

110 Ibid., 101.

111 This was a common sentiment among western female immigrants. One eastern woman who immigrated to Kansas described the difference, stating that in the East "you had to have your pedigree … to be accepted anywhere, but [out West] it didn't matter a bit who your ancestors were or what you did for a living; if you were nice you were nice." This same woman also noted the appeal of being able to work and still be considered respectable. Specifically, what impressed her most "was the fact that [in the West] a girl could work in an office or a store, yet that wouldn't keep her from being invited to the nicest homes or marrying one of the nicest boys. This freedom to work seemed to me a wonderful thing." Luchetti, *I Do!*, 159.

112 See Shanna Stevenson, "Here Come the Suffragists: The Role of the Mercer Girls in the Washington Woman Suffrage Movement" (Washington State Historical Society), http://www.washingtonhistory.org/files/library/HereCometheSuffragists.pdf.

113 See ibid.

114 The British mainland north of the forty-ninth parallel had remained unincorporated since the signing of the Oregon treaty and was primarily controlled by the Hudson Bay Company and the native tribes. See Peter Johnson, *Voyages of Hope: The Saga of the Bride-Ships* (Victoria, BC: Touchwood Editions, 2010), 18.

115 See Brown's Belmont Website, "Social Studies 10, Unit 6 Readings: British Columbia: Colony to Confederation," http://belmontbrown.weebly.com/uploads/7/9/4/2/7942726/ch6_reading.pdf.

116 Donald J. Hauka, *McGowan's War: The Birth of Modern British Columbia on the Fraser River Gold Fields* (Vancouver: New Star Books, 2004).

117 The act was introduced by Edward Bulwer Lytton, Britain's new colonial secretary. In addition to his political career, Lytton was also a writer, authoring such lines as "the pen is mightier than the sword" and the opening lines "it was a dark and stormy night." Edward George Bulwer Lytton, *Paul Clifford* (London: Henry Colburn and Richard Bentley, 1830), 1.

118 Allan Christensen, ed., *The Subverting Vision of Bulwer Lytton: Bicentenary Reflections* (Newark: University of Delaware Press, 2004), 220.

119 Great Britain Colonial Office, *British Columbia: Papers Relative to the Affairs of British Columbia*, pt. 1 (London: George Edward Eyre and William Spottiswoode, 1859), 49–50, https://books.google.com/books?id=WsdEAQ AAMAAJ&pg=RA1-PA93&lpg=RA1-PA93&dq=British+Columbia:+Papers +Relative+to+the+Affairs&source=bl&ots=ppMa-NasG3&sig=Pch8z100N YozqQCY9Jei1r_cunA&hl=en&sa=X&ei=uKVsVYeoDcihNuiTg_gJ&ved= 0CEsQ6AEwCQ#v=onepage&q=foreigners&f=false.

120 The free land available in Oregon under the Donation Land Act had ended in 1855. Will Bagley, *With Golden Visions Bright before Them: Trails to the Mining West* (Norman: University of Oklahoma Press, 2012), 407.

121 Adele Perry, *On the Edge of Empire: Gender, Race, and the Making of British Columbia, 1849–1871* (Toronto: University of Toronto Press, 2001), 141 (noting that it was estimated that men exceeded women "by some 277 percent").

122 Matthew Macfie, *Vancouver Island and British Columbia: Their History, Resources, and Prospects* (London: Longman, Green, Longman, Roberts, & Green, 1865), 497, https://ia700407.us.archive.org/17/items/vancouverisland-00macf/vancouverislandoomacf.pdf.

123 Jean Barman, *The West beyond the West: A History of British Columbia*, rev. ed. (Toronto: University of Toronto Press, 1996), 90,

124 Adele Perry, "'Fair Ones of a Purer Caste': White Women and Colonialism in Nineteenth-Century British Columbia," *Feminist Studies* 21 (Autumn 1997): 512. The *Colonist* was also an active promoter "of a homesteading law that would provide cheap land and thus encourage transients to become settlers." Ibid., 504.

125 Nancy Millar, *Once upon a Wedding: Stories of Weddings in Western Canada, 1860–1945, for Better or Worse* (Calgary: Bayeux Arts, 2000), 24.

126 Adrienne Mason, *Tales from the West Coast: Smugglers, Sea Monsters, and Other Stories (Amazing Stories)* (Alberta: Altitude, 2003), 14–15. Canadian papers had also been writing about the need for more white women. In a letter to the editor of the *British Columbian* dated June 7, 1862, the writer discussed the need

for more female immigration, particularly the "introduction of fair ones of a purer caste," which he believed was necessary to end the practice of interracial marriages. Perry, "'Fair Ones of a Purer Caste,'" 508n38.

127 Johnson, *Voyages of Hope*, 9.

128 Ibid., 10.

129 Perry, "'Fair Ones of a Purer Caste,'" 505.

130 Ruth W. Sandwell, ed., *Beyond the City Limits: Rural History in British Columbia* (Vancouver: University of British Columbia Press, 1999), 162.

131 Perry, "'Fair Ones of a Purer Caste,'" 501.

132 Mason, *Tales from the West Coast*, 16.

133 Perry, "'Fair Ones of a Purer Caste,'" 505.

134 Ibid. See also Adele Perry, "'Oh! I'm Just Sick of the Faces of Men': Gender Imbalance, Race, Sexuality and Sociability in Nineteenth Century British Columbia," *BC Studies: The British Columbia Quarterly* 105–106 (Spring/ Summer 1995): 34. There were also significant fears regarding the children of mixed marriages, and these fears were seemingly confirmed after the 1869 armed resistance of the Métis, the term for people of mixed white and aboriginal ancestry. The uprising was a response to increasing British governmental control. Perry, "'Fair Ones of a Purer Caste,'" 506. For a history of Métis rebellions, see George F. G. Stanley, *The Birth of Western Canada: A History of the Riel Rebellions* (Toronto: University of Toronto Press, 1960).

135 Cynthia R. Comacchio, *The Infinite Bonds of Family: Domesticity in Canada, 1850–1940* (Toronto: University of Toronto Press, 1999), 46.

136 Van Kirk, "From 'Marrying-In' to 'Marrying-Out,'" 4.

137 Ibid., 5.

138 *Jones v. Fraser* (1886), 2 C.N.L.C 203 (S.C.C.). Similarly in 1899, the Supreme Court for the Northwest Territories decided that the children of these "informal" marriages could not inherit. Catherine A. Cavanaugh and Randi R. Warne, eds., *Telling Tales: Essays in Western Women's History* (Seattle: University of Washington Press, 2001), 76.

139 Perry, "Oh! I'm Just Sick of the Faces of Men," 34.

140 William Rathbone Greg, *Why Are Women Redundant?* (London: N. Trübner, 1869), 5.

141 Johnson, *Voyages of Hope*, 22.

142 Ibid., 23.

143 The surplus woman debate stemmed from fear that female middle-class employment would drive down wages for men, and it was widespread in America as well as England. See Jacqueline Jones, *American Work: Four Centuries of Black and White Labor* (New York: Norton, 1998), 309. See also Maxine L. Margolis, *Mothers and Such: Views of American Women and Why They Changed* (Berkeley: University of California Press, 1985), 195.

In his inaugural speech, Massachusetts Governor John Andrews stated that gender disparity

> disorders the market for labor, it reduces women and men to an unnatural competition for employments fitted for men alone, tends to increase the number both of men unable to maintain families, and of women who must maintain themselves unaided. In civilized, refined society, it is the office and duty of man to protect woman, to furnish her a sphere, a support, a home. . . . Where women are driven to the competitions of the market with men, or where men are left unsolaced and unrefined by the presence of women, society is alike weakened and demoralized.
>
> I know of no more useful object to which the Commonwealth can lend its aid than that of a movement adapted in a practical way to open the door of emigration to young women who are wanted for teachers, and for every other appropriate as well as domestic employment in the remote West, but who are leading anxious and aimless lives in New England.

Abrams, "Hidden Dimension," 1382.

144 Julia Bush, *Edwardian Ladies and Imperial Power* (London: Leicester University Press, 2000), 149. This was not the first time the group had had to adjust its focus. The FMCES was initially founded to aid the immigration of middle-class women, but the lack of middle-class jobs in British Columbia forced the group to focus most of their efforts on the emigration of working-class women. Marie Rye, secretary of FMCES, stated, "I am fully aware . . . that none but *working* women are wanted in British Columbia." Perry, *On the Edge of Empire*, 152.

145 Mason, *Tales from the West Coast*, 20.

146 Millar, *Once upon a Wedding*, 25.

147 Johnson, *Voyages of Hope*, 145.

148 Mason, *Tales from the West Coast*, 22.

149 Johnson, *Voyages of Hope*, 145.

150 Perry, "'Fair Ones of a Purer Caste,'" 513.

151 Johnson, *Voyages of Hope*, 146.

152 Ibid., 169.

153 Although the Victoria Female Emigration Society (this was the society formed to help the women upon arrival) recommended a rate of only about twenty-five pounds per year, even this was 50 percent above the average rate in England. Moreover, it appears that, despite this recommendation, the average wages were considerably more. Lorraine C. Brown, "Domestic Service in British Columbia 1850–1914" (master's thesis, University of Victoria, 2007), 25.

154 Mason, *Tales from the West Coast*, 24–25.

155 Ibid., 25.

156 Philippa Levine, ed., *Gender and Empire* (Oxford: Oxford University Press, 2004), 162. See also Johnson, *Voyages of Hope*, 146 (noting that when "one

woman was asked about her employment preferences, she responded that she would like to be placed with "an American family where I should be on a footing of equality").

157 Johnson, *Voyages of Hope*, 146. Susannah Moodie's autobiography depicting her time in the Canadian bush during the 1830s and 1840s is similar. Moodie, who was middle-class, describes the social inversion of the frontier, noting the resentful comments of the lower class Mrs. Joe who, upon watching Moodie wash her own clothes for the first time, remarked, "I am glad to see you brought to work at last. I hope you may have to work as hard as I have … I hate you all, and I rejoice to see you at the wash-tub, and I wish that you may be brought down upon your knees to scrub the floors." Susanna Moodie, *Roughing It in the Bush* (London: Richard Bentley, 1852), 142.

158 Johnson, *Voyages of Hope*, 197.

CHAPTER 5. ADVERTISING FOR LOVE

1 Frank Luther Mott, *A History of American Magazines, Vol. II: 1850–1865* (Cambridge, MA: Harvard University Press, 1938), 206 (noting that "*Porter's Spirit of the Times* was almost alone in taking a lenient view of [matrimonial advertisements] as a 'slick and convenient mode of popping the question,' quite suitable to 'this progressive, dashing, gay, and frisky old nineteenth century'").

2 Francesca Beauman, *Shapely Ankle Preferr'd: A History of the Lonely Hearts Advertisement* (London: Chatto & Windus, 2011), 10.

3 *Poor Robin* focused entirely on matters of marriage and sex. In fact, "poor robin" was actually a slang term for penis. Ibid., 10.

4 Ibid., 1.

5 Ibid., 2.

6 Ibid., 1. This is a decent fortune; at today's rates, three thousand pounds is the equivalent of nearly half a million dollars!

7 Ibid.

8 Until this point, all such ads had been jests, including an entire satirical catalogue, published in *Poor Robin's Intelligence*, which had advertised husbands and wives for sale. Ibid., 10.

9 Ibid., 3.

10 Ibid.

11 Ibid., 14.

12 See "People in Place: Families Households and Housing in London 1550–1720," http://www.history.ac.uk/cmh/pip/pip.html.

13 Such jobs included "seamstresses, handicraftswomen, and servants." Helen M. Berry, *Gender, Society and Print Culture in Late-Stuart England: The Cultural World of the* Athenian Mercury (Aldershot: Ashgate, 2003), 168.

14 Ibid., 11. Another shocking admission was that the *Athenian Mercury* also endorsed women's intellectual capabilities. The magazine publically rejected

the widely held view regarding the "natural imbecility of the female sex" and instead stated that any difference between the two was "not due to natural stupidity ... but to their lack of education." Ibid., 111.

15 Ibid., 168.

16 Coontz, *Marriage, a History*, 5. According to Coontz, the rise of the love match was the result of two "seismic social changes" occurring in the seventeenth and eighteenth centuries. The first was the increased financial independence of young people, which made them less dependent on their parents, and the second was the belief in free choice. Ibid., 146.

17 Berry, *Gender, Society and Print Culture*, 190.

18 However, eighteenth-century parents were far from willing to cede control over marriage to their children, and the single biggest obstacle to marriage was the withholding of parental consent. In fact, this impediment was featured in two-fifths of all questions under the heading of "Constraints." Berry, *Gender, Society and Print Culture*, 248.

19 C. C. Langdell, *A Selection of Cases on the Law of Contracts: With References and Citations* (Boston: Little, Brown, 1871), 798–99.

20 *Drury v. Hooke*, 1 Vern. 412, 22 E.R. 900 (1686); *Hall and Keene v. Potter*, 3 Lev. 411, 83 E.R. 756 (1699).

21 The reasons are unclear, but it is possible that her parents' displeasure with the marriage caused them to reduce her fortune.

22 *Drury v. Hooke*, 1 Vern. 412n.2.

23 Ibid.

24 *Hall and Keene v. Potter*, 3 Lev. 411.

25 As this case demonstrated, the problem with marriage brokerage contracts was more than a concern regarding their potential to victimize particular individuals. During this period, marriage brokers were viewed as inherently corrupt because it was believed that brokers' desire for profit would inevitably cause them to encourage bad marriages. See *Crawford v. Russell*, 62 Barb. 92, 98 (1872).

26 *Hall and Keene v. Potter*, 411.

27 Although Lady Ogle was nobility and the heiress to a great fortune, there were a number of contingencies to her inheritance. In contrast, Thinne was in possession of his estate and, although not nobility, he was a member of a "great family." Ibid.

28 The court describes the match as "convenient, i.e., suitable." Ibid.

29 *Hermann v. Charlesworth*, 2 K.B. 123, 125 (1905).

30 Erica Harth, "The Virtue of Love: Lord Hardwicke's Marriage Act," *Cultural Critique* 9 (Spring 1988): 125.

31 Roger Lee Brown, "The Rise and Fall of the Fleet Marriage," in *Marriage and Society: Studies in the Social History of Marriage*, ed. R. B. Outhwaite (New York: St. Martin's, 1981), 118, 133.

32 R. B. Outhwaite, *Clandestine Marriage in England, 1500–1850* (Rio Grande, OH: Hambledon Press, 1995), 70.

33 The Fleet Prison "was the prison in which formerly all prisoners for debt from the entire kingdom were, or could demand to be, confined." However, the accommodations of the prison were far too small to house all the debtors that congregated there, and as a result "it became customary to allow those who could give security for appearance in the prison when summoned to take private lodgings or set up private establishment anywhere within the 'rule of liberties' of the Fleet—a portion of London of considerable area and well defined limits." George Elliott Howard, *A History of Matrimonial Institutions: Chiefly in England and the United States with an Introductory Analysis of the Literature and the Theories of Primitive Marriage and the Family* (Chicago: University of Chicago Press, 1904), 1:437, http://www.gutenberg.org/files/49107/49107-h/49107-h.htm#Page_435.

34 Ibid., 1:443.

35 Ibid., 1:436. There is actually some debate as to how many of these marriages were performed by incarcerated ministers. According to Robert Brown, most of these ministers entered the Fleet on a voluntary basis. Brown, "Rise and Fall of the Fleet Marriage," 120.

36 Brown, "Rise and Fall of the Fleet Marriage," 116 (estimating that there were between 200,000 and 300,000 Fleet Street marriages between 1694 and 1754).

37 Howard, *History of Matrimonial Institutions*, 1:441.

38 Leneman, *Promises, Promises*, 2. See also Outhwaite, *Clandestine Marriage in England*, 72.

39 Outhwaite, *Clandestine Marriage in England*, 72.

40 Brown, "Rise and Fall of the Fleet Marriage," 117. One of the reasons such earlier bills failed to pass is that they were piecemeal and did little to prevent the Fleet marriages. Outhwaite, *Clandestine Marriage in England*, 72.

41 As Henry Swinburne wrote in his *Treatise of Spousals or Matrimonial Contracts: Wherein All the Questions Relating to That Subject Are Ingeniously Debated and Resolved* (London: S. Roycroft, 1686), 194, "[S]eeing secret Contracts cannot be proved, it is all one in effect, as if they were not."

42 During the eighteenth century, if one party disputed a marriage, supporting evidence, such as a written document or at least two witnesses of good character, was required to prove the marriage. See Rebecca Probert, *Marriage Law and Practice in the Long Eighteenth Century: A Reassessment* (Cambridge: Cambridge University Press, 2009), 32. However, Fleet marriages with their false or nonexistent records and lack of witnesses offered little protection to the participants, particularly the women. Brown, "Rise and Fall of the Fleet Marriage," 130–31.

43 Parental consent was needed for marriage by license. However, marriage by banns did not require affirmative parental permission, only that there was no formal parental objection. Probert, *Marriage Law and Practice*, 227.

44 Howard, *History of Matrimonial Institutions*, 1:458.

45 See Esther Webber, "Gretna Green: The Bit of Scotland Where English People Go to Get Married," *BBC News*, August 19, 2014, http://www.bbc.com/news/magazine-28679430.

46 Harth, "Virtue of Love," 135.

47 This idea was expressed in Richardson's famous novel of the period, *Clarissa*, in which Clarissa's brother refers to daughters as "chickens for the tables of other men." Samuel Richardson, *Clarissa, or, the History of a Young Lady: Comprehending the Most Important Concerns of Private Life* (London: Printed for S. Richardson, 1748), 77.

48 Harth, "Virtue of Love," 40.

49 David Lemmings, "Marriage and the Law in the Eighteenth Century: Hardwicke's Marriage Act of 1753," *Historical Journal* 39, no. 2 (June 1996): 354. See also Harth, "Virtue of Love," 140.

50 Mary Vermillion, "*Clarissa* and the Marriage Act," *Eighteenth Century Fiction* 9, no. 4 (July 1997): 404.

51 Harth, "Virtue of Love," 128.

52 Kirstin Olsen, *Daily Life in the 18th-Century England* (Westport, CT: Greenwood, 1999), 35.

53 Some women began speaking out against the practice of arranged marriage. Lady Mary Wortley Montagu, who was the subject of an attempted arranged marriage, issued a scathing critique of such marriages. She wrote, "People in my way are sold like slaves, and I cannot tell what price my masters will put on me." Montagu eventually eloped rather than marry her father's chosen suitor. Roy Porter, *The Penguin Social History of Britain: English Society in the Eighteenth Century* (London: Penguin, 2001), 21.

54 Bridget Hill, *Women, Work and Sexual Politics in Eighteenth-Century England* (Oxford: Basil Blackwell, 1989), 225. See also Olwen Hufton, *The Prospect Before Her: A History of Women in Western Europe, 1500–1800* (London: HarperCollins, 1995), 64.

55 In fact, the number of unmarried women in these groups tripled. Hill, *Women, Work and Sexual Politics*, 225. See also Bridget Hill, ed., *Eighteenth Century Women: An Anthology* (New York: Routledge, 1984), 71.

56 Jamie Doward, "New Romantics? No, the Poldark Era Cared More for Rich Brides: Open University Study Finds Marriage Was a Mercenary Affair in the 18th Century," *Guardian*, March 28, 2015, http://www.theguardian.com/lifeandstyle/2015/mar/29/poldark-era-new-romantics-rich-brides-18th-century.

57 Berry, *Gender, Society and Print Culture*, 30 (noting that there were "77 men to every 100 women in London in 1694").

58 See "People in Place," describing the bachelor population of Cheapside.

59 Hardwicke's Act applied only until age twenty-one, and did not affect inheritance. However, in at least "one case the daughter was not entitled to inherit until she reached the age of thirty, unless she married with the specified consents." Rebecca Probert, "Control over Marriage in England and Wales, 1735–1823: The Clandestine Marriages Act of 1753 in Context," *Law and History Review* 27, no. 2 (Summer 2009): 433 (citing *Parnell v. Lyon*, 35 E.R. 186 [1813]). See also *Crommelin v. Crommelin*, 30 E.R 313 (1796).

60 Beauman, *Shapely Ankle Preferr'd*, 50. Technically, the first female-authored ad actually appeared in 1727. According to the *People's Almanac*, Helen Morrison, "a lonely spinster," placed this matrimonial ad. However, this endeavor did not end well. No one considered the ad legitimate, and Morrison's actions were actually considered so crazy that the mayor had her sent to an insane asylum for four weeks. See Alexis Abb, "Gentleman Seeketh Matrimony: A Brief History of Personal Ads," *Metroland*, February 9, 2012, http://metroland. net/2012/02/09/gentleman-seeketh-matrimony/.

61 Beauman, *Shapely Ankle Preferr'd*, 51.

62 Ibid., 50.

63 Ibid., 61.

64 See ibid., 189.

65 Sarah Gardner, *The Matrimonial Advertisement, or a Bold Stroke for a Husband* (London, 1777), 52. The independence of the widow is also apparent from her warning, "remember I WILL BE OBEYED." This line is dropped from later versions of the play presumably because it was seen as too forceful a declaration by a woman. Isobel Grundy, "Sarah Gardner: 'Such Trumpery' or 'A Lustre to Her Sex?,'" *Tulsa Studies in Women's Literature* 7 (Spring 1988): 22.

66 However, the independence created by matrimonial ads was far from universally embraced. In later versions of the play, Gardner was forced to change her defense of matrimonial ads to the bland "I shall say nothing in defence of the mode." Grundy, "Sarah Gardner," 22.

67 Ibid., 18.

68 Women in desperate circumstances also turned to matrimonial advertisements. One of the most poignant of these types of ads was placed in the *Times* in 1788, by a lady named Eleanora who wrote the following:

> MATRIMONY. A Lady, about 25 years of age, who has been flattered with the idea of possessing an agreeable person, and who, without any flattery at all, is in the actual possession of an independent fortune, solicits the attention of any young gentlemen of birth, education, and personal consequence. The ill usage of her relations had obliged her to separate herself from them; and they, in revenge, not only employ their utmost malice to disturb her repose, but threaten prosecutions to deprive her of her fortune.

> Any such Gentleman, therefore, who will stand forth as her protector, to save her from the tyranny of her family on the one hand, and the impositions of lawyers on the other, shall be rewarded with the object he has protected and the fortune he has preserved.

Beauman, *Shapely Ankle Preferr'd*, 45.

69 H. G. Cocks, *Classified: The Secret History of the Personal Column* (New Zealand: Random House Books, 2009), viii.

70 *New England Courant*, January 29, 1722, cited in Charles Wyllys Elliott, *The New England History: From the Discovery of the Continent by the Northmen, A.D. 986, to the Period When the Colonies Declared Their Independence, A.D. 1776* (New York: Scribner, 1857), 1:22–23. The paper was owned by Franklin's older brother.

71 "To the Author of the *New-England Courant*," *New England Courant*, April 23, 1722, http://www.ushistory.org/franklin/courant/issue39.htm.

72 Coontz, *Marriage, a History*, 68. Coontz also notes that during the Middle Ages, most marriages, whether urban or rural, were perceived as a "business partnership." Ibid., 114.

73 Howard, *History of Matrimonial Institutions*, 2:152.

74 Ibid., 2:153.

75 *Putnam's Monthly Magazine of American Literature, Science, and Art, Vol. VI: July to December, 1855* (New York: Dix & Edwards, 1855), 61.

76 Howard, *History of Matrimonial Institutions*, 2:153.

77 Ibid. A similar law was also in place in Rhode Island. Ibid.

78 Ibid., 2:153.

79 Ruth H. Bloch, *Gender and Morality in Anglo-American Culture 1650–1800* (Berkeley: University of California Press, 2003), 79.

80 Rosemary O'Day, *Women's Agency in Early Modern Britain and the American Colonies* (New York: Routledge, 2007), 63.

81 Howard, *History of Matrimonial Institutions*, 2:162.

82 Ibid., 2:165.

83 Bloch, *Gender and Morality in Anglo-American Culture*, 81.

84 By the end of the seventeenth century, nearly all the colonies had laws requiring parental consent. For example, New Jersey passed laws requiring parental consent in 1668; Pennsylvania passed a version of these laws in 1676. In addition, such laws were not confined to the English colonies. In fact, New Netherland, the former Dutch colony that included parts of the current New York, New Jersey, Pennsylvania, Maryland, Connecticut, and Delaware, had one of the strictest parental consent laws. They required parental consent even in the case of second marriages, if the widowed daughters were underage. Ibid., 80.

85 Ibid., 82.

86 Apparently the fine did little to deter the couple because in 1667 Rowland was again fined five pounds for his "disorderly and unrighteous endeavor[] to obtain the affections of Mistress Elizabeth Prence." He was then put under a bond of fifty pounds to "refrain and desist." However, eventually the governor must have relented because the couple was married in the spring of 1668. Howard, *History of Matrimonial Institutions*, 2:163. See also Richard Middleton and Anne Lombard, *Colonial America: A History to 1763*, 4th ed. (Hoboken, NJ: Wiley-Blackwell, 2011).

87 Lisa Grunwald and Stephen Adler, *The Marriage Book: Centuries of Advice, Inspiration, and Cautionary Tales from Adam & Eve to Zoloft* (New York: Simon & Schuster, 2015), 344.

88 Reprint of an English newspaper article recounting the humiliating fraud.

89 "Matrimonial Hoax at Leeds," *New York Daily Times*, October 5, 1852, http://query.nytimes.com/mem/archive-free/pdf?res=950CE6D71738E334BC4D53DFB6678389649FDE.

90 "Romantic Rascality: A Lion among the Ladies—Something about Matrimonial Advertisements and Governesses," *New York Daily Times*, December 13, 1856, http://query.nytimes.com/mem/archive-free/pdf?res=9B02E7D81039E134BC4B52DFB467838D649FDE.

91 Ibid.

92 Ibid.

93 "A Warning to the Ladies—Matrimonial Advertisements," *New York Times*, December 16, 1856, http://query.nytimes.com/mem/archive-free/pdf?res=9A00E5D81039E134BC4E52DFB467838D649FDE.

94 Ibid.

95 "Panurge Answers the Matrimonial Advertisements," *New York Daily Times*, June 10, 1856, http://query.nytimes.com/mem/archive-free/pdf?res=9806EEDF1339E134BC4852DFB066838D649FDE.

96 Reprinted in "Thieving as a Science," *Nashville Union and American*, April 23, 1858, http://chroniclingamerica.loc.gov/lccn/sn85038518/1858-04-23/ed-1/seq-2.pdf.

97 Such treatment of matrimonial hoaxes demonstrates that, by this point, these types of scams were being grouped with the large number of other swindles that were common in the mid-nineteenth century. The letter warning of the old hag appeared directly after a letter detailing a get-rich-quick scheme in which the victims were enticed to send in a small amount of money in return for which they were promised that their money would shortly be greatly multiplied. Ibid.

98 Ibid.

99 "Matrimony. Matrimonial Correspondence, New Series: ANNIE," *Water-Cure Journal*, January 1855, 18, https://books.google.com/books?id=Xz4TAAAAYAAJ&pg=PA41&lpg=PA41&dq=vegetarian+and+hydropath,+wear+the+bloom

ers&source=bl&ots=jGG9MwVfF1&sig=MItRkgUfqR4SmGMG6QpPjDkF
Oxo&hl=en&sa=X&ei=OrBxVf-
9NYilNqPagMgH&ved=0CCUQ6AEwAg#v=onepage&q=I%20am%20
thirty-one%20years%20of%20age&f=false.

100 "Matrimony. Matrimonial Correspondence, New Series: GERTRUDE,"
   Water-Cure Journal, March 1855, 65, https://books.google.com/books?id=Xz4T
   AAAAYAAJ&pg=PA41&lpg=PA41&dq=vegetarian+and+hydropath,+wear+th
   e+bloomers&source=bl&ots=jGG9MwVfF1&sig=MItRkgUfqR4SmGMG6Q
   pPjDkFOxo&hl=en&sa=X&ei=OrBxVf-
   9NYilNqPagMgH&ved=0CCUQ6AEwAg#v=onepage&q=singing%20
   angel&f=false.

101 "Wives! Seven Wives Wanted: Miss Maria Lovewell's Answer to the Seven
   Gentlemen Wanting Wives," *Jeffersonian Republican*, January 4, 1843, http://
   chroniclingamerica.loc.gov/lccn/sn86053954/1843-01-04/ed-1/seq-1/#date1=
   1836&index=0&rows=20&words=LOVEWELL+MARIA&searchType=basic
   &sequence=0&state=&date2=1922&proxtext=%22maria+lovewell%22&y=-
   219&x=-1003&dateFilterType=yearRange&page=1.

102 Ibid.

103 Ibid.

104 "Ladies' Department," *Ashland (OH) Union*, February 4, 1857, http://chroni-
   clingamerica.loc.gov/lccn/sn83035173/1857-02-04/ed-1/seq-4.pdf.

CHAPTER 6. WANTED — CORRESPONDENCE

 1 Nancy L. Rhoades and Lucy E. Bailey, eds., *Wanted—Correspondence: Women's
   Letters to a Union Soldier* (Athens: Ohio University Press, 2009), 6.

 2 Gail Hamilton, "A Call to My Country-Women," *Atlantic Monthly* 11 (March
   1863): 345–49.

 3 Ibid., 346.

 4 Rhoades and Bailey, *Wanted—Correspondence*, 28.

 5 Ibid., 180–81. Sending a photograph was considered risqué since, unlike letters,
   which contained their own words, women had no control over what was said
   about their photos.

 6 For many men and women, war stirred romantic feelings. Ibid., 55.

 7 *Advertising for Love: A Collection of Funny, Strange, Poignant and Just Plain
   Bizarre Personal Ads from the Nineteenth Century*, http://www.advertisingfor-
   love.com/2009/09/love-of-travelin-soldier.html.

 8 Ibid.

 9 Ibid.

10 For example, "A young soldier stationed at Fortress Monroe, Va., wishes to
   correspond with some young lady to relieve the tedium of camp life; also with
   a view for matrimony, if the fortunes of the war should prove. Address
   Augustus B. St Lawrence, Old Point Comfort, VA." Ibid.

11 Rhoades and Bailey, *Wanted—Correspondence*, 34–35.

12 In addition, many of those who did survive were no longer attractive marital candidates. Many had physical disabilities due to the war, a significant number returned from the war addicted to drugs and alcohol, and many thousands of others had acquired venereal disease. Abbott, *History of Marriage*, 223 (noting that more than 73,000 union soldiers were treated for syphilis and more than 109,000 were treated for gonorrhea).

13 "Married Women in Kansas," *Fremont (OH) Journal*, December. 7, 1855, http:// chroniclingamerica.loc.gov/lccn/sn85026050/1855–12–07/ed-1/seq-2/#date1=1 836&index=0&rows=20&words=disposal+ever+husband+made+subject&sea rchType=basic&sequence=0&state=&date2=1922&proxtext=%22ever+be+ma de+subject+to+the+disposal+of+the+husband%2C+%22&y=-219&x=- 1017&dateFilterType=yearRange&page=1.

14 In contrast, only 71 percent of southern states had separate estate laws, only 47 percent had separate trader laws, and only 41 percent had earnings laws. B. Zorina Kahn, "Married Women's Property Laws and Female Commercial Activity: Evidence from United States Patent Records 1790–1895," *Journal of Economic History* 56, no. 2 (June 1996): 364.

15 "Invitation to Female Emigrants," *Anti-Slavery Bugle*, December 15, 1855, http:// chroniclingamerica.loc.gov/lccn/sn83035487/1855–12–15/ed-1/seq-3.pdf.

16 The entrepreneur, Fred Harvey, specifically linked the idea of love and the railroad when he began staffing his whistlestop cafes with "Harvey Girls," young rural women of "good character, attractive, and intelligent," who promised to "remain single for one year, live in chaperoned dormitories, and entertain callers in 'courting parlors.'" By the turn of the century, nearly five thousand had found husbands through their work as Harvey Girls. David J. Wishart, ed., *Encyclopedia of the Great Plains* (Lincoln: University of Nebraska Press, 2004), 332, https://books.google.com/books?id=rtRFyFO4 hpEC&q=%22Harvey+Girls%22#v=snippet&q=%22Harvey%20 Girls%22&f=false.

17 Abrams, "Hidden Dimension," 1406.

18 Ibid., 1406–7.

19 T. A. Larson, *History of Wyoming* (Lincoln: University of Nebraska Press, 1965), 81n11 (originally published in *Galaxy* 13 [June 1872]: 755–60).

20 The newspaper also complimented the legislature on "a shrewd advertising dodge ... a cunning device to obtain for Wyoming a widespread notoriety." Ibid., 80.

21 Michael A. Massie, "Reform Is Where You Find It: The Roots of Woman Suffrage in Wyoming," *Annals of Wyoming* 62, no. 1 (Spring 1990): 12, https:// ia700704.us.archive.org/16/items/annalsofwyom621231990wyom/annalsof-wyom621231990wyom.pdf. The author, Robert Morris, was actually the son of Wyoming's first female judge. Larson, *History of Wyoming*, 90.

22 T. A. Larson, "The Woman Suffrage Movement in Washington," *Pacific Northwest Quarterly* 67, no. 2 (April 1976): 50.

23 Joyce Litz, *The Montana Frontier: One Woman's West* (Albuquerque: University of New Mexico Press, 2004).

24 See Edward Hawkins Sisson, *America the Great* (2014), 1083, https://books.google.com/books?id=2BL2AwAAQBAJ&printsec=frontcover&source=gbs_ge_summary_r&cad=0#v=onepage&q&f=false.

25 See National Constitution Center, *Centuries of Citizenship: A Constitutional Timeline* (map of women's voting rights), http://constitutioncenter.org/timeline/html/cw08_12159.html. See also B. Zorina Khan, *The Democratization of Invention: Patents and Copyrights in American Economic Development, 1790–1920* (New York: Cambridge University Press, 2005), 166, https://books.google.com/books?id=cdoKqQ6rxfEC&pg=PA166&lpg=PA166&dq=by+1890,+82+percent+of+Western&source=bl&ots=PvU48tyWSW&sig=5eQwHQ3oLGd4GRlMmgo6QWp2ZOk&hl=en&sa=X&ei=UI91VbOBDYqgNuaYgqAI&ved=0CB8Q6AEwAA#v=onepage&q=by%201890%2C%2082%20percent%20of%20Western&f=false.

26 Enss, *Object Matrimony*, 33.

27 Ibid., 33. The history of African American mail-order brides deserves further research. There is very little known about these women or the particular challenges they faced as marital immigrants.

28 Lawrence M. Friedman, "Crimes of Mobility," *Stanford Law Review* 43 (1990–1991): 654.

29 In Britain, between 1863 and 1887, infanticide reached epidemic proportions. During these years, 3,225 intentional deaths of children under the age of one were recorded, and it is likely that many more were never discovered. Ibid., 654. In the United States, it was poverty rather than shame that was the primary motivation for neonaticide. Lita Linzer Schwartz and Natalie K. Isser, *Child Homicide: Parents Who Kill* (Boca Raton, FL: CRC Press, 2007), 32.

30 Friedman, "Crimes of Mobility," 656.

31 Ibid. The pregnant mail-order bride is a recurring character in Western fiction. Stories like "Second Chance Bride" by Carolyn Davidson (in Cathy Maxwell, Ruth Langan, and Carolyn Davidson, *Wild West Brides* [Don Mills, ON: Harlequin, 2002]), *Last Chance Bride* by Jillian Hart (Don Mills, ON: Harlequin, 1998), and *Gifts of Love* by Theresa Michaels (Don Mills, ON: Harlequin, 1992) feature such women. In other stories, such as "Object, Matrimony" (Lane, "Object, Matrimony," 5–7, 57–58), the men suspect that the woman's reason for wanting a quick marriage is her pregnancy.

32 For example, some women used it to extract concessions from their would-be husbands. It was not uncommon for a mail-order bride to have her prospective husband sign an agreement that he would not abuse or mistreat the

bride-to-be. She, in turn, would often sign an agreement not to "nag." Enss, *Hearts West*, 108.

33 "The Course of True Love," *Daily Yellowstone Journal*, September 18, 1887, http://chroniclingamerica.loc.gov/lccn/sn86075021/1887–09–18/ed-1/seq-1. pdf.

34 Reprinted in "Black Hills (Dakota Territory)," *New York Times*, January 27, 1887, http://search.proquest.com/docview/94569096/820B07FF470A4B7DPQ/21 ?accountid=13965.

35 According to the article, the man was not discouraged; he "intends to keep trying until he is successful." "The Young Man Failed to Suit," *Virginia City Enterprise*, reprinted in *New York Times*, December 21, 1890, 16, http:// timesmachine.nytimes.com/timesmachine/1890/12/21/103287578. html?pageNumber=16.

36 It turns out that this was fortunate. "The next day the gentleman was arrested as a mail robber." "A New York Young Lady," *Western Advance*, June 27, 1874, 1, http://chroniclingamerica.loc.gov/lccn/sn85033535/1874–06–27/ed-1/seq-1. pdf.

37 "She Lives in Bingville," *Shiner Gazette*, July 21, 1910, 6 (reprinted from *Kansas City Star*), http://texashistory.unt.edu/ark:/67531/metapth111840/m1/6/ zoom/?q=short%20pants.

38 "Local Men 'Panned' by Girls Seeking Husbands," *Klamath Falls (OR) Evening Herald*, March 2, 1916, 4, http://chroniclingamerica.loc.gov/lccn/ sn99063812/1916–03–02/ed-1/seq-4.pdf.

39 Laura J. Schaefer, *Man with Farm Seeks Woman with Tractor: The Best and Worst Personal Ads of All Time* (New York: Thunder's Mouth Press, 2005), 13.

40 "Looking for a Wife: Mississippi Man Sends Complete Description of Himself," *Goodwin's Weekly*, April 18, 1903, 15, http://udn6.lib.utah.edu/cdm/ compoundobject/collection/goodwins1/id/6125/rec/49. The first ad was published in 1855 and the second nearly fifty years later. However the difference is unlikely due to time. It is hard to imagine any woman from any time period finding the first ad particularly enticing.

41 Pam Ilyse Epstein, "Selling Love: The Commercialization of Intimacy in America, 1860s–1900s" (PhD diss., Rutgers, State University of New Jersey, 2010), 50, https://rucore.libraries.rutgers.edu/rutgers-lib/30047/pdf/1/. See Arthur MacDonald, *Abnormal Woman: A Sociologic and Scientific Study of Young Women, Including Letters of American and European Girls in Answer to Personal Advertisements with a Bibliography* (Washington, DC: published by author, 1895), 77, 79, 92, 103, http://www.unz.org/Pub/MacDonaldArthur-1895.

42 Epstein, "Selling Love," 51.

43 Ibid., 52.

44 Ibid.

45 Ibid., 53.

46 "The Organ of the Concert Saloons: An Appeal to the Legislature," letter to the editor, *New York Times*, January 26, 1862, http://www.nytimes.com/1862/01/26/news/the-organ-of-the-concert-saloons-an-appeal-to-the-legislature.html.

47 Junius Henri Browne, *The Great Metropolis, a Mirror of New York* (Hartford, CT: American, 1869), 595, https://archive.org/stream/greatmetropolismoobrow#page/594/mode/2up.

48 "An Amusing Matrimonial Hoax: How a Glasgow Merchant Was Imposed Upon—Searching after a Wife in Manchester," *New York Times*, October 25, 1876, http://query.nytimes.com/mem/archive-free/pdf?res=9907E6DD1038EE3BBC4D51DFB667838D669FDE.

49 "Extraordinary Marital Hoax," *New York Times*, October 15, 1877, http://query.nytimes.com/mem/archive-free/pdf?res=9905E6DA103FE63BBC4D52DFB667838C669FDE.

50 *Hoch v. People*, 29 Ill. 265, 269 (1905).

51 Ibid.

52 One of the killers was actually a woman; Belle Gunness also used matrimonial advertisements to murder multiple husbands. It is estimated that Gunness killed more than forty people, including all her husbands and children. See Janet L. Langois, *Belle Gunness: The Lady Bluebeard* (Bloomington: Indiana University Press, 1985). The second was Harry Powers, "the West Virginia Bluebeard," who also used matrimonial advertisements during the 1930s to find and kill his victims. Ron Charles, "'Quiet Dell' by Jayne Anne Phillips, Is Too Tepid to Be Another 'In Cold Blood,'" *Washington Post*, October 15, 2013.

53 "Insane from Courting: Victim of Matrimonial Correspondence Paper," *Iola (KS) Register*, June 6, 1902, 3, http://chroniclingamerica.loc.gov/lccn/sn83040340/1902-06-06/ed-1/seq-3.pdf.

54 This was particularly true in the swiftly growing cities, where it is estimated that 20 to 40 percent of urban dwelling men were unmarried. Rachel F. Moran, "How Second-Wave Feminism Forgot the Single Woman," *Hofstra Law Review* 33 (2004): 247.

55 Michael Grossberg, *Governing the Hearth: Law and the Family in Nineteenth-Century America* (Chapel Hill: University of North Carolina Press, 1988), 38.

56 Melissa Murray, "Marriage as Punishment," *Columbia Law Review* 112 (2012): 5 (citing N.Y. Penal Code § 330 [Albany: Weed, Parsons, 1865]).

57 Grossberg, *Governing the Hearth*, 45.

58 Ibid., 45–46.

59 Ibid., 45.

60 Ibid., 45–46.

61 *Wells v. Padgett*, 8 Barb. 323, 325 (1850).

62 Murray, "Marriage as Punishment," 17n78.

63 Grossberg, *Governing the Hearth*, 47.

64 Murray, "Marriage as Punishment," 5.

65 Lettmaier, *Broken Engagements*, 19–27 (noting a similar trend in England).

66 Timothy Walker, *Introduction to American Law: Designed as a First Book for Students*, 2nd ed. (Cincinnati: Derby, Bradley, 1846), 223, https://ia600306. us.archive.org/11/items/introductiontoamoowalkuoft/introductiontoam-oowalkuoft.pdf. See also *Garmong v. Henderson*, 114 Me. 75 (1915) (awarding $116,000 in damages); *Clevenger v. Castle*, 237 N.W. 542 (Mich. 1931) (awarding damages of $450,000).

67 Neil G. Williams, "What to Do When There's No 'I Do': A Model for Awarding Damages Under Promissory Estoppel," *Washington Law Review* 70 (1995): 1026.

68 *Meister v. Moore*, 96 U.S. 76 (1877).

69 Ariela R. Dubler, "In the Shadow of Marriage: Single Women and the Legal Construction of Family and the State," *Yale Law Journal* 112 (2003): 1659.

70 Ibid., 1656–57.

71 J. G. Sutherland and John R. Berryman, *A Treatise on the Law of Damages Embracing an Elementary Exposition of the Law, and Also Its Application to Particular Subjects of Contract and Tort*, 2nd ed. (Chicago: Callaghan, 1893), 3:320, https://archive.org/stream/atreatiseonlawdoounkngoog#page/n7/ mode/2up.

72 "Her Affection Misplaced: A Matrimonial Advertisement Ends in a Breach of Promise Suit," *New York Times*, December 1, 1884, http://query.nytimes.com/ mem/archive-free/pdf?res=9A00E6D71038E033A25752C0A9649D94659FD 7CF.

73 Ibid.

74 *Kaufman v. Fye*, 42 S.W. 25 (1897).

75 Ibid., 30.

76 *People v. Adams*, 162 Mich. 371 (1910).

77 At one point, Adams even told her that, if she referred to him as her husband, "he would pull his trunk and leave." Ibid., 376.

78 Ibid., 382.

79 The paper was established to "promote honorable matrimonial engagements and true conjugal felicities." "Marital Expectations," http://www.trailend.co/ marital-expectations.html.

80 *American Newspaper Directory, Containing a Description of All the Newspapers and Periodicals Published in the United States, Dominion of Canada and Newfoundland, and of the Towns and Cities in Which They Are Published*, 25th ed. (New York: Geo. P. Rowell, 1893), 1066.

81 See, e.g., "She Wants Her Husband and Money," *New York Times*, September 10, 1887, http://query.nytimes.com/gst/abstract.html?res=9C0CEFDD1530E633A 25753C1A96F9C94669FD7CF; "Romance Ended Sadly," *Marietta Daily Leader*, April 18, 1899, http://chroniclingamerica.loc.gov/lccn/

sn87075213/1899–04–18/ed-1/seq-3.pdf; "Alleged Bigamist Arrested: Monroe Is
Said to Have Wives in Half a Dozen Cities," *New York Times*, November 14,
1899, http://query.nytimes.com/mem/archive-free/pdf?res=9907E0DF1230E
E32A25757C1A9679D94689ED7CF; and "A Matrimonial Fraud: She Was a
Refined and Cultivated Young Lady," *Los Angeles Herald*, October 15, 1893, 2,
http://chroniclingamerica.loc.gov/lccn/sn85042461/1893–10–15/ed-1/seq-2.
pdf.

82 In 1895, the editor of the well-known matrimonial magazine *Heart and Hand*
was arrested for offering to put men in touch with fake "heiresses for 25 cents a
piece, three for half a dollar." This only confirmed that matrimonial ads were
seen as exploitive. "Used the Mails to Defraud," *Maysville (KY) Evening Bulletin*,
March 19, 1895, 4, http://chroniclingamerica.loc.gov/lccn/sn87060190/1895–
03–19/ed-1/seq-4.pdf. See, e.g., "*Heart and Hand*: It Caught Suckers in
Logansport by the Score," *Logansport (IN) Reporter*, March 23, 1895, 6, http://
www.newspapers.com/newspage/4225520/ (stating that "it may be news to
many suckers in Logansport to learn that Warren F. Thompson, the matrimonial agent, who claims to be able to supply wives of dazzling beauty and
unlimited wealth was arraigned in the United States' court at Chicago yesterday
for using the mails to defraud").

83 "If Gullible, Fine Him: Judge Regrets He Cannot Punish Victims of
Matrimonial Advertisements," *New York Times*, November 5, 1907, http://
query.nytimes.com/mem/archive-free/pdf?res=9F05E4D9103EE033A25756C
0A9679D946697D6CF.

CHAPTER 7. MARRIAGE AT THE BORDER

1 The Chinese Exclusion Act was a U.S. federal law signed by President Chester
A. Arthur on May 6, 1882. It was one of the most significant restrictions on free
immigration in U.S. history, prohibiting all immigration of Chinese laborers.

2 Moreover, further amendments to Chinese Exclusion Act also meant that if a
laborer left the United States to marry and return with his wife, he would be
excluded from reentry as a laborer. See Scott Act of 1888.

3 The act essentially limited Chinese immigration to a handful of merchants and
their wives. Bill Ong Hing, *Making and Remaking Asian America through
Immigration Policy, 1850–1990* (Stanford: Stanford University Press, 1993), 45.
American-born Chinese men could still bring in Chinese wives, but this
number was small. Erika Lee, *At America's Gates: Chinese Immigration during
the Exclusion Era, 1882–1943* (Chapel Hill: University of North Carolina Press,
2003), 92.

4 In fact, it was the desire to alleviate such unrest that convinced the government
to finally permit immigration. See Paul R. Spickard, *Japanese Americans: The
Formation and Transformations of an Ethnic Group* (New Brunswick, NJ:
Rutgers University Press, 2009), 11.

5 Ibid., 13.

6 Ibid.

7 Ibid., 14. Consequently, as much as 20 percent of the Japanese immigration that occurred between 1885 and 1908 consisted of single women immigrating on their own and not as wives. Ibid., 18.

8 In the period between the Gentlemen's Agreement and the 1924 Exclusion Act, "more than 20,000 Japanese women, not all of them picture brides, emigrated to the mainland and Hawaii." Roger Daniels and Otis L. Graham, *Debating American Immigration, 1882–Present* (Lanham, MD: Rowman & Littlefield, 2001), 9.

9 Many of these marriages were initiated by the prospective groom using a go-between, but many of the picture brides also arranged their own marriages.

10 This fact often led American immigration authorities to question whether the women had given true consent. Midge Ayukawa, "Good Wives and Wise Mothers: Japanese Picture Brides in Early Twentieth-Century British Columbia," *BC Studies*, nos. 105–6 (Spring/Summer 1995): 109, http://ojs.library.ubc.ca/index.php/bcstudies/article/viewFile/979/1017. See also Pamela Haag, *Consent: Sexual Rights and the Transformation of American Liberalism* (Ithaca, NY: Cornell University Press, 1999), 114.

11 Ayukawa, "Good Wives and Wise Mothers," 109. See also Donna R. Gabaccia, *Seeking Common Ground: Multidisciplinary Studies of Immigrant Women in the United States* (Westport, CT: Praeger, 1992), 125–26 (describing how these marriages were arranged, discussing the women's motivations).

12 Ayukawa, "Good Wives and Wise Mothers," 110.

13 With less land to grow food, Okinawans were forced into "an increasingly dependent situation where they grew sugarcane for cash so they could buy foodstuff from Japan." Setsu Shigematsu and Keith Camacho, eds., *Militarized Currents: Toward a Decolonized Future in Asia and the Pacific* (Minneapolis: University of Minnesota Press, 2010), 99.

14 Ibid.

15 See Steve Rabson, "Being Okinawan in Japan: The Diaspora Experience," *Asia-Pacific Journal: Japan Focus*, http://www.japanfocus.org/-Steve-Rabson/3720.

16 Taku Suzuki, *Embodying Belonging: Racializing Okinawan Diaspora in Bolivia and Japan* (Honolulu: University of Hawai'i Press, 2010), 25. See also Jon Lie, *Multiethnic Japan* (Cambridge, MA: Harvard University Press, 2004), 98. In fact, by 1907, Okinawan immigrants made up nearly 20 percent of all Japanese immigrants in Hawaii. See Brian Niiya, ed., *Japanese American History from A-7, 1868 to the Present* (New York: Facts on File, 1993), 33. In addition, they composed nearly 15 percent of all Japanese immigration to the United States. See Y. Scott Matsumoto, "Okinawa Migrants to Hawaii," 26, http://evols.library.manoa.hawaii.edu/bitstream/handle/10524/476/JL16133.pdf.

17 Gabaccia, *Seeking Common Ground*, 127.

18 Hing, *Making and Remaking Asian America*, 66. After Korea was annexed by Japan, Korea was subject to the same Gentlemen's Agreement, with the same picture bride exception. Consequently, like Japanese women, Korean picture brides could emigrate by marrying Korean immigrants already in the United States.

19 Technically, Korea was colonized while Okinawa was annexed.

20 Anne Soon Choi, *Korean Americans* (New York: Infobase, 2007), 36.

21 Shirley Hune and Gail M. Nomura, eds., *Asian/Pacific Islander American Women: A Historical Anthology* (New York: New York University Press, 2003), 108.

22 Many of the grooms intentionally deceived the women about their age, appearance, and financial prospects. See Gordon Morris Bakken and Brenda Farrington, eds., *The Gendered West: The America West* (New York: Routledge, 2013), 347.

23 Ibid. The women could also attempt to replace their lackluster fiancés with more appealing candidates, but given the short time period before they were deported, few women were able to take advantage of this option. Spickard, *Japanese Americans*, 35.

24 Spickard, *Japanese Americans*, 36–37.

25 Mei Nakano, *Japanese American Women: Three Generations 1890–1990* (Sebastopol, CA: Mina Press, 1990), 26 (quoting from a 1917 picture bride's letter).

26 Yong-ho Ch'oe, ed., *From the Land of Hibiscus: Koreans in Hawai'i, 1903–1950* (Honolulu: University of Hawai'i Press, 2006), 29.

27 Hune and Nomura, *Asian/Pacific Islander American Women*, 106.

28 Many of these women had received a modern education as part of the modern movement that took place in Korea around the turn of the century. Yen Le Espiritu, *Asian American Women and Men: Labor, Laws, and Love*, 2nd ed. (Lanham, MD: Rowman & Littlefield, 2008), 34. In addition, many had been influenced by American women missionaries who taught them to seek "political, religious and personal freedom." Gabaccia, *Seeking Common Ground*, 126.

29 "Most of these women became actively involved in nationalistic causes by organizing and participating in a number of organizations, such as the Korean Ladies' Relief Society and the Yŏngnam Women's Business League." See Ch'oe, *From the Land of Hibiscus*, 30. See also Soo-Young Chin and Dora Yum Kim, *Doing What Had to Be Done: The Life Narrative of Dora Yum Kim* (Philadelphia: Temple University Press, 1999), 21.

30 Rumi Yasutake, *Transnational Women's Activism: The United States, Japan, and Japanese Immigrant Communities in California, 1859–1920* (New York: New York University Press, 2004), 125.

31 Gabaccia, *Seeking Common Ground*, 130. (This was particularly common in places like Hawaii, where there were large numbers of picture brides living in close proximity.)

32 Timothy J. Lukes and Gary Y. Okihiro, *Japanese Legacy: Farming and Community Life in California's Santa Clara Valley* (Cupertino: California History Center, De Anza College, 1985), 75; Yasutake, *Transnational Women's Activism*, 125.

33 See Yasutake, *Transnational Women's Activism*, 125.

34 Frequently, this meant the hiring of *Tsubens*, bilingual Japanese who performed legal work for Japanese immigrants. Ibid., 125.

35 Ibid. This was a divorce rate of 6 percent, which was higher than the national average of approximately 8 divorces per 1,000 couples. U.S. Department of Health, Education, and Welfare, National Vital Statistics System, "100 Years of Marriage and Divorce Statistics, United States, 1867–1967" (December 1973), 9, http://www.cdc.gov/nchs/data/series/sr_21/sr21_024.pdf.

36 Yasutake, *Transnational Women's Activism*, 125. (In almost all of these cases, the women had jobs as barmaids or waitresses and were economically independent.)

37 Significantly less than half this population was female. Yoon K. Pak, *Wherever I Go, I Will Always Be a Loyal American: Schooling Seattle's Japanese Americans during World War II* (New York: RoutledgeFalmer, 2002), 47.

38 Kazuhiro Oharazeki, "Japanese Prostitutes in the Pacific Northwest, 1887–1920" (PhD diss., State University of New York at Binghamton, 2008), 152, ProQuest (AAT 3320155), http://search.proquest.com/docview/304326828.

39 Ibid.

40 Ibid., 152. See also Bakken and Farrington, *Gendered West*, 329.

41 Oharazeki, "Japanese Prostitutes," 155.

42 The desertion of husbands by wives, called *kakeochi* in Japanese, was fairly common, and many of these men would place kakeochi ads in Japanese newspapers listing rewards for their wives' return. See Yasutake, *Transnational Women's Activism*, 119. See also Niiya, *Japanese American History*, 195.

43 Bakken and Farrington, *Gendered West*, 331.

44 Oharazeki, "Japanese Prostitutes," 149–50.

45 Not surprisingly, Japanese American papers from the period routinely decried the "Americanization" of Japanese immigrant women. They criticized American society's tendency to treat "women with excessive respect," which they believed made women vain and arrogant. They bemoaned the fact that Japanese women were abandoning the "supreme virtues" of obedience and chastity. Yasutake, *Transnational Women's Activism*, 125. See also Oharazeki, "Japanese Prostitutes," 157.

46 Kerry Abrams, "Peaceful Penetration: Proxy Marriage, Same-Sex Marriage, and Recognition," *Michigan State Law Review* 2011 (2011): 146. See also Martha

Gardner, *Qualities of a Citizen: Women, Immigration, and Citizenship, 1870–1965* (Princeton, NJ: Princeton University Press, 2009), 40.

47 Gardner, *Qualities of a Citizen*, 40.

48 Ibid., 39.

49 U.S. citizenship laws prevented Asian immigrants from naturalizing. However, the Fourteenth Amendment was clear that the American-born children of Japanese immigrants were citizens. See *United States v. Wong Kim Ark*, 169 U.S. 649 (1898).

50 Sidney L. Gulick, "The Contributors' Column," *Atlantic Monthly* 127 (January–June, 1921): 718, https://books.google.com/books?id=n4A3AQAAMAAJ&pg =PA718&lpg=PA718&dq=Sidney+Gulik,+contributors%27+column&source= bl&ots=ngZOVt1mNV&sig=g_cyh4JwsLEtx7cnohNxMk_w_BI&hl=en&sa= X&ved=0CC4Q6AEwAmoVChMIpLOKnKeUxgIVy48NCh29dwec#v=onepa ge&q=Sidney%20Gulik%2C%20contributors%27%20column&f=false. Similarly, in a 1920 congressional hearing on Japanese immigration, Kiichi Kanzaki (general secretary of the Japanese Association of America) noted the earlier statements of Senator Phelan, who had "made a very sensational statement concerning the number of Japanese 'picture brides,' and in that statement he included all Japanese women brought in as wives. I think only one-sixth or one-seventh of the total number were really picture brides." U.S. Congress, House of Representatives, *Administration of Immigration Laws: Hearings before the Committee on Immigration and Naturalization, House of Representatives, Sixty-Sixth Congress, Second Session* (Washington, DC: Government Printing Office, 1920), 663, https://books.google.com/books?id= wxU9AAAAYAAJ&pg=PA674&lpg=PA674&dq=Kanzaki,+General+Secretary +of+the+Japanese+Association+of+America&source=bl&ots=GKVWCVo07 c&sig=teTgiR8UTRKm4V4OQVpwzs_hlrI&hl=en&sa=X&ved=0CCoQ6AE wBGoVChMI3dqZsrGUxgIVhJUNCh2sjgB4#v=onepage&q= one-sixth&f=false.

51 Gulick, "Contributor's Column," 718.

52 In addition, some picture marriage opponents, such as the San Francisco Labor Council, claimed the women were actually laborers in disguise who were immigrating to displace white farmers. Abrams, "Peaceful Penetration," 148.

53 Erika Lee and Judy Yung, *Angel Island: Immigrant Gateway to America* (New York: Oxford University Press, 2010), 130.

54 Ibid., 132. By this point it was already too late. Although the Japanese government issued the Ladies Agreement in 1920, in which it promised to stop issuing passports to picture brides, the exclusionists were still not satisfied with anything less than an outright ban. Ibid.

55 In the early 1920s, American officials took the substantial step of declaring that "any marriage performed when one of the parties was in the United States and the other in a foreign country was invalid for immigration purposes." Japan

then stopped the practice and would issue passports only to women who married a Japanese man physically present in Japan. Nancy F. Cott, *Public Vows: A History of Marriage and the Nation* (Cambridge, MA: Harvard University Press, 2002), 154.

56 Foreign-born Japanese and other Asians were ineligible for naturalization at this time. They could acquire citizenship only through jus soli (birth in America) or potentially through jus sanguinis (birth to an American citizen), but the latter was extremely difficult. See Kristin A. Collins, "Illegitimate Borders: *Jus Sanguinis* Citizenship and the Legal Construction of Family, Race, and Nation," *Yale Law Journal* 123 (2014): 2235. See also Karen J. Blair, ed., *Women in the Pacific Northwest History: An Anthology*, rev. ed. (Seattle: University of Washington Press, 2001), 303 (noting that after 1924, "no new immigrants from Japan, male or female, arrived"). Included in this act was the National Origins Act, which "defined 'wife' and 'husband' for immigration purposes as not including wife and husband by reason of picture marriage." Abrams, "Peaceful Penetration," 154.

57 The first immigration restrictions were the 1875 Page Act, which allowed immigration officials to exclude any Chinese women they determined were immigrating for "lewd or immoral purposes." Gardner, *Qualities of a Citizen*, 52.

58 Immigration Act, Forty-Seventh Congress, 22 Stat. 214, Sess. 1, Chap. 376 (August 3, 1882), 214, http://library.uwb.edu/guides/usimmigration/22%20 stat%20214.pdf. The government now had the capability to expel immigrants based on criteria delineated in the act.

59 Immigration Act, 22 Stat. 214 (August 3, 1882).

60 Immigration Act 1891, 26 Stat. 1084, Fifty-First Congress, Sess. 2, Chap. 551 (March 3, 1891), 1084, http://library.uwb.edu/guides/usimmigration/26%20 stat%201084.pdf.

61 Immigration Act 1903, 32 Stat. 1213, Fifty-Seventh Congress, Sess. 2, Chap. 1012 (March 3, 1903), 1213, http://www-rohan.sdsu.edu/dept/polsciwb/brianl/ docs/1903ImmigrationAct.pdf. (It also now costs two dollars for each passenger.)

62 The prime example would be women who had sexual relations outside of marriage. Immigration Act of 1907, 34 Stat. 898, Fifty-Ninth Congress (February 20, 1907), 5, https://ia600406.us.archive.org/1/items/ cu31924021131101/cu31924021131101.pdf.

63 Immigration Act of 1910, 36 Stat. 265, Sixty-First Congress, Sess. 2, Chap. 128 (March 26, 1910), https://a.next.westlaw.com/Link/Document/Blob/ If56a0991cba111d8a44800065ba32aee.pdf?targetType=us-statlrg&originationC ontext=document&transitionType=DocumentImage&uniqueId=4cf2 1eb6–60f9–4abb-ae13-c82e07feoaf8&contextData=%28sc. UserEnteredCitation%29. See also Gardner, *Qualities of a Citizen*, 74.

64 Gardner, *Qualities of a Citizen*, 87.

65 Ibid., 93.
66 The inspectors were skeptical that Vera's sister could manage the financial burden she represented, and they breezily dismissed Vera's own claims to self-sufficiency noting, "she is frail and undersized." Ibid., 95.
67 Ibid., 97.
68 Ibid., 19.
69 Ibid., 84.
70 Ibid.
71 Marie Hall Ets, *Rosa: The Life of an Italian Immigrant* (Madison: University of Wisconsin Press, 1970), 163, https://books.google.com/books?id=vT2zcRDOh-YC&pg=PA3&lpg=PA3&dq=Ets,+Rosa,+the+life+of+an+Italian+immigrant&source=bl&ots=vU_aa_QVh_&sig=cbilDAm_odf76BDOfCDeJqKojeo&hl=en&sa=X&ei=q92CVcqcHcemgwTFpYLgDQ&ved=0CBoQ6AEwADge#v=onepage&q=Lombardo&f=false.
72 Virginia Yans-McLaughlin, *Family and Community: Italian Immigrants in Buffalo, 1880–1930* (Champaign: University of Illinois Press, 1977), 70, https://books.google.com/books?id=qdnsgKKyVGoC&q=chaperone#v=snippet&q=chaperone&f=false. The fear of traveling alone was quite prevalent at this time, and there was a tremendous concern that unsuspecting single women would be trafficked into "white slavery." For this reason, it was not uncommon for some European mail-order brides to have their fiancés return home and marry them before the journey so that they could make the journey together. Suzanne M. Sinke, *Dutch Immigrant Women in the United States, 1880–1920* (Champaign: University of Illinois Press, 2002), 21.
73 Gabaccia, *Seeking Common Ground*, 74.
74 Sinke, *Dutch Immigrant Women*, 18 (in contrast, in America, only 1 percent of Dutch women remained unmarried).
75 The marital prospects were particularly dire for young domestic workers. Ibid., 19.
76 Rachel Calof, *Rachel Calof's Story: Jewish Homesteader on the Northern Plains*, ed. J. Sanford Rikoon (Bloomington: Indiana University Press, 1995), 6. According to Calof, "In Russia at that time, the occupations of butcher, tailor, shoemaker, or musician were considered inferior trades and those engaged in such work were socially unacceptable." Ibid., 6.
77 Sydney Stahl Weinberg, *The World of Our Mothers: The Lives of Jewish Immigrant Women* (Chapel Hill: University of North Carolina Press, 1988), 128.
78 Calof, *Rachel Calof's Story*, 10.
79 Clare Savage Littledale, "Picture-Brides and Love at First Sight," *New York Times*, August 20, 1922, http://query.nytimes.com/mem/archive-free/pdf?res=9503E0DB1E3FE432A25753C2A96E9C946395D6CF.
80 "200 Picture Brides Come Here to Wed: Greek and Armenian Girls Met at Pier by Their Prospective Husbands. Twelve Left Uncalled For. They Will Have to

Return Unless They Are Claimed—Many Bring Gifts," *New York Times*, August 3, 1922, 32, http://query.nytimes.com/mem/archive-free/pdf?res=9902E4DF1 339EF3ABC4B53DFBE668389639EDE.

81 In fact, one of the passengers on the ship was Captain E. A. Yarrow, one of the directors of the Near East Relief Organization, which was founded to help the survivors of the Armenian Genocide, and it is likely he was escorting some of these survivors. Ibid. See also "Ernest Yarrow, Christian Missionary and Witness to the Armenian Genocide," Horizonweekly.ca, February 24, 2015, http://www.horizonweekly.ca/news/details/62227 (describing the numbers killed).

82 "200 Picture Brides."

83 Susan Zeiger, *Entangling Alliances: Foreign War Brides and American Soldiers in the Twentieth Century* (New York: New York University Press, 2010), 53. Similarly, many of the would-be grooms were also survivors of the Armenian Genocide. For example, in a letter from a factory worker to his intended bride, the man wrote the following: "I have received your photo consenting to be my fiancée. I love you and I am keeping your photo in my right pocket. We are joining our fate and destiny to each other, and as our pure hearts are joined together, we must know each other well. I am sure I will find in you all the qualities that I have hoped for. I know that you are an unattached person; as for me; I was married in my homeland but during the devastating world war my family was all killed." Isabel Kaprielian-Churchill, "Armenian Refugee Women: The Picture Brides, 1920–1930," *Journal of American Ethnic History* 12, no. 3 (Spring 1993): 7, http://www.jstor.org/stable/27501061?seq=1#page_scan_tab_contents. See also Natalie De Bogory, "Adventurers in Marriage," *Outlook*, 618–20, http://www.unz.org/Pub/Outlook-1921aug17-00618?View=PDF.

84 Gardner, *Qualities of a Citizen*, 27–28.

85 Helen Irving, "When Women Were Aliens: The Neglected History of Derivative Marital Citizenship," Legal Studies Research Paper no. 12/47 (Sydney Law School, July 2012), 4, http://papers.ssrn.com/sol3/papers.cfm?abstract_id=2110546.

86 Ibid., 4–5.

87 Governments argued such naturalization was a benefit to women, but the presumption of such benefit was deeply questionable. It applied only if a woman lived, and remained, in her husband's country. It applied only if his country accorded rights to women citizens. And most importantly, it applied only if, in fact, a denaturalized woman acquired her husband's citizenship. All of these conditions applied to women marrying American men, and thus immigrant women benefited from American naturalization laws, while these laws often harmed native-born women. Such indignities were further highlighted during World War I when "hundreds of native-born women were required to register as alien enemies because of the status of the men they had

married." Linda K. Kerber, *No Constitutional Right to Be Ladies: Women and the Obligations of Citizenship* (New York: Hill & Wang, 1998), 42.

88 In 1922, Congress passed the Cable Act, also known as the Married Women's Independent Nationality Act, which enabled American women to keep their American citizenship even after marriage to a foreigner. However, American women and men were still not treated equally. American women continued to lose their citizenship if they married a man ineligible for citizenship such as an Asian, polygamist, or anarchist. In contrast, men faced no such restrictions, and this inequality was not remedied until the 1930s. See Cott, *Public Vows*, 165.

89 Candice Lewis Bredbenner, *A Nationality of Her Own: Women, Marriage, and the Law of Citizenship* (Berkeley: University of California Press, 1998), 80–81.

90 See Cott, *Public Vows*, 140.

91 Dirk Hoerder and Jörg Nagler, eds., *People in Transit: German Migrations in Comparative Perspective, 1820–1930* (New York: German Historical Institute/ Cambridge University Press, 1995), 241. Of course, many immigrants were very active in the women's rights movement. See, e.g., David E. Edwards, *Yesterday's Dreams, Upper Michigan Memories* (Honolulu: Edwards Enterprises, 1988), 61. See also Lisa A. Alzo, *Slovak Pittsburgh* (Mount Pleasant, SC: Arcadia, 2006), 18.

92 De Bogory, "Adventurers in Marriage," 619. De Bogory also received notoriety as the first English translator of the Russian anti-Semitic screed, *The Protocols of the Learned Elders of Zion*, by Sergei Nilus. See Neil Baldwin, *Henry Ford and the Jews: The Mass Production of Hate* (Cambridge, MA: Perseus Books, 2001), 82.

93 De Bogory, "Adventurers in Marriage," 619. See also Zeiger, *Entangling Alliances*, 53.

94 Zeiger, *Entangling Alliances*, 39.

95 Ibid., 9.

96 Ibid., 130.

97 Ibid.

98 Ibid., 130–31.

99 Ibid., 131.

100 Gardner, *Qualities of a Citizen*, 137. It was argued that by excluding Chinese female immigrants, Chinese male citizens were resorting to interracial marriages.

101 See Rose Cuison Villazor, "The Other *Loving*: Uncovering the Federal Government's Racial Regulation of Marriage," *New York University Law Review* 86 (2011): 1367.

102 Caroline Chung Simpson, *An Absent Presence: Japanese Americans in Postwar American Culture, 1945–1960* (Durham, NC: Duke University Press, 2001), 167.

103 Paul R. Spickard, *Mixed Blood: Intermarriage and Ethnic Identity in Twentieth-Century America* (Madison: University of Wisconsin Press, 1989), 139.

104 Ibid., 139–40.

105 Ibid., 140.

106 People who did not marry were considered "'narcissistic,' 'deviant,' 'infantile,' or 'pathological.'" Coontz, *Marriage, a History*, 230.

CHAPTER 8. MAIL-ORDER FEMINISM

1 Betty Friedan, *The Feminine Mystique* (New York: Norton, 2001), 100.

2 Coontz, *Marriage, a History*, 242.

3 Ibid., 250.

4 For example, in 1972, Title IX of the Education Act was passed, prohibiting sex discrimination in any program receiving federal aid; in 1973, *Roe v. Wade* was decided, recognizing women's right to abortion; and in 1975, it was no longer legal to require a married woman to have her husband's written permission in order to get a loan or credit card.

5 Patricia Coffin, ed., "The Shulmans Have a 50–50 Marriage Agreement That's Down in Writing," *Life: The Marriage Experiments*, April 28, 1972, https://books.google.com/books?id=_1YEAAAAMBAJ&pg=PA43&lpg=PA43&dq=Alix+Kates+Shulman,+Life+magazine&source=bl&ots=nCmqprjaHD&sig=bGHMjoo4ioojioQckabfalLh8Cw&hl=en&sa=X&ei=2lmEVeXeN8OXNqXasPgE&ved=0CFcQ6AEwCDgK#v=onepage&q=Alix%20Kates%20Shulman%2C%20Life%20magazine&f=false.

6 Coontz, *Marriage, a History*, 255.

7 Ibid., 254.

8 Ibid., 265.

9 Anne VanderMey, "The Mail-Order Bride Boom," *Fortune*, April 9, 2013, http://fortune.com/2013/04/09/the-mail-order-bride-boom/.

10 See Lisa Anne Simons, "Marriage, Migration, and Markets: International Matchmaking and International Feminism" (PhD diss., University of Denver, 2001), 48. See also Jonathon Narducci, *Love Me—The Documentary* (2014), http://www.lovemethedocumentary.com/filmmakers.php.

11 Lera Loeb, "Yes, This Woman Is a 'Mail Order Bride,'" *Glamour*, June 1, 2009, http://www.glamour.com/sex-love-life/2009/06/yes-this-woman-is-a-mail-order-bride.

12 Adrian Chen, "New York's Most Famous Mail-Order Bride May Conquer All Media," *Gawker*, December, 10, 2009, http://gawker.com/5423895/new-yorks-most-famous-mail-order-bride-may-conquer-all-media.

13 Loeb, "Yes, This Woman Is a 'Mail Order Bride.'"

14 Chen, "New York's Most Famous Mail-Order Bride."

15 Ibid.

16 Lynn Visson, *Wedded Strangers: The Challenges of Russian-American Marriages* (New York: Hippocrene Books, 1998), 209.

17 Ibid., 209.

18 "Indie Feature: Mail Order Bride," *Back Stage* 4, no. 7 (February 18, 2000), http://business.highbeam.com/3907/article-1G1–60139532/indie-feature-mail-order-bride.

19 Mila Glodava and Richard Onizuka, *Mail Order Brides: Women for Sale* (Fort Collins, CO: Alaken, 1994), 26. Glodava wrote the book based on her experiences with thirty mail-order brides. After concluding that the majority of them were in exploitative and abusive relationships, she created the Mail Order Bride Legal Aid Fund, with support from the Asian Pacific Development Fund, to help free mail-order brides from abusive relationships. This book is part of her advocacy work on behalf of mail-order brides. She teamed up with Richard Onizuka, the former clinical director of the Asian/Pacific Center for Human Development, to write the book. She hoped that together, they would fill in the "sketchy and incomplete" information people have regarding mail-order marriages. Ibid., xiii.

20 Ibid., 31.

21 Nicole Constable, *Romance on a Global Stage* (Berkeley: University of California Press, 2003), 79.

22 See Simons, "Marriage, Migration, and Markets," 6, 16.

23 See, e.g., Vergara, "Abusive Mail-Order Bride Marriage," 1553n34 (acknowledging that "[t]here is no direct data on the incidence of abuse in mail-order marriage because the INS does not keep a record of how immigrant spouses meet their sponsoring spouses").

24 Tahirih Justice Center, "Abuse and Exploitation through the International Marriage Broker (IMB) Industry," http://www.tahirih.org/mission/the-issues/abuse-and-exploitation-through-the-international-marriage-broker-imb-industry/.

25 Tahirih Justice Center, "Frequently Asked Questions: International Marriage Broker Regulation Act of 2005 (IMBRA)," 2, http://www.tahirih.org/site/wp-content/uploads/2009/03/FAQs-IMBRA-101013.pdf.

26 See Simons, "Marriage, Migration, and Markets," 8–11; Roxanne Sims, "A Comparison of the Laws in the Philippines, the U.S.A., and Belarus to Regulate the Mail-Order Bride Industry," *Akron Law Review* 42 (2009): 611n32. See also Kerry Abrams, "Immigration Law and the Regulation of Marriage," *Minnesota Law Review* 91 (2007): 1654.

27 Simons, "Marriage, Migration, and Markets," 13 (noting that most scholarly articles claiming high levels of abuse cite journalists). I myself contributed to this trend. In May 2012, I wrote an article for the *New Republic* magazine in which I supported my assertion that these relationships have higher levels of abuse by citing the U.S. governmental report on matchmaking, which in turn cited a newspaper article, "Here Come the Brides" (John Krich, "Here Come the Brides: The Blossoming Business of Imported Love," *Mother Jones* 11, no. 2 [February–March 1986]: 34–37, 43–46). See also Marcia Zug, "The Latest

Victim of GOP Intransigence? Mail-Order Brides," *New Republic*, May 17, 2012, http://www.newrepublic.com/article/politics/103338/vawa-brides-violence-women-adams.

28 In her dissertation, Simons summarizes a government study on mail-order brides stating that the "[f]indings of the report indicate that these concerns—fraud and abuse—are *not significantly tied to matchmaking* as a form of immigration." Simons, "Marriage, Migration, and Markets," 39–40.

29 Ibid., 11.

30 See Sims, "Comparison of the Laws," 610.

31 For example, a study of intimate partner homicide in New York found 51 percent of the victims were foreign-born, while 45 percent were born in the United States. New York City Department of Health and Mental Hygiene, "Femicide in New York City: 1995–2002" (2004), http://www.nyc.gov/html/doh/downloads/pdf/ip/femicide1995–2002_report.pdf. See also National Coalition Against Domestic Violence, "Immigrant Victims of Domestic Violence," http://www.learningtoendabuse.ca/sites/default/files/dv_immigrantvictims.pdf; Futures Without Violence, "The Facts on Immigrant Women and Domestic Violence," https://www.futureswithoutviolence.org/userfiles/file/Children_and_Families/Immigrant.pdf. In addition, this abuse also appears to be worse for married immigrant women. According to studies, 59.5 percent of married immigrant women experience abuse, compared to 49.8 percent of unmarried immigrant women. See Mary Ann Dutton, Leslye E. Orloff, and Giselle Aguilar Hass, "Characteristics of Help-Seeking Behaviors, Resources, and Service Needs of Battered Immigrant Latinas: Legal and Policy Implications," *Georgetown Journal on Poverty Law and Policy* 7, no. 2 (Summer 2000): 259, http://niwaplibrary.wcl.american.edu/cultural-competency/research-publications/CULTCOMP_Georgetown-Imm-Victim-Helpseeking 2000.pdf.

32 Giselle Aguilar Hass, Nawal Ammar, and Leslye Orloff, "Battered Immigrants and U.S. Citizen Spouses," *Legal Momentum*, April, 24, 2006 (on file with the author).

33 My argument that American immigration law protects mail-order brides from abuse is bolstered by the fact that higher levels of mail-order bride abuse are seen in countries that do not afford these women similar immigration/citizenship protections. For example, a report compiled by Norwegian women's shelters indicated that compared to their number in the overall population, mail-order brides "were overrepresented as shelter residents." Maria Eriksson, Marianne Hester, Suvi Keskinen, and Keith Pringle, eds., *Tackling Men's Violence in Families: Nordic Issues and Dilemmas* (Bristol: Policy Press, University of Bristol, 2005), 94. However, a mail-order bride's status under Norwegian law is quite different from that of an American mail-order bride. Bjørn Hvinden and Håkan Johansson, eds., *Citizenship in Nordic Welfare*

States: Dynamics of Choice, Duties and Participation in a Changing Europe (New York: Routledge, 2007), 117.

34 U.S. Citizenship and Immigration Services, Immigration and Nationality Act of 1952, § 101(a)(15)(K)(i), 8 U.S.C. § 1101(a)(15)(K)(i) (2000), http://www.uscis.gov/iframe/ilink/docView/SLB/HTML/SLB/act.html.

35 A conditional resident has the right to work, to travel abroad, and to reenter the country. See Title 8, Code of Federal Regulations § 216.1 (2008).

36 Specifically, she cannot be deported for ending her marriage, but until she has full citizenship, she can still be deported for certain crimes.

37 Pub. L. No. 104–208 § 301, 110 Stat. 3009–546 (1996), which was codified at 8 U.S.C.A. § 1182(a)(9)(B) (Westlaw 2008). See Daniel González, "U.S. Immigration Law Drives Husband, Wife Apart: U.S. Man's Mexican Wife Forced to Leave Country," *Arizona Republic*, February 17, 2008, http://www.azcentral.com/news/articles/0217illegalbride0217.html; see also Wendy Koch, "'Mixed Status' Tears Apart Families," *USA Today*, April 25, 2006, A3, http://www.usatoday.com/news/nation/2006-04-25-mixed-status_x.htm; Cindy Gonzalez, "A Family Broken at the Border," *Omaha World Herald*, December 17, 2007, http://www.detentionwatchnetwork.org/node/502.

38 Individuals who entered the country without a valid visa will not be able to apply for a green card without returning to their home country first, regardless of their marriage to a U.S. citizen. Once such individuals have left the country, those who were in the United States for more than 180 days will face a multi-year bar on reentry. In addition, although unlawful presence waivers are possible, their availability is limited. Unlawful presence must be the only inadmissibility ground, and more problematic, the applicant must be able to demonstrate that the U.S. citizen spouse or child would experience "extreme hardship" if the waiver is not granted.

39 The 2014 DACA expansion would permit the undocumented parents of American-born children to apply for deferred action. Specifically, under the proposed expansion, parents of U.S. citizens and lawful permanent residents would be able "to request deferred action and employment authorization for three years, . . . provided they have lived in the United States continuously since January 1, 2010, and pass required background checks." See U.S. Citizenship and Immigration Services, "Executive Actions on Immigration," http://www.uscis.gov/immigrationaction. However, due to a federal court order, DACA expansion, which was supposed to begin on February 18, 2015, did not go into effect as scheduled. If and when this executive action will go forward remains to be seen. Ibid.

40 8 U.S.C. § 1154(b)(ii) (2001).

41 Committee on Foreign Relations, U.S. Senate, *Human Trafficking: Mail Order Bride Abuses*, 108th Congress, 2nd Sess., July 13, 2004, http://niwaplibrary.wcl.

american.edu/reference/additional-materials/vawa-legislative-history/
miscellaneous/Human%20Trafficking%20Mail%20Order%20Bride%20
Abuses.pdf/view?searchterm=INS%20%22Mail%20Order%20Bride%22%20
Report.
42 In 1996, the Immigration and Nationality Service estimated that there were
between 4,000 and 6,000 mail-order marriages per year and that these
marriages represented 2.7 to 4.1 percent of all immigration involving female
spouses. Robert J. Scholes, "Appendix A: The 'Mail-Order Bride' Industry and
Its Impact on U.S. Immigration" (2006), 4, http://www.aila.org/File/Related/
mailorder-a.pdf. See also Robert J. Scholes, "AF ISO WM: How Many
Mail-Order Brides," *Immigration Review* 28 (Spring 1997): 7–10, http://www.
cis.org/sites/cis.org/files/articles/1997/IR28/IR28.pdf. Moreover, due to the
explosive use of the Internet, these numbers are likely much higher today. See
Committee on Foreign Relations, *Human Trafficking*. See also Suzanne H.
Jackson, "To Honor and Obey: Trafficking in 'Mail-Order Brides,'" *George
Washington Law Review* 70 (2002): 493.
43 INS, "International Matchmaking Organizations: A Report to Congress, Part II
7" (1999), http://library.niwap.org/wp-content/uploads/2015/IMM-Art-
IntrtnlMatchmaking.ReportCongrees.pdf. The lack of evidence indicating
higher rates of abuse for mail-order brides is particularly telling given the fact
that mail-order brides are specifically informed of their right to self-petition in
cases of abuse. Interviews with the women demonstrate that even before they
immigrate, many mail-order brides understand that that domestic violence is
illegal in the United States and that there are ways for abuse victims to receive
help. Simons, "Marriage, Migration, and Markets," 69.
44 Leslye E. Orloff, Mary Ann Dutton, Giselle Aguilar Hass, and Nawal Ammar,
"Battered Immigrant Women's Willingness to Call for Help and Police
Response," *University of California, Los Angeles Women's Law Journal* 13 (2003):
60 (all of these rates were still substantially lower than the reporting rates for
U.S. citizen women).
45 Because those who come over as fiancées have conditional status for two years,
their immigration is less secure than a legal permanent resident. However, it is
likely higher than Orloff's second category, those on temporary nonimmigrant
visas. Thus, Orloff's research suggests that their legal and relatively stable
immigration status should make abused mail-order brides more likely to report
incidents of domestic violence than undocumented women.
46 See City of Seattle, Office of Immigrant and Refugee Affairs, "Immigrant and
Refugee Commission Annual Report, June 2013–June 2014," http://www.
seattle.gov/Documents/Departments/ImmigrantAndRefugeeCommission/2
014IRCommissionAnnualReport.pdf. See also Leigh Goodmark, *A Troubled
Marriage: Domestic Violence and the Legal System* (New York: New York
University Press, 2011), 72–73; see also Shankar Vedantam, "Call for Help Leads

to Possible Deportation for Hyattsville Mother," *Washington Post*, November 1, 2010, http://www.washingtonpost.com/wp-dyn/content/article/2010/11/01/AR2010110103073.html.

47 8 U.S.C.A. § 1375a(a). They receive a copy of the informational pamphlet, U.S. Visas, "Rights and Protections for Foreign-Citizen Fiancé(e)s and Spouses of U.S. Citizens and Spouses of Lawful Permanent Residents: Important Pamphlet : For K-1, K-3, IR-1/CR-1, and F2A Immigrant Visa Applicants (International Marriage Broker Regulation Act)," http://travel.state.gov/content/visas/english/general/IMBRA.html. The pamphlet was released in October 2010.

48 Ibid.

49 8 U.S.C.A. § 1375a(d)(2)(A)(i) (West Supp. 2006).

50 8 U.S.C.A. § 1375a(d)(2)(B). See also Violence Against Women Reauthorization Act of 2013, Pub. L. No. 113–4 § 127 Stat. 54, 807 (2013).

51 The purpose of this is to reduce the likelihood that mail-order marriages can provide men with an easy way to use and abuse multiple women. Violence Against Women Act of 2005, Pub. L. No. 109–162, § 832(a)(1), 119 Stat. 2960, 3066–67 (2006) (codified at 8 U.S.C. § 1184).

52 Simons, "Marriage, Migration, and Markets," 70.

53 This ban was lifted after six months. See Lee Kyung-sook, "To Prevent Human Trafficking, Cambodia Bans International Marriages to Koreans," *Asia Foundation: Weekly Insight and Analysis in Asia*, March 31, 2010, http://asiafoundation.org/in-asia/2010/03/31/to-prevent-human-trafficking-cambodia-bans-international-marriages-to-koreans/; "Cambodia Bans Marriage to Korean Men," *Chosunilbo*, March 22, 2010, http://english.chosun.com/site/data/html_dir/2010/03/22/2010032200462.html.

54 Lee Kyung-sook, "To Prevent Human Trafficking."

55 Constable, *Romance on a Global Stage*, 64.

56 Simons, "Marriage, Migration, and Markets," 70. See also Jackson, "To Honor and Obey," 481 (citing a study conducted by the CIA which criticized IMOs for failure to screen clients and allowing underage women to advertise, but conceding that such companies were not traffickers).

57 Simons, "Marriage, Migration, and Markets," 70.

58 See U.S. Census Bureau, "2010 Census Briefs: Age and Sex Composition" (2010), http://www.census.gov/prod/cen2010/briefs/c2010br-03.pdf.

59 Melissa Murray, "Black Marriage, White People, Red Herrings," *Michigan Law Review* 111 (2013): 997. See also Pamela Haag, *Marriage Confidential: Love in the Post-Romantic Age* (New York: Harper, 2011), 29.

60 For example, 75 percent of children raised in single-parent homes experience poverty before they turn eleven, as compared with only 20 percent of children from two-parent households. See Ralph Richard Banks, *Is Marriage for White People? How the African American Marriage Decline Affects Everyone* (London:

Plume, 2012), 24. In addition, having an involved father produces children who "tend to be smarter, have better psychological health, do better in school and get better jobs." Dan Kindlon and Michael Thompson, *Raising Cain: Protecting the Emotional Life of Boys* (New York: Random House, 1999), 98. See also June Carbone and Naomi Cahn, "Is Marriage for Rich Men?," *Nevada Law Journal* 13 (2012–13): 401.

61 See *United States v. Windsor*, 133 S. Ct. 2675 (2013).

62 D'vera Cohn, Jeffrey S. Passel, Wendy Wang, and Gretchen Livingston, *Barely Half of U.S. Adults Are Married—A Record Low* (Washington, DC: Pew Research Social and Demographic Trends, December 14, 2011), http://www.pewsocialtrends. org/2011/12/14/barely-half-of-u-s-adults-are-married-a-record-low/.

63 Aja Gabel, "The Marriage Crisis: How Marriage Has Changed in the Last Fifty Years and Why It Continues to Decline," *University of Virginia Magazine,* Summer 2012. See also Kathryn Edin and Maria J. Kefalas, *Promises I Can Keep: Why Poor Women Put Motherhood before Marriage* (Berkeley: University of California Press, 2005).

64 This is not true for all countries. In many parts of Europe, it is common for couples to maintain long-term, stable family relationships regardless of marriage. See, e.g., Banks, *Is Marriage for White People?*, 129. See also "Marriage in America: The Fraying Knot," *Economist*, January 12, 2013, http://www. economist.com/news/united-states/21569433-americas-marriage-rate-falling-and-its-out-wedlock-birth-rate-soaring-fraying.

65 Marriages continue to be the most stable relationships. Marriage is therefore good for families and particularly good for children. Banks, *Is Marriage for White People?*, 128–29.

66 *Perry v. Schwarzenegger*, 704 F. Supp. 2d 921, 970 (N.D. Cal. 2010), *aff'd sub nom. Perry v. Brown*, 671 F.3d 1052 (9th Cir. 2012).

67 *Perry v. Schwarzenegger*, 704 F. Supp. 2d at 994.

68 Ibid.

69 Ibid., 970. One of the ironic results of this high regard for marriage is that it lowers marriage rates. Richer couples use marriage as a stepping stone for the more "difficult and expensive task of raising a family." However, lower-class couples often have their families in reverse order; they have children before marriage, because they view marriage as the ultimate commitment and want to wait until they are both financially and emotionally stable. In addition, having children before marriage can put extra pressure on relationships and make them more likely to fail, thus further decreasing marriage rates among lower-income families. Guy Garcia, *The Decline of Men: How the American Male Is Tuning Out, Giving Up, and Flipping Off His Future* (New York: HarperCollins, 2008), 69.

70 The same-sex marriage debate has focused national attention on the concept of marriage as important and desirable. Proponents of same-sex marriage cite the

hundreds of legal benefits that attach to marriage, but they also note that the social and emotional benefits that attach to marriage are at least as important. Similarly, same-sex marriage critics also confirm the continuing importance of marriage when they express fears that this important institution will be devalued or discarded by permitting same-sex marriage. See "Interview with Dr. James Dobson," *Larry King Live* (CNN television broadcast, November 22, 2006) (transcript), http:// transcripts.cnn.com/transcripts/0611/22/lkl.01. html. See also Holning Lau, "Would a Constitutional Amendment Protect and Promote Marriage in North Carolina? An Analysis of Data from 2000 to 2009," *Cardozo Law Review De Novo* (2012): 173n3, http://www.cardozolawreview. com/Joomla1.5/content/denovo/Lau.DOMA.2012.FINAL.pdf.

71 Banks, *Is Marriage for White People?*, 24 (noting that "white follows black").

72 Garcia, *Decline of Men*, xii.

73 Ibid.

74 Hanna Rosin, *The End of Men and the Rise of Women* (New York: Riverhead Books, 2012), 149–60.

75 Ibid., 8.

76 Garcia, *Decline of Men*, 19.

77 Rosin, *End of Men*, 4.

78 See also Garcia, *Decline of Men*, xiv.

79 Rosin, *End of Men*, 2.

80 Ibid. In an interview with one poor mother who kicked out her children's father, the woman explained her decision by stating, "He's not around no more. I got rid of him. ... He was only here to sleep—didn't want to pay no bills, didn't want to do nothing." Edin and Kefalas, *Promises I Can Keep*, 77 (internal quotation marks omitted). According to Edin and Kefalas, "few mothers are willing to endanger the resources they and their children desperately need just to keep the baby's father around." Ibid., 81.

81 Rosin, *End of Men*, 91.

82 Ibid., 68.

83 Ibid.

84 Ibid., 8–9 ("They lost the old architecture of manliness, but they have not replaced it with any obvious new one").

85 Garcia, *Decline of Men*, 139.

86 Ibid., xv. See also Rosin, *End of Men*, 68.

87 Garcia, *Decline of Men*, xiii. Moreover, as Garcia warns, this situation is not just bad for men; it is bad for women. He notes that marginalized men are more likely to "seek solace in the hypermasculine rituals of violence and aggression with an ugly undercurrent of homophobia, misogyny, and masochism." Ibid., xiii–xiv. See also Edin and Kefalas, *Promises I Can Keep*, 81.

88 Visson, *Wedded Strangers*, 46.

89 Kate O'Rourke, "To Have and to Hold: A Postmodern Feminist Response to the Mail-Order Bride Industry," *Denver Journal International Law and Policy* 30 (2002): 479.

90 This is the conclusion reached by Ericka Johnson, a researcher at Linkoping University in Sweden, who conducted hundreds of interviews with men and women contemplating mail-order marriage, and who stated that she initially "found the vehemence with which the men discredited American women in their letters a little surprising, but it came up so frequently that . . . I could only assume they were responding to what must be a very frustrating dating scene for them. Obviously they were not finding the type of woman they wanted to marry in America, and maybe they were not even finding women who want to get married to them at all." Ericka Johnson, *Dreaming of a Mail-Order Husband: Russian-American Internet Romance* (Durham, NC: Duke University Press, 2007), 27.

91 Ibid., 26.

92 Constable, *Romance on a Global Stage*, 67.

93 Simons, "Marriage, Migration, and Markets," 199–20.

94 Constable, *Romance on a Global Stage*, 19.

95 Simons, "Marriage, Migration, and Markets," 97.

96 Johnson, *Dreaming of a Mail-Order Husband*, 21.

97 Simons, "Marriage, Migration, and Markets," 112.

98 Haag, *Marriage Confidential*, 29.

99 Constable, *Romance on a Global Stage*, 67.

100 Visson, *Wedded Strangers*, 220.

101 Wanwadee Larsen, *Confessions of a Mail Order Bride: American Life through Thai Eyes* (Far Hills, NJ: New Horizon Press, 1989), 141.

102 Ibid., 178.

103 Thus, rather than disparaging these marriages, women's advocates should consider supporting them. See, e.g., Bonnie Erbe, "Let's Ban Imports of Brides," *Deseret News*, October 22, 2006 ("Let's not just make it tougher for American men to hook up with 'mail order brides' over the Internet and import them, let's ban the practice altogether"), http://www.deseretnews.com/article/650200348/Lets-ban-imports-of-brides.html?pg=all. See also "China Takes Fight to the Internet! Begins Banning Mail-Order Bride Websites," *Catholic Online*, September 17, 2014, http://www.catholic.org/news/international/asia/story.php?id=56930.

104 This is the idea of the male breadwinner and female homemaker. See, e.g., Jody Lyneé Madeira, "The Family Capital of Capital Families: Investigating Empathetic Connections Between Jurors and Defendants' Families in Death Penalty Cases," *Michigan State Law Review* 2011 (2011): 879.

105 Simons, "Marriage, Migration, and Markets," 84. Some have suggested it may also be confining for American women as well. See Haag, *Marriage*

Confidential, 71 (noting that the laziest husbands "are all acutely, self-consciously feminist, seeing themselves as fully liberated—thoughtful, smart, open to new ideas about gender, willing to subvert the norms. It's paradoxical, that a feminist sensibility in a marriage kindles a pre-feminist inequality").

106 Visson, *Wedded Strangers*, 49–50.

107 In fact, in certain areas of Russia, Siberia in particular, women are deciding that doing it all by themselves is simply impossible and are pushing for the legalization of polygamy, reasoning that "half a good man is better than none at all." Mira Katbamna, "'Half a Good Man Is Better Than None at All': A Study of Polygamy in Russia Suggests We Have a Lot to Learn about How to Beat the Recession," *Guardian*, October 26, 2009, http://www.theguardian.com/education/2009/oct/27/polygamy-study-russia-central-asia.

108 Constable, *Romance on a Global Stage*, 65. Many critics of mail-order marriage appear to have fully embraced Betty Friedan's critique of marriage. In the *Feminine Mystique* (203), Friedan wrote that "[s]urely there are many women in America who are happy at the moment as housewives. ... But happiness is not the same thing as the aliveness of being fully used."

109 Constable, *Romance on a Global Stage*, 20.

110 Johnson, *Dreaming of a Mail-Order Husband*, 26. According to mail-order bride researcher Ericka Johnson, "as negatively as feminism is viewed in Russia, its counterpart, the concept of women's solidarity is very strong, both politically and in daily practice. The term 'feminist' is an insult but many women are comfortable professing solidarity with other women." Ibid., 30.

111 Ibid., 25.

112 Simons, "Marriage, Migration, and Markets," 92 (noting that the women expressed the common themes of "the disenfranchised the world over" such as the inability to use their own "power and creative potential to effect change in their lives and/or improvements in their community or nation").

113 Ibid., 92.

114 Visson, *Wedded Strangers*, 207.

115 Rosin, *End of Men*, 61.

116 Ibid., 61.

117 Simons, "Marriage, Migration, and Markets," 91.

118 Visson, *Wedded Strangers*, 53.

119 Johnson, *Dreaming of a Mail-Order Husband*, 53.

120 Visson, *Wedded Strangers*, 216.

121 Ibid., 218.

122 Ibid., 217.

123 Constable, *Romance on a Global Stage*, 163–64.

124 Johnson, *Dreaming of a Mail-Order Husband*, 52.

125 Ibid., 55.

126 Simons, "Marriage, Migration, and Markets," 109. See also Johnson, *Dreaming of a Mail-Order Husband*, 151.

127 Simons, "Marriage, Migration, and Markets," 69.

128 Visson, *Wedded Strangers*, 218.

129 Ibid., 52.

130 Constable, *Romance on a Global Stage*, 134.

131 Simons, "Marriage, Migration, and Markets," 83.

132 Ibid., 163.

133 Cott, *Public Vows*, 150. See also Abbott, *History of Marriage*, 103.

134 Robert S. Lynd and Helen Merrell Lynd, *Middletown: A Study in American Culture* (New York: Harcourt Brace & World, 1929), quoted in Cott, *Public Vows*, 150.

135 Jane Austen wrote some of the most enduring romantic novels and is famous for saying "[a]nything is to be preferred or endured rather than marrying without Affection." At the same time, she also famously noted that "single women have a dreadful propensity for being poor—which is one very strong argument in favour of Matrimony." Abbott, *History of Marriage*, 83–84.

136 According to Stephanie Coontz, love was often seen as increasing marital equality. For example, Nathaniel Hawthorne declared to his wife Sophia that although he expected her to follow his guidance and do his bidding, "I possess this power only so far as I love you." Coontz, *Marriage, a History*, 181.

137 Rev. Daniel Wise, *The Young Lady's Counsellor: Or Outlines and Illustrations of the Sphere, the Duties, and the Dangers of Young Women. Designed to Be a Guide to True Happiness in This Life and to Glory in the Life Which Is to Come* (New York: Phillips & Hunt, 1851), 232, https://ia902501.us.archive.org/27/items/youngladyscounseoowise/youngladyscounseoowise.pdf.

138 Coontz, *Marriage, a History*, 187.

139 See ibid., 186 (noting that "[n]ot until the late twentieth century did a majority of women tell pollsters that love outweighed all other considerations in choosing a partner").

140 Haag, *Marriage Confidential*, 12.

141 Deborah Stone, "For Love nor Money: The Commodification of Care," in *Rethinking Commodification: Cases and Readings in Law and Culture*, ed. Martha M. Ertman and Joan C. Williams (New York: New York University Press, 2005), 273.

142 Ibid., 275.

143 Visson, *Wedded Strangers*, 231.

144 Ibid.

145 It can also help men. As many of these examples have shown, the men often benefited from their wives' wages and financial management. Consequently, it was actually the romanticization of marriage and the rise of the cult of

domesticity that devalued men who could not conform to the middle-class idea of the male provider. See Coontz, *Marriage, a History*, 188.

146 See Margaret Jane Radin, "Contested Commodities," in Ertman and Williams, *Rethinking Commodification*, 89 (likening marriage to prostitution, but noting that wives, unlike prostitutes, do not realize they're selling their sexual services. Women in such relationships "try to understand what they are doing as giving, as equal sharing, while their sexuality is actually being taken from them").

147 Robin West, *Caring for Justice* (New York: New York University Press, 1999), 120.

148 Ibid., 121.

149 Ibid., 122.

150 For example, feminist scholar Martha Nussbaum has argued that the real question is how to expand the options and opportunities for women workers. She is also focused on "how to increase the humanity inherent in their work and how to guarantee that workers of all sorts are treated with dignity." Consequently, Nussbaum has argued that if prostitution increases options for women and provides them with more dignified opportunities than other types of work, it should be favored. A similar argument can be made with mail-order marriage. Such marriages have the potential to increase opportunities for women by providing them with the means of financial remuneration for their work as a housewife. The problem, as Nussbaum would see it, is not in the sale of their marriage or wifely services, but in guaranteeing their dignity and protection. Martha Nussbaum, "Taking Money for Bodily Service," in Ertman and Williams, *Rethinking Commodification*, 247.

151 Visson, *Wedded Strangers*, 57.

CONCLUSION

1 Visson, *Wedded Strangers*, 213.

2 Johnson, *Dreaming of a Mail-Order Husband*, 63.

3 See National Healthy Marriage Resource Center, "Remarriage Trends in the United States: A Fact Sheet," 2, http://www.healthymarriageinfo.org/resource-detail/index.aspx?rid=2994 (noting that "20% of first marriages end in divorce within five years").

4 Remarriages have a significantly higher divorce rate after five years. A statistic that includes second marriage, 25 percent of which end in divorce within five years, would put the five-year divorce rate at greater than 20 percent. Ibid.

5 Department of Homeland Security Press Office, "Statement by Secretary of Homeland Security Janet Napolitano on the Implementation of the Supreme Court Ruling on the Defense of Marriage Act," July 1, 2013, http://www.dhs.gov/news/2013/07/01/statement-secretary-homeland-security-janet-napolitano-implementation-supreme-court.

6 Moni Basu, "Love Wins in Gay Couple's 40-Year Immigration Fight," CNN, June 28, 2014, http://www.immigrationequality.org/cnn-love-wins-in-gay-couples-40-year-immigration-fight/.

7 See, e.g., "Recount: 75 (or 79) Countries Where Homosexuality Is Illegal," 76 Crimes, May 23, 2015, http://76crimes.com/2015/05/23/recount-75-or-79-nations-where-homosexual-is-illegal/.

8 Heather Cassell, "Russian LGBTs Seek Asylum in US," *Bay Area Reporter*, February 20, 2014, http://www.ebar.com/news/article.php?sec=news&article=69501.

9 Gay Marriage Agency, Golden Boys, "Welcome to Gay Marriage Agency 'Golden Boys'!," http://gaymarriageagency.com/.

10 Ibid.; "U.S. Lawmakers Criticized Ukraine," http://gaymarriageagency.com/2013/u-s-lawmakers-criticize-ukraine/ (copy on file with author).

11 "Free Introduction Letter," http://gaymarriageagency.com/free-introduction-letter/.

12 Gay Fiancés, "Gay Marriage Moves On," May 30, 2013, http://gayfiances.com/gay-marriage-moves-on.html#more-118.

13 Interestingly, in May 2015, the Philippines, which already had a mail-order marriage ban, specifically revised the law so that it applied to both women and men. Presumably, this change was in response to the possibility of same-sex mail-order marriage. Maricel Cruz, "Mail-Order Bride Bill Gets House OK," *Standard*, May 14, 2015, http://manilastandardtoday.com/2015/05/14/mail-order-bride-bill-gets-house-ok/.

14 In *Marriage, a History*, Stephanie Coontz argues that the defining feature of modern marriage is love. In fact, the full title of her book is *Marriage, a History: From Obedience to Intimacy or How Love Conquered Marriage*. However, her argument regarding what defines modern marriage is more nuanced than this title suggests. Coontz notes that it was changing beliefs about free choice and specifically a growing belief in the right to choose one's spouse that led to the rise of the love match. Coontz thus shows that it is free choice, even more than love, that is the defining characteristic of modern marriage.

INDEX

ABOUT THE AUTHOR

Marcia A. Zug grew up in New York City and attended Dartmouth College and Yale Law School. She is Associate Professor at the University of South Carolina School of Law. Her work focuses on the intersection of family law and immigration law.

9 780814 771815